CRITICAL PROBLEMS IN CHILDREN AND YOUTH

**CONTEMPORARY CHRISTIAN
COUNSELING**

CRITICAL PROBLEMS IN CHILDREN AND YOUTH

GRANT L. MARTIN, Ph.D.

CONTEMPORARY CHRISTIAN COUNSELING

General Editor

GARY R. COLLINS, PH.D.

Library of Congress Cataloging-in-Publication Data:

Martin, Grant L.
    Critical problems in children and youth: counseling techniques for
    problems resulting from attention deficit disorder, sexual abuse,
    custody battles, and related issues/Grant L. Martin.
        p.   cm.   —(Contemporary Christian counseling; 5)
    Includes bibliographical references and index.
    ISBN 0-8499-0886-8:
        1. Youth—Pastoral counseling of.   2. Children—Pastoral counsel-
    ing of.   3. Christian life—1960–   4. Church work with
    youth.   5. Church work with children.   I. Title.   II. Series.
    BV4447.M318   1992   92–26621
    253.5—dc20   CIP

23459   LBM   987654321

Printed in the United States of America

Contents

Introduction

CHILD SEXUAL ABUSE, RITUAL ABUSE, custody battles, parent alienation syndrome, defiant and oppositional disorders. "What's a nice counselor like you doing working with problems like this?" "Surely a Christian counselor isn't going to have to get down and get dirty with the darker side of human conflict."

Well, I only wish this were true. The reality of our times is that we have no choice. Our conflicted society, with all of its turmoil and struggle, demands our participation against all that is painful and destructive. Every day children are being harmed and abused. That abuse comes in sexual, ritualistic, educational, and legal contexts. If we choose to work with children, we have made a commitment to be an advocate for them in matters within our training and experience. This book is written for those Christian psychologists, counselors, pastors, and students who want to be an instrument to point hurting children and families to the source of hope and health.

I have spent more than twenty-six years working as a psychologist. When I first entered private practice I was one of only a few Christian licensed psychologists in my area working with children. At that time I believed I could handle most of the problems of childhood that people might bring my way. After all, I had completed eight years of college, several internships, and had served on the staff at one of the leading child study centers in the country. What else was there to learn? The answer was, "Almost everything!"

I had some expertise in educational problems, which included learning disabilities, behavior problems, and special education instructional procedures. Those were areas I would often explore with parents and their children.

Then some curves were thrown at me. Inquiries came to my office asking if I worked with abused children. I was subpoenaed as a witness in a custody battle. Parents gave me descriptions of horrendous dreams, drawings, and symptoms in their five-year-old child. An abused wife asked my help in keeping her battering husband from getting sole custody of their children.

These were not problems covered in my training. (Nor were they included in most graduate schools of my era.) So I set out, case by case, trauma by trauma, to enroll in the postdoctoral "school of hard knocks." This course has included thousands of hours of clinical contact with children, innumerable workshops, many books, and countless conversations with colleagues.

I am much wiser now. That means I am much more aware of how much I don't know. Yet I believe my experience allows me to share some ideas with others who have the privilege and challenge of working with children and teens. In the chapters ahead I draw freely from experts in these fields. I have done so because their ideas and procedures have helped me deal more effectively with children and their families.

This book examines the issues of attention-deficit hyperactivity disorder in enough detail to carry out a competent evaluation and intervention. Appropriate references and resources are provided to allow further study of both the scope and detail of the subject. The same is true on the topic of identification and treatment of child sexual abuse. Here, too, enough substance is given to provide an understanding of the mechanics and flow of the procedures, and references are given for further study. Chapter five includes discussion of ritual abuse, a problem which is being seen with tragic frequency. A summary of traumagenic states is given as the concept applies to sexual and ritualistic abuse, and words of caution are included about investigative objectivity in the discussion of signs and symptoms of satanic ritualistic abuse.

Finally, chapters six and seven discuss how to apply the "sword of Solomon" to the difficult process of custody evaluations. My own experiences, documented by research and experts in the field, are shared for your inspection and use. Not all of you will choose to work with parenting plan assessments, and these two chapters will help you decide whether to expose yourself to the hassles related to this type of forensic work.

I cannot speak for what God has called you to become, but let me share a portion of my journey. For twenty-six years I have worked with children and their families. About ten years ago I began seeing increasing numbers of abused children. Through various open doors, I felt God calling me to become more aptly qualified in the area of family violence.

Now, I come from a relatively violence-free background. I also have a staunch Quaker heritage with a strong emphasis on peacemaking. While I am fairly competitive and reasonably assertive, I am not usually highly confrontive or aggressive. Believe me, I was dragged into the field of family violence, kicking and screaming. It is not my natural style. I do not like having to interview abused children or suspected abusers. I know my passions are involved because it is with a sense of righteous indignation, and sometimes holy rage, that I continue in this field.

I enjoy writing, speaking, and teaching; I don't enjoy being cross-examined by an attorney as part of an expert testimony on a child abuse trial or custody battle. I don't know where else God might eventually lead me, but for now I believe God is asking me to become the most competent child psychologist I can be. On this mandate, I continue to research the best ways to be an advocate for children and their families.

Christ has called us to translate our personal faith into compassionate and wise excellence in our profession. In the Old Testament, excellence is associated with the concept of wisdom. For example, Isaiah 28:29 tells us, "This also comes from the LORD of hosts; he is wonderful in counsel, and excellent in wisdom" (RSV).

The Parable of the Talents (Matthew 25:14–30) helps us understand that "doing one's best" must take into consideration the opportunities and resources available to each of us as stewards of God's gifts. Not everyone has the same opportunities, thus we will be judged by the individual gifts and resources at our disposal. We are to become the best that we can be according to the purpose to which we have been called. This means we should acquire the best training available. We should desire to show the highest of professional standards, not for personal glory, but because God calls us to the highest level that can be reached as we hunger and thirst after those things which are of God.

Grant L. Martin, Ph. D.
Seattle, Washington

Chapter One

Initial Interviews with Children and Youth

THE CONSENSUS IS THAT FROM 5 TO 15 percent of all children in the United States have problems that require mental health services. This means that from 3 to 9 million children need qualified professional care.[1] The most frequent complaint heard from parents involves negative behaviors, including noncompliance, temper tantrums, bossy and demanding behavior, crying, whining and aggression. The next most frequent category of parental concern involves toileting problems, enuresis, and encopresis. Additional issues include concerns for personality problems, school, sleep, developmental, sibling/peer, and divorce/separation problems. Though these categories are certainly not the only sources of negative behavior, they account for about 75 percent of all childhood problems.[2]

What these figures don't tell us is the cause or source of the problems. Why does the child have bad dreams, academic problems, or bed wetting symptoms? The reasons, of course, are many, but present day statistics indicate that a majority of these complaints relate directly to or are attributable to attention deficit disorder, abuse, and divorce. These are the key subjects that will be discussed in the following chapters. They are certainly not the only sources of negative behavior, but they are important areas of concern for contemporary Christian counselors. But first, let's lay the groundwork by considering the characteristics of the child therapist and the tools or materials and supplies that facilitate his or her work.

CHARACTERISTICS OF A CHILD THERAPIST

Certainly, there is no stereotype of the "successful" children's counselor. Personality and training can merge in many different ways to yield a competent children's mental health professional, however, there are basic qualities that probably do distinguish a person who can learn to work well with children from one who cannot.

Crucial to the counseling process is the ability to establish a good realtionship with a child. This depends on the counselor's ability to convey interest, warmth, sincerity, and respect for the youngster. The counselor must like being with children. Most of the time, working with children is challenging, even exhausting, yet also fun. The counselor should be comfortable being with children and relating to children. This means having the self-confidence to roll up your sleeves and paint up a storm without worrying about how silly you look or whether your next adult client will notice the tempura paint under your fingernails. If children make you nervous, and you just cannot allow yourself to be spontaneous and childlike, then this type of work may not be for you.

The other side of this characteristic is the need to balance childlike freedom and playfulness with professional objectivity and self-control. It will not help the child if the counselor is so wrapped up in creating a fantastic piece of artwork that the diagnostic value of the experience is overlooked. The counselor must learn to be a part of the experience with the child, while maintaining an awareness of the hypothesis-testing and data-gathering components of the experience.

This is no different from a relationship with an adult client; it's just that the context and activities are designed for a child or a teen-ager.

A youth or children's counselor needs to have his or her own issues of childhood well resolved. A therapist with a history of abuse or having divorced parents can help with the empathy and rapport of a relationship, but this works only in the absence of significant amounts of current contamination. The counselor needs to be healthy enough that the child's important issues and topics are not avoided simply because the therapist isn't ready to deal with them.

Communication is another crucial factor in counseling children. The child therapist must have a desire to relate to, talk to, and find out about children. Ask yourself if you tend to notice and reach out to children when they are around you. Do you take the time to find out what a child is thinking? If his or her version of an event is confusing, do you tend to gloss over it and go on, or do you take the time to help clarify the story? A successful counselor of children will see humor and merit in the seemingly disjointed reports of a child and will have the patience to encourage reporting in a way that affirms the child.

In working with children, artwork and other creative expressions can be extremely important to the process of successful assessment and treatment. The counselor needs to have, or should develop, some appreciation of children's art.

Two aspects of an artistic appreciation are significant here. First, the counselor should have an interest in and ability to understand and use the media that children enjoy: painting, drawing, molding, and constructing. The successful therapist will feel comfortable using these techniques with children. This does not mean the counselor must be a great artist; it means the counselor will allow the child to be expressive in a form he or she finds comfortable. If you find these activities boring, threatening, or even demeaning, then this area of work may not be a good fit for you.

The second implication of the artistic or visual modality of learning relates to learning *style*. Children learn by processing what they hear, see, and touch. A singularly verbal or auditory mode of communication is not sufficient in the child-counseling process. The counselor needs to be able to draw pictures or use some other type of visual means to communicate ideas and principles. I have to admit, I am a rather poor artist in the sense of making recognizable figures and objects on a piece of paper, but I can usually think of some simple stick figure or basic graphic medium to illustrate my point. Another therapist may be more comfortable working with poetry, music, or storytelling. Many approaches are used. The key is to implement some system of creative expression, appropriate for the individual child, in the youth counseling process.

It is also important to use all channels of learning with a child. If you are a strong one dimensional learner (most men are visual learners; most women are auditory learners), you may need to learn to compensate for this in your work with children. Consider, too, the strong possibility that at times you will need to work with a child who is disabled in one or more of his or her learning modalities. In this instance it will be crucial for you to expand your techniques to encompass the needs of that child.

SUPPLIES AND MATERIALS

The physical surroundings of the child counselor's office should be interesting and comfortable for children. (Teen-agers require different items than do young children, and usually do better in a typical office setting.) For younger children, a separate playroom with adequate storage is a distinct advantage. A "wet" area with sink and tiled floor is best for art projects and other activities that tend to get messy.

A separate carpeted area or a throw rug are handy so you can get down at floor level with the child and play or talk. Beanbag chairs are not only comfortable, they are great icebreakers. It helps with rapport building if the counselor can flop into a beanbag next to the child so they can play with building blocks or read a book together. Tables and chairs are a helpful addition, particularly for art, crafts, or drawing activities. Many play therapists recommend a sand tray. The following list includes additional suggestions.

Art supplies
  Felt tip pens (Many children like the scented kind)
  Crayons, pencils, eraser, ruler
  Newsprint, construction paper, paper bags
  Glue
  Blunt scissors
  Easel with ledge for paints, brushes, and water
  Protective aprons or smocks
Play-Doh®
Dollhouse, furnished with family figures of various
  ages and both sexes
Sand tray with toy animals, human figures, ve-
  hicles, and buildings. Some therapists like water
  available to create mud (and messes).
Toys for various ages and interests. Both boy and
  girl interests need to be represented, e.g., build-
  ing blocks, dolls with nursing bottles and
  clothes, miniature soldiers and army equipment,
  playhouse supplies, dishes and utensils, peg-
  pounding set with mallet, cars, trucks, airplanes,
  rubber knife, toy gun, balls (soft, pliable)
Puppets—helpful to have variety such as family,
  royalty, occupations, and animals
Play telephones
Plain mask (Lone Ranger type), sun glasses
Feeling cards
Punching bag
Various books dealing with childhood problems
  such as divorce, death, and attention deficits

Toys and materials to avoid include sharp, pointed, or glass items which could hurt the child; elaborate, expensive, complicated, battery-operated, or mechanical toys; highly structured materials that require extensive, lengthy involvement for completion; and items that break readily or have parts that are easily lost, such as puzzles. Children enjoy these toys, but it's frustrating to end up with lost pieces.

I have found therapeutic games a useful component in both the assessment and treatment phases. While chess and checkers

have been around for years, therapeutic games are a more recent development. A number of games have been developed to
deal with everything from preventing abuse to managing anger.[3]

Board games like Gardner's "Talking, Feeling, and Doing
Game" can be quite valuable.[4] This game is similar in format
and appearance to many of the board games that are familiar
to most children. It is based on Talking, Feeling, and Doing cards
which require a specific response. They contain nonthreatening
to moderately-threatening questions covering a broad range
of human experiences. They usually elicit beneficial discussion.[5] The child receives a reward chip for each response
provided. The counselor can focus on the questions and answers as points of departure for a therapeutic exchange.

I use this type of game with children who are fairly
nonverbal and when I am having trouble getting sufficient
diagnostic responses. I also use games during the treatment
stage of therapy. Of course, I select the game and content to
fit the therapeutic needs of the particular child and situation.

The rationale for incorporating game media in therapy with
children includes the following concepts.

1. Compared to other therapeutic procedures, games are a
   more natural medium of self-expression, experimenta-
   tion, and learning for children.
2. The child feels "at home" and safe in a game setting and
   can readily relate to the game and "play out" concerns,
   feelings, and thoughts.
3. Games can serve as projective assessment tools.
4. A game medium facilitates communication and expression.
5. A game medium allows for a cathartic release of feelings, frustrations, and anxieties.
6. Game playing experiences can be educational, renewing,
   wholesome, and constructive. For example, a situation
   can be presented in which anxiety about certain conditions can be confronted and resolved.
7. Games offer children an opportunity to learn to deal
   with the "rules of the game." This can be an analogy to
   living responsibly in relationship to others.

8. Games allow a child's playfulness and fantasy activity to emerge, releasing creative potential for living and problem solving.
9. An adult can more fully and naturally understand the world of a child by observing children playing games.
10. The game context can assist in building rapport.[6]

THE COUNSELING PROCESS—ASSESSMENT

When dealing with problems of children, assessment is a critical and complex component of the treatment process. Assessment has several obvious purposes, including determining the nature and cause of the presenting problem(s), and providing guidelines for intervention and treatment. Parents come to a counselor for expert assistance in determining why their child is acting up and failing in school. Once a diagnosis is made, the family further expects direction on how to resolve the problem.

How can we best accomplish these functions? It's not a simple process. Initially, the counselor must make direct observations of the child's behavior taking into account social, cultural, spiritual, biological, and developmental influences on the child. Assessment of any person is difficult, but with children the task can be a greater challenge because they lack the maturity and insight to adequately express what is going on inside them. Yet, these very "deficiencies," coupled with a lack of cultural conditioning, allow children to be free, honest, and spontaneous with their feelings and ideas. Naturally, the counselor will have to distinguish between truth and fantasy, recognizing that fantasy also has meaning. And just when we have made sense of the child's fantasy, we discover that he or she drew all the family figures in black simply because there were only black crayons in the box! The process keeps us on our toes.

Three kinds of information are necessary to make an adequate assessment and diagnosis of children. The first is an adequate knowledge of general theories and principles of psychological assessment, including how to evaluate and select assessment methods, conduct an assessment, and communicate findings.

The second is a knowledge of normal child and family development. The third category is information about the incidence, prevalence, developmental characteristics, biological influences, and other characteristics of specific problems.

PROCESS OF ASSESSMENT

To accomplish the goals of assessment, it is helpful to work within an established framework: a method of systematically collecting and organizing information to assimilate the formal and informal data gathered during the assessment process. The assessment structure also helps the counselor choose the tools or techniques for gathering, interpreting, and summarizing the data.

Assessment begins with a *clarification* of the reason for the referral. The counselor and referral source (usually the parent, but sometimes the teacher, another mental health professional, or an agency) must eventually agree on the issues and behaviors to be investigated. This may not be an easy first step. Parents may come to the counselor with vague concerns for their child, or perhaps the teacher has suggested to the parents that the child needs help from a counselor. If the parents bring a child and give only general descriptions of complaints, the counselor will have to elicit information to clarify what is happening with the child in the context of the home, as well as the school. Eventually, this first step will result in a statement of the *presenting problem* that is acceptable to the clinician and agreed to by the parents.

The next step is to determine what *assessment process* is necessary to answer the questions being asked. If there are major concerns about school achievement and ability level, cognitive and achievement measures will probably be needed. In contrast, if the presenting problem seems related to family stressors or trauma, measures of the child's internal emotional dynamics will be used.

Occasionally, the initial interview does not yield sufficient information to define the problem or dictate the assessment procedures. Under these circumstances various questionnaires, rating scales, and interviews will be necessary to complete an initial clarification of what needs to be diagnosed. Information can be obtained from the child's school, former teachers, family members, and others, as well as from the child or adolescent under consideration, to provide a clearer description of the problem. This preassessment process helps the counselor and the family obtain a sharper sense of direction in the diagnostic stage and later when it becomes necessary to suggest intervention strategies that will stand a chance of actually being implemented. The family that has a difficult time defining the problem may also have a difficult time implementing changes.

Once the assessment objectives are clarified, as the counselor, you must decide whether your skills and training ethically allow you to accept responsibility for that particular counseling process. If not, an appropriate referral must be made.

As the assessment process proceeds, the counselor needs to determine the child's *developmental status* in emotional, social, intellectual, and spiritual areas. Taken into consideration are the characteristics of the parents and extended family, environmental influences, and medical or health history and status.

Based on the conclusions reached from all this information, a *diagnostic description* is made and areas of intervention determined. (The later chapters of this book present details for carrying out the assessment process for the problem areas of attention disorders, sexual abuse, and custody disputes.)

CHALLENGES OF INTERVIEWING CHILDREN AND ADOLESCENTS

Conducting clinical interviews with children and teens is very different from working with adults, and the younger the child, the more challenging this work can be. There are several reasons for this.

Obviously, the cognitive and language skills of a child are less developed than those of the adults with whom most of us associate and communicate. Trying to communicate clearly and precisely with a child who does not have the verbal skills or conceptual abilities of an adult makes the job of assessment difficult. It is like talking with someone who speaks a foreign language that you have never learned! The experience can be most frustrating.

Further, children and adolescents seldom come to a counselor of their own volition; they are usually brought in by a parent. The parent observes a problem and is taking steps to correct it. This often indicates a lack of awareness or ownership of a problem by the child. This lack of ownership, in turn, creates barriers and defenses that may not be present with someone who is self-referred.

Frequently young people are taken to a counselor because of alleged misconduct—they are fighting with their siblings or failing in school, so they have to see a "shrink." This can add to children's resistance since they assume the therapist will side with their parents and add to their burden of shame.

Sometimes children are programmed by their parents to have a negative view of counseling. Maybe the child has been told, "The counselor will give you a good talking to," or "We are going to take you to a Christian counselor who will show you how God expects you to behave." This view of counseling, as punishment for being bad, can add to the barriers and make honest expression difficult.

Adolescents, particularly, may have negative misconceptions about mental health professionals. They may assume only "crazy" people see a therapist and may be embarrassed or ashamed when they or their family must seek professional help. If a child has been called "nuts" or a "weirdo," having to see a counselor may serve to confirm his or her worst fears.[7]

Consider also that the nature of the difficulty can itself be a barrier to communication. Learning and language disabilities, attention disorders, excessive parental dependence, traumatic fear, or phobias, can definitely interfere with the process of evaluation. The child may not be able to put thoughts or feelings into words that adequately convey the problem to the counselor.

NEED TO BE FLEXIBLE

These inherent difficulties require a flexible approach to effectively interview children. The clinician must be versatile (rigid procedures simply do not work) and alert to both verbal and nonverbal feedback from the child. Then, based on the child's responses, it may be necessary to adapt the method of interaction with the child. Although you will probably have an agenda in mind when you ask the child to draw a person or complete a picture story, you need to be adaptable in maintaining that general agenda in order to accommodate the child's emotional state, unique responses, and expressed desires and interests.

For example, normally you wouldn't probe regarding suspected sexual abuse in the initial phase of an interview. On the other hand, suppose that while playing with the doll house during the first fifteen minutes of the session, the child spontaneously mentions, "My daddy touched my bottom." You certainly would want to alter your planned sequence to follow up on the child's comment. In another situation a child may be firmly resistant to talking about abuse details even after several sessions. Although you would not want to forego exploring the topic of abuse, you might use indirect options, such as talking on play telephones, to help draw out the child. It is important to respect the child's right to limit discussion of particular topics or to withhold information. In counterbalance, it is also necessary to protect the child, and other possible victims, by getting as many details as efficiently as possible.

Establishing Rapport

Rapport with a child is more than trust. It is a state of understanding, harmony, and accord: a mutual understanding and positive regard for the other. When rapport is established, the child has some level of understanding that the counselor wants to help. The child feels valued by the counselor and believes the counselor has his or her best interests at heart. Normally, when this happens, any defensive attitude begins to weaken and the child becomes more willing to reveal personal hurts and thoughts. At this point a commitment to the change process has been established.

Building rapport begins even before the child comes into the counseling office. It is influenced by what the parents have told the child prior to the session. In this regard, parents often ask me what they should tell their child about coming to see a counselor. I suggest several metaphors that can be used to explain the counseling process to the child.

One idea is to compare seeing a psychologist to a visit with the dentist. When your tooth hurts, you see a dentist. The dentist looks at your teeth, sometimes takes x-rays, and does things to help the pain go away. A counselor is like a dentist wanting to help with the pain in the child's life, only this pain is evidenced by bad dreams, lack of friends, or difficulty in school. The psychologist will talk to the child and the parents, and since counselors can't take x-rays of feelings, they use games, stories, pictures, and talking about the pain to find out why it hurts. The counselor wants to find out what can be done to make the pain go away. One good thing about going to a counselor is that there are no shots with big needles or bad tasting medicine to take like there often is when going to a dentist or physician.

The idea of a coach and an athlete can also be used. The coach's job is to get to know the child and help figure out exactly what has happened to make the team have difficulties. The child can be told:

- The coach does his or her job by being a guard who stands by and protects you so you can figure things out without being scared or bothered.
- The coach is fun and playful so you can learn about yourself and others.
- The coach will be in charge and sometimes will push you to do your work, but will also make sure you have some fun when the work gets too hard.
- The coach will be gentle so that you can be quiet and thoughtful. And the coach will be wise to guide us on this journey together and make our team strong and healthy.[8]

A detective metaphor can be used with older children and teens. The counselor and child work together like detectives on TV to solve the problem of why things are out of control. Perhaps they will need to discover who or what stole the child's happiness.

The parents can use these and other metaphors prior to the first session, and the counselor can use them as part of the explanations given in the first interview. The idea is to take away the negative connotations about seeing a counselor by substituting a problem-solving word-picture that gives the child hope and self-respect. The American Psychological Association has published a booklet to help explain therapy to children. *A Child's First Book About Play Therapy*[9] can be given to the parent for reading to the child, or it can be used by the counselor as a conversation guide.

The next step in building rapport takes place in the waiting room. The first few moments of interaction can be crucial. Both verbal and nonverbal elements are important. Greet the child with a warm, cheerful voice. I usually try to make a positive comment about something the child is wearing or was doing when I first came into the room. If I know the names of other family members, I will greet everyone by name, looking for an opportunity to include a tension-breaking comment.

Sometimes I will say something silly like, "I really like your blue dress," when it is obviously bright red. The child will usually correct me and in the process has learned that Dr. Martin can be a tease. It helps to make comments that reveal you are familiar with people or events in the child's area of interest. If the child is wearing a sweatshirt from a local sports team, offer an observation about how the team is doing. If the child has a school textbook or a hobby item such as a folder of sports cards, ask questions or offer personal stories or experiences relevant to the item. Immediately, the child or adolescent learns that the counselor knows about things that interest kids and likes some of those same things.

With teen-agers, I sometimes ask to talk to the teen alone first. This can be particularly important if there are behavioral or legal problems. This gives the adolescent a chance to tell his or her side of the story before I have been "contaminated" by the parents' version. This confirms to teenagers that I have the best interests in mind, and that I won't immediately jump on their case before learning both sides.

I'm not sure how important the counselor's physical appearance and mode of dress are to children. Because my practice includes both children and adults, I don't make a point of dressing specifically for children. I maintain a routine traditional style that usually includes a coat and tie, or a sweater and tie. I haven't found dress to be a negative factor. I suspect the most important issue is how comfortable the therapist is in conveying openness and acceptance to the child. Also important are the continued actions of the counselor. If I were to wear a suit and maintain a very rigid posture and verbal stance in the interview or playroom, the child would have a more difficult time seeing me as flexible. So, once in the playroom, I tend to take off my coat, plop down on the beanbag, and enter into the activities of the child. It is the relaxed and playful, yet purposeful, manner of the counselor that is more important than a specific mode of dress.

Rapport can also be promoted by matching or pacing the behavior of the child. This is done by mirroring the child's postures, movements, speed of talking, voice tone, and volume.[10] If done, this technique should be carried out sensitively with a sincere desire to communicate and understand. Anything less will come across as manipulation and deception.

Another standard rapport building technique includes accepting the views of the child without challenging them. The client needs to experience the freedom of issuing opinions and values free of challenges and corrections, which can come after the therapeutic phase begins. In the beginning, though, the child needs to be accepted without implied agreement or approval.

Exploring the child's or teen-ager's area of expertise can also be another rapport-builder. To use this technique the counselor admits to being less knowledgeable or skillful than the child in an area mastered by the child. By expressing puzzlement or lack of knowledge, the counselor can provide an opportunity for the child to have a "superior moment."

Another approach is to use video games. Most children are significantly better than adults at playing electronic games. I have an old computer in the playroom, and besides being an excellent icebreaker and reward, it serves as an opportunity for my young clients to display skills and competency. Various card and board games can be used for this same purpose.

As mentioned earlier, talking about experiences and interests you have in common with the child can also build rapport. Hobbies, sports, pastimes, travel, or school subjects are examples of topics that can be shared. This type of conversation helps reveal a human side of the counselor that is emphathetic to the child's experiences and feelings.

Rapport building doesn't end twenty minutes into the first interview. Rather, it must be enhanced and maintained throughout the relationship. And as with any relationship, rapport will ebb and flow. But the wise counselor will always give it high priority and never become so focused on diagnosis and problem solving that the rapport is allowed to disintegrate.

The Reluctant Child

The reluctant child may show up in the waiting room refusing to accompany the counselor to the office or playroom. When this occurs, there are several remedies to the situation. If the child clings to the parent and acts frightened, I sometimes mention the toys and "fun things" in the playroom. About 80 percent of the fearful children let go of their parents at this thought. If that doesn't work, I ask the parent to go with us to the playroom. Then I go ahead with my normal interview procedures with the parent present. Depending on my assessment of the child's limits, I may suggest that the parent return to the waiting room after a few minutes of activities. With some very traumatized children, I have had the parent stay in the room for three to five sessions before the child could tolerate the parent's absence.

A variation on this technique is the use of an observation room next to the playroom. Fearful, dependent children who will not tolerate leaving the parent, are shown how the one-way mirror works. Then the parents are asked to go to the observation room. If the light is left on in the observation area, the child can still see that the parent is present, but distance has been gained.

If rapport still seems to be lacking after trying several methods, it is wise to assess the communication and conduct of the parents. It may be that the child is receiving conflicting messages. Perhaps the mother is encouraging therapy but the father is opposed to it. As a result of this tension, the child may be attempting to avoid the counseling process. Or perhaps the child is in middle childhood, or older; he or she may come but refuse to participate. The conflict at home must be resolved before the child can be expected to cooperate with the process.

In my practice, I have had only three or four teen-age clients who actually lived up to the threats they made to their parents that they would not talk to the counselor. I use this information to encourage parents who tell me their teen-ager has agreed to come but refuses to talk. Usually I can use safe topics, humor, and nonverbal activities to encourage even the most reluctant teen-ager to talk. The fact is, most teens have a lot to say when they find the counselor to be safe and understanding.

ILLUSTRATION

I had to use a unique approach to solve this problem with one unusually resistant teen-ager. Although socially immature for a high school freshman, Andy was extremely bright. His parents were in Christian ministry, but there had been much conflict in the home. The boy was filled with anger, and wouldn't talk to me. I sensed that most of his reluctance was due to fear and anxiety, not rebellion and obstinance. He simply found talking to a stranger (particularly a counselor) so overwhelming that he froze.

With a high level of interest and skill in computers, he would join me eagerly in computer activities. He also completed some nonverbal tasks such as sentence completion and drawing. Based on my initial impressions, I told the parents I thought their son was emotionally frozen. I also told them I believed he could be "thawed out" if they were willing to allow the process to take a long-term course. This involved a highly challenging adventure computer game—one that can require several weeks to decode all the messages, discover the clues, and come up with a solution.

I began building rapport by spending the entire session working on that adventure game. Andy would engage in simple nods or make occasional brief comments in response to our mutual effort to figure out the game. As we played the game over the succeeding weeks, he volunteered more and more comments. After a couple of months, he had developed enough freedom that we could play the game for just half of the session and talk about school, hobbies, and other nonthreatening topics the rest of the time. Gradually, I introduced questions about family and personal issues. We eventually moved from the playroom to my office.

After six months, we still hadn't figured out the final solution to the game, but we were spending the whole session in dialogue about therapeutic issues. The computer game was no longer necessary; it had served as an invaluable tool in helping this young man to open up. I'm not sure any other process would have been so successful. The final outcome of our sessions together was definitely positive.

CONFIDENTIALITY

All children, particularly teen-agers, are concerned about what the counselor might reveal to their parents. Two types of information may be subject to transmittal. The first is the diagnostic opinion about the status and needs of the young person. The parents will want to know if the child is depressed and what they should do about it. The counselor will almost always need to share this information.

The second type of information is the content of the interviews: the details and comments that the child has actually said or revealed to the counselor during the course of assessment and treatment. When I counsel young people, I explain that the specific details of the interviews will be confidential, but that the general impressions and recommendations will be given to the parents. I always tell adolescents that they can flag any discussion as confidential even if it fits within these general guidelines.

Sometimes there are exceptions to these guidelines, such as custody or court-ordered evaluations. In these cases, the client should be told that essentially everything will be subject to transmittal to requesting authorities.

State laws also require that the client be informed of the counselor's duty to inform others if the client is a danger to himself or others. In addition, mental health professionals must report suspected instances of abuse. An adolescent needs to know that the counselor cannot allow young people to place themselves in dangerous situations (i.e., suicide plans and schemes to run away) without informing their parents and/or authorities.

Every state mandates a general disclosure statement regarding the elements of confidentiality within a therapeutic relationship. Make sure you follow the disclosure requirements of your state.

Since the requirements vary, make sure you are aware of and follow the information release regulations for your legal jursidiction. An example is the state of Washington, which recently amended the laws on confidentiality; this changed procedures, forms, and recordkeeping policies. Technically, a child over the age of thirteen has the authority to release his or her confidential therapy records. As a matter of practice, the parents, as legal guardians of a minor, still sign the release forms. Usually I ask the teen-ager to sign them also.

INTERVIEW GUIDELINES

This section looks at general considerations and procedures for interviewing children and youths. Since ideas about building rapport were discussed earlier, this section deals with some of the remaining features of the initial or assessment phase of working with children.

INTERVIEWING YOUNG CHILDREN

1 Corinthians 13:11 is most relevant when interviewing young children. "When I was a child, I talked like a child, I thought like a child, I reasoned like a child. When I became a man, I put childish ways behind me." For most of us, childhood was quite some time ago. We have forgotten much of the detail of what it was like to be a child. As a result, we may have difficulty relating to young children.

Infants and toddlers are usually best seen in interaction with their parents. I seldom see a child under three years of age unless the mother or father is also present. The primary focus in this context is the bonding and parent-child interaction. (See the discussion about parent-child observation procedures described in chapter seven.) Another way to gather diagnostic data is by observing children at play. Many scales and techniques have been devised to measure and objectify the behavior of children at play. *Play Diagnosis and Assessment* is a comprehensive resource for these procedures.[11] Selecting the best approach for a given child involves constantly responding to feedback.

There are many ideas to keep in mind when dealing with children from about age five to thirteen. Children with average or higher intelligence and good verbal skills can be asked standard questions about family, school, friends, hobbies, and pets, gradually shifting questions to the nature of the problem, and how they think and feel.

Children respond best to a soft tone of voice, simple phrases, and short, clear sentences. Of course, playfulness and a sense of humor are common bridges to successful communication. A pat on the back or a hug (given with caution and discretion) can be worth a great deal, though care must be exercised. For example, the abused child may be fearful, and physical touch should be avoided until sufficient trust is established. Respect the child's limits; do not force yourself, either physically or emotionally, into the private space of the young person.

Many times I use structured drawing tasks like a Draw-A-Person, Family Drawings or the House-Tree-Person. I almost always give the Bender Gestalt test, which can be scored for emotional indicators or visual motor development.[12] In my practice I have seen hundreds of protocols, so I can deduce a great deal simply by the way the child goes about the task and how long it takes to complete the designs, as well as by how each design is drawn.

Often I give one of several sentence completion tasks where the child is asked to complete a stem such as, "I get angry when. . . ." Sometimes I use this task as a discussion guide to talk about the response with the child. Standard questions include: If you had three wishes, what would they be? If you could be any kind of animal you wanted, what would you be? If you could go anywhere in the world, where would you go and who would you take with you? These types of questions reveal information about the child's goals, desires, fears, and needs. The responses are most useful clinically when compared to objective test or rating scale data, but they are also useful to help direct further inquiry in the interview.

Most children like to play. So, whether the initial verbal interview has been successful or not, I usually take the child to the playroom. Some children rush enthusiastically into the room calling it a wonderful place and exclaiming, "What a neat bunch of toys!" Other children remain unmoved by the games and toys. They may even express disappointment in the toys, or may deny wanting to play with anything. Each type of response says something about the child.

The withdrawn child enters the room hesitantly and only gradually engages in play, often needing encouragement. In contrast, the hyperactive child bolts from item to item, talking a mile a minute. To observe the child in action let him or her select the toys and determine their use, then be responsive when asked for help and watch for opportunities to instruct and encourage the child in independent problem solving.

Adults frequently tell children to sit still and stop fiddling when someone is talking to them. My reaction is—let the child fiddle! The toys provide a means to keep little hands busy while you talk. This source of nonverbal behavior can provide a measure of the child's anxiety and stress.

Some children find both the therapist's office and the playroom threatening. In that case a walk in a nearby park or around the building may prove more suitable. Other possibilities include a nearby cafeteria or a fast-food restaurant, but be sure to confirm such variations in routine with the child's parents and verify any dietary limitations that might be pertinent to the outing.

At times, children are brought to the office with a lunch or snack to finish. Permitting them to bring it to the playroom usually allows them to feel relaxed, and the crumbs are no worse than the usual mess children make.

At the beginning of the session, it is a good idea to let the child, particularly an older child, know how much time is available for the interview. Often I give the child five or ten minutes advance notice that the session is going to end. If clean-up is necessary, it is important for the child to participate. The child's response to the request to tidy up can also be diagnostic. Seldom have I had a child refuse to comply. During the assessment phase I may test the child's limits some but will let the child leave without forcing the issue. During the treatment phase, I have more opportunity to encourage compliance, often with the help of the parent.

INTERVIEWING ADOLESCENTS

If interviews with family members will be part of the counseling process, it is often best to talk to the adolescent first. Some therapists suggest that arrangements for the initial interview should even be made directly with the adolescent, rather than with the parent.[13] This recognition that the teenager has a right to organize his or her own time may help the unwilling, defiant adolescent respond more positively. By contrast, when the parents are seen first, the adolescent can readily conclude that an unfavorable report has been given to the counselor before even having a chance to state his or her own point of view. This is often a situation where the whole family should be seen together.

From the perspective of Jay Haley, author of *Problem-Solving Therapy*, the first interview with the family is an opportunity to negotiate to define the problem that needs attention.[14] Through the process the therapist endeavors to have all family members participate, to have each family member identify the changes he or she wants, and to define the family problem as completely as possible before making interventions.

Using a total family approach for the initial session allows the adolescent to hear what the parents are saying and provides an opportunity for the teen to offer his or her alternative point of view. The initial responses of the counselor are also shared jointly by the entire family. This helps the counselor avoid being quoted out of context when family members compare notes during the next argument.

Confidentiality is crucial for the adolescent. As discussed earlier, the limits and nature of the confidentiality should be spelled out clearly between the teen-ager and the counselor. When possible, I make it clear to young people that everything they tell me will remain confidential, except those things that I am required by law to tell. I also explain that if I ever have to tell their parents something, I will first inform the teen-ager of my intentions.

Respect is another significant factor for adolescents. Often they are being seen because of conflicts with adults. There are probably very few adults whom they trust. Most likely their experiences have included a great deal of criticism and disap-proval. Naturally they expect the same response from the therapist and may even try to elicit or provoke a negative re-sponse to prove the validity of that distrust. Remember too, that adolescents react to an imaginary audience. When they feel self-critical, they assume others are equally critical of them. To counteract this, the counselor must convey a sincere desire to build a relationship with the young person regardless of mode of dress, hair style, or language.

Some young people will try to shock the counselor with course language or vulgar stories. The wise counselor will ac-cept this sort of thing calmly and uncritically. Above all, the assessment phase demands an accepting response from the therapist. During treatment there will be ample opportunities for feedback and confrontations, but the initial response of the therapist needs to be nonjudgmental.

Telling the young person, "I want to respect your privacy," and "If there are things you don't want to talk about today, I will honor your wishes,"will open up the conversation. These statements may even have the effect of a paradoxical injunction. That is, while young persons may resist doing things when they are pressured to do them, removing the pressure frees them to do precisely what they have resisted doing. The result can be an open discussion from an otherwise resistant teen.[15]

Do not hesitate to communicate clearly the purpose of the interview. Ask adolescents why they think they are in the counselor's office; ask who set up the appointment and why that person brought them to the counselor. Does the young person believe the reasons that person gave for coming were the true ones? What does the teen-ager expect out of the coun-seling process? Does the teen believe there is a problem which requires the attention of a counselor? The answers to these questions can help assess the attitude and emotional condition of the young person.

Another part of the assessment process includes exploration, in some depth, of the nature of the adolescent's peer group. Who are his friends? What do her friends do? What are their values and expectations for each other? The counselor is trying to identify the subgroup culture and make an assessment about the health and developmental status of the teen's social skills and that of his or her group.

Also, remember that most adolescents are attuned to negative reactions from others. If they are depressed, the whole world—present, past, and future—is colored black. They recall unpleasant memories much more readily than pleasant ones, and they underplay the positive feedback they receive while overemphasizing the negative. In a discussion like this, the counselor tries to focus on the positive, mirroring hopeful feelings and using supportive approaches. This doesn't mean you agree with the teen's values or approaches to relationships, but you can communicate and demonstrate that a person can be loved and affirmed, in spite of disagreement with their opinions or some of their behavior.[16]

Finally, self-disclosure is another helpful means of facilitating discussion with adolescents. Here it is helpful to share some in-depth background about yourself, either from the present or from when you were a teen. I have a number of stories about awkward, stressful, or humorous situations, including examples of failure, that I tell on myself to communicate my fallibility along with an optimistic hope that negative experiences can be followed by more positive ones.

TREATMENT GUIDELINES

So far this chapter has been devoted to assessment and the initial interview. The details of diagnosis and treatment are discussed in later chapters. Before moving on, however, a summary of the whole process will help give the big picture before going into the details in the rest of the book.

1. The process begins by conducting a comprehensive evaluation of the child or adolescent and his or her family.
2. The counselor must make a careful differential diagnosis.

3. A specific treatment plan is then developed with clearly stated objectives.
4. Throughout assessment and treatment both the child and parents or caregivers should be treated as respected partners in treatment—partners who will actively assist in the planning and implementation of the therapeutic work. The additional involvement of teachers, coaches, pastors, and extended family, among others, will be needed.
5. It is very important to develop and maintain a strong, positive relationship with the child.
6. A combination of directive and nondirective, cognitive-behavioral, affective, and experiential techniques will be needed to assist the child and his or her family in carrying out the appropriate interventions.
7. Initial treatment will end when the stated objectives are met, not necessarily when all problems are solved.
8. Termination of the initial treatment should be open ended. It should be clear that the counselor is available for consultation to the parent or child any time help is needed.
9. Signs or warning signals should be identified, that will help the child and parent know when some type of clinical booster session is needed.[17]

SUMMARY

As mentioned at the opening of this chapter, 5 to 15 percent of all children have problems severe enough to require mental health services. There are unique challenges in working with children and adolescents, and these require unique skills and characteristics of a child therapist. Successful counseling often involves the use of playroom supplies and materials, which can be quite varied. In addition to typical toys and materials, therapeutic games for children can be helpful.

Assessment is the first phase of interviewing children and youths. Assessment serves to determine the nature and cause of the presenting problem and to guide in planning treatment.

It is not a simple process, and many factors must be considered. The clinician must have an adequate knowledge of general theories and principles of psychological assessment, along with a knowledge of normal child and family development. The counselor must also have information about the incidence, prevalence, and other characteristics of specific problems.

Assessment begins with a clarification of the reason for referral, followed by an outlining of the assessment process, which leads to a determination of the child's developmental status. Based on this information, a diagnostic description is made and areas of intervention are determined. There are proven methods of establishing and maintaining rapport with children, and specific techniques for interviewing children and adolescents.

Issues of confidentiality must be addressed honestly, especially when dealing with adolescents.

NOTES

1. A. E. Kazdin, "Developmental Psychopathology: Current Research, Issues, and Directions," *American Psychologist* 44 (1989): 180–187.

2. B. N. Schroeder, et al., "Managing Children's Behavior Problems in Pediatric Practice," *Advances in Developmental and Behavioral Pediatrics*, ed. M. Wolraich and D. K. Routh, (Greenwich, Conn.: JAI Press, 1983) 4: 69.

3. Many of these games are available from Childsplay/Childswork. See also E. T. Nickerson, "It's Fun, but Will it Work? The Use of Games as a Therapeutic Medium for Children and Adolescents," *Journal of Clinical Child Psychology* 9.1 (1980): 78–81.

4. Richard A. Gardner, "The Talking, Feeling, and Doing Game," *Handbook of Play Therapy*, ed. Charles E. Schaefer and Kevin J. O'Conner (New York: John Wiley & Sons, 1983) 259–273.

5. Gardner, *The Talking, Feeling, and Doing Game*, (Cresskill, N.J.: Creative Therapeutics, 1973).

6. Eileen T. Nickerson and Kay S. O'Laughlin, "The Therapeutic Use of Games," *Handbook of Play Therapy*, ed. Charles E. Schaefer and Kevin J. O'Conner (New York: John Wiley & Sons, 1983).

7. Philip Barker, *Clinical Interviews with Children and Adolescents* (New York: W. W. Norton & Co., 1990), 5–7

8. Beverly James, *Treating Traumatized Children: New Insights and Creative Interventions* (Lexington, Mass.: Lexington Books, 1989), 61–65.

9. Available from Childswork/Childsplay, Center for Applied Psychology, 441 N. 5th St., Third Floor, Philadelphia, Penn. 19123. Phone: 1–800–962–1141.

10. Barker, *Interviews with Children*, 31–37.

11. Charles E. Schaefer, Karen Gitlin, and Alice Sandgrund, eds., *Play Diagnosis and Assessment* (New York: John Wiley & Sons, 1991).

12. E. M. Koppitz, *The Bender Gestalt Test for Young Children* vol. 2, of *Research and Application, 1963–1973* (New York: Grune & Stratton, 1975).

13. A. H. Esman, "Assessment of the Adolescent," *Handbook of Clinical Assessment of Children and Adolescents*, C. J. Kestenbaum and D. T. Williams, eds., vol. 1 (New York: Universities Press, 1988).

14. Jay Haley, *Problem-Solving Therapy* (San Francisco: Jossey-Bass, 1976).

15. Barker, *Interviews with Children*, 58.

16. William Van Ornum and John B. Mordock, *Crisis Counseling with Children and Adolescents* (New York: Continuum, 1990), 41–52.

17. James, *Treating Traumatized Children*, 8–9.

Chapter Two

Attention-Deficit Hyperactivity Disorder: Assessment

Mary daydreams in class and seldom seems to know how to do her assignment."

"Matthew doesn't listen, and is often irritable and moody."

"Steve can't sit still in class, but he can play video games for hours. I've tried everything—rewards, punishments, lectures, prayer—nothing seems to work."

"Eric appears to want to do his work and stay out of trouble, but he says he just can't help it."

These comments typify the frustrations experienced regularly by parents of children with attention disorders. No matter how much they love their child or how hard they try to do the right thing, problems persist. Being a parent is difficult work with any child; but the frustration increases with a child who fails to respond to the methods used successfully with other children; who continues to struggle with school; who finds friendships difficult to maintain; and who becomes increasingly discouraged. Notes from the teacher, complaints from other parents, and "helpful" comments by relatives about the inattentive and overactive child, though well-intentioned, only add to the stress of the family. An assumption underlying the attitudes of most people outside the family is that "consistent and firm discipline would straighten that child out."

"Let me have that defiant and fidgety child for a few days, and I'll shape him right up," is uttered by the impatient church member as Jeffery meanders across the stage examining the manger during the Christmas pageant. Meanwhile, Jeffery's mother is punishing herself for having taken the risk to let her son participate in the children's choir. She vows to make an appointment with the psychologist as soon as possible. This parent is desperate for help and comes to you with tears of pain. Will you be able to help?

Attention-deficit Hyperactivity Disorder (ADHD) is a diagnostic category for children who have problems with attention, impulse control, and overactivity. It is one of the most common reasons children are referred to mental health professionals and may be one of the most prevalent problems of childhood. Because of this extensive occurrence and a problematic history of definition and diagnosis, it is a topic that needs to be addressed and understood. Most counselors or pastors who work with children will invariably counsel with parents expressing comments like those quoted above.

Professional differences of opinion about a strict definition of ADHD make it difficult to diagnose accurately but the consensus seems to be that approximately 3 to 5 percent of the childhood population has ADHD.[1] This means that on the average, every classroom will have at least one ADHD child. Boys with ADHD outnumber girls about six to one.[2] The higher incidence in males suggests a sex-linked mechanism in the expression of the disorder. Girls with ADHD are considerably less likely to manifest aggressive behavior or conduct problems. But in all other features, girls and boys are quite similar in their presenting symptoms.

ADHD is one of the most frequently studied childhood disorders, and there is ample information a counselor can share with the parents. We now know a great deal about the prevalence, developmental nature, prognosis, and treatment. There is no known cure, but enough is understood about management to make the life of an ADHD child much less frustrating and the lives of the parents relieved of unnecessary guilt and anxiety.

Our discussion of this topic will begin with an overview of definitions followed by a description of basic assessment procedures. The next chapter presents a summary of ADHD management and treatment concepts.

DEFINITIONS

HISTORY OF TERMS

Perhaps one of the earliest descriptions of the symptoms of ADHD is found in a character named Fidgety Phil, who appeared in a children's story written in 1848 by Dr. Heinrich Hoffman, a German physician. George Still wrote the first scientific paper on the subject in 1902, describing a set of problems that included inattention, impulsivity, and difficulty benefitting from life experiences. He clearly described children we would call ADHD.

Consistent with the medical understanding and social climate of the turn of the century, he referred to these children as having problems with "defects in moral control" and "volitional inhibition."[3] Still was one of the first to observe that the inattentive and distractible features of these children were not characteristic of normal developmental patterns. This suggested an age-referenced criteria that was an important consideration for diagnosis. From his clinical study of twenty children he also observed that this disorder occurred more frequently in males than females. Still postulated that the causes of these problems included heredity, trauma, and learning history. He was very pessimistic about treatment for these children, recommending institutionalization at an early age.

Following a world outbreak of encephalitis in 1917 and 1918, researchers noted symptoms of restlessness, inattention, overarousal, and hyperactivity in children who had otherwise recovered from encephalitis. Described as *postencephalitic disorder,* these patterns of behavior were thought to stem from some degree of brain injury.

In 1937, Charles Bradley experimented with stimulant drugs. Emotionally disturbed children were given benzedrine, and for a time they calmed down, were less oppositional, and paid attention better. Very little additional research was done on this topic until the 1950s and 1960s.

In the fifties, psychotropic medications became a significant part of the treatment for institutionalized persons, allowing many hospitalized adults to function satisfactorily in society. This success brought about a renewed interest in the use of stimulant medications for children with attention problems. At that time the primary problem emphasized was hyperactivity, with limited attention span and impulsivity being secondary. The hyperactivity problems were thought to be a result of brain injury. One of the main terms used to describe the disorder was *hyperkinetic impulse disorder.*

The research shifted, however, so that by the 1970s the core problem was seen as inattention rather than excessive activity. Further research in this decade determined that most children with verifiable brain injuries did not develop hyperactivity. Additionally, hard evidence of structural brain damage was only found in fewer than 5 percent of hyperactive children. *Minimal brain damage* became the diagnostic label of the sixties and early seventies even though there was very little corroborating evidence of central nervous system damage.

A huge amount of research was devoted to the disorder in the seventies. Over two thousand studies were published by 1979. The decade ended with the prevailing view that poor attention span and impulse control were at least of equal importance to hyperactivity.[4] Also, brain damage was thought to have a relatively minor role in the cause of the disorder. Other brain mechanisms such as underarousal, brain neurotransmitter deficiencies, or neurological immaturity were viewed as possible contributors to the problem. Researchers also began to consider diet and child rearing as important factors.

Research continued in the 1980s, making the topic the most researched problem of childhood. By the end of that decade most professionals viewed ADHD as a developmentally handicapping condition, usually chronic in nature. It has a strong biological or hereditary predisposition and has a significant negative impact on academic and social outcomes for many children.[5]

Over the years, many terms have been used to describe this condition: organic driveness, postencephalitic behavior disorder, minimal brain damage, minimal brain dysfunction, hyperkinesis, hyperkinetic impulse disorder, hyperactivity, attention deficit disorder, and attention deficit disorder with or without hyperactivity. The current official term is *Attention-deficit Hyperactivity Disorder* (ADHD). But, as more knowledge is gained this term may be replaced by yet another.

CURRENT DEFINITIONS

To some degree, professional debate continues as to the exact features of ADHD. Most authorities agree that the characteristics of inattention, impulsivity, and overactivity must be included.

Russell Barkley, a major contributor to this field, favors the theory that the manner in which behavior is regulated by its consequences is the fundamental problem in ADHD. He hypothesizes that ADHD children have a deficiency in rule-governed behavior relative to their developmental level, along with other deficits in sensitivity to consequences. ADHD is a deficit in the functional relationship between child behavior and environmental events, rather than a problem in cognitive constructs or capacities. In other words, Barkley believes ADHD children have a biologically determined deficiency in their ability to follow rules and be positively influenced by consequences. The focus is on motivational deficits rather than attentional ones. To define ADHD, he says,

> ADHD consists of developmental deficiencies in the regulation and maintenance of behavior by rules and consequences. These deficiencies give rise to problems with inhibiting, initiating, or sustaining responses to tasks or stimuli, and adhering to rules or instructions, particularly in situations where consequences

for such behavior are delayed, weak, or nonexistent. The deficiencies are evident in early childhood and are probably chronic in nature. Although they may improve with neurological maturation, the deficits persist in comparison to same-age normal children, whose performance in these areas also improves with development.[6]

There are several clinical implications to this conceptualization of ADHD. First, the assumption that these deficits are largely biologically based should direct family and teachers to stop blaming these children for not behaving appropriately. They are not intentionally lazy, naughty, or unwilling to obey.

Second, this notion should help relieve parents and teachers from believing they are guilty of mismanaging these children. The other side of this coin, however, is that this is a permanent and, presently, incurable disorder.

Third, this view of ADHD specifies the type of environment that will best assist this child in behaving more appropriately. Clear, external rules with immediate, meaningful, and frequent reinforcements are needed. Conversely, numerous rules that are vaguely defined and intermittently reinforced will cause additional problems in compliance and attention. The design of classroom instruction, child management, and parenting skills will need to be impacted by this understanding of ADHD children.

Fourth, since this is a permanent condition, consistency, perseverance, and longsuffering are necessary. The problem will not go away after just a few months of intervention and attention. According to the latest information available, ADHD will remain with the child, to some degree, forever. The removal of short-term efforts will likely result in the child returning to the pretreatment forms of behavior. As counselors, we need to give the family a realistic forecast about the current and future demands of an ADHD child, and then be ready to stand with the family through the myriad, arduous situations they will encounter.

A fifth implication of this understanding is the need for assessment procedures to take into account the great variations across settings and caregivers, as well as across time, that result from such deficits. For example, clear rules and consequences may apply in one setting, but not another. This necessitates a comprehensive and holistic approach to diagnosis.

OTHER DEFINITIONS

Goldstein and Goldstein have presented a common sense definition of attention disorder based on the Douglas hypothesis that attention-disordered children experience a constitutional predisposition to experience problems with attention, effort and inhibitory control, poorly modulated arousal, and a need to seek stimulation.[7] Their approach says attention disorder is a pervasive problem affecting all areas of the child's interaction with his environment. Children experiencing attention deficit hyperactivity disorder commonly present difficulty in four broad areas.

Inattention and Distractibility. ADHD children have difficulty remaining on task and focusing attention in comparison to other children of similar chronological age. Deficit attention skills are believed to include selection, beginning, sustaining, focusing, dividing, and vigilance. These children have difficulty beginning activities, sustaining attention until the activity is completed successfully, and focusing attention on two stimuli at the same time, such as watching the teacher write on the board while simultaneously taking notes. Finally, they have trouble being vigilant or ready to respond to the subsequent cue or prompt necessary for instruction or direction.

As they attempt to attend to a task, these children tend to have problems selecting and screening important from unimportant features of their immediate surroundings. ADHD students may also be distracted internally by their own thoughts. These difficulties in inattention and distractibility create a dual problem for the child and yield poor and inconsistent performances in many school, home, and social situations.

Overarousal. Many ADHD children are excessively restless, overactive, and easily aroused. They have difficulty controlling the movement of their bodies, especially when they are required to sit still for a long time. Also, the extremes and volatility of their emotions are greater and more intense than the same features of their peers. Whether happy or sad, their feelings are expressed clearly for everyone to notice. This child becomes frustrated very quickly, often over minor incidents, then will forget the upsetting event just as quickly. This can be frustrating to a parent who is still bothered by the outburst and can't understand why the child is no longer agitated. Because of this volatility, the assumption is often made that these children are lacking in conscience.[8]

Impulsivity.   ADHD children appear to act without thinking. They have trouble weighing the consequences of their actions, planning future actions, and following rule-governed behavior. They may know the rule and be able to explain it to you, but ten minutes later, when you are not looking, the child is unable to control his or her behavior. These children have a strong need for immediate gratification and are unable to stop and evaluate consequences for repeated offenses. This results in impetuous, nonthinking behavior and, from all appearances, the child never seems to learn from his or her experience. Parents tend to label this behavior as willfully disobedient, inconsiderate, and oppositional. This child requires excessive supervision and frustrates parents and teachers because of this inability to benefit from experience.

Difficulty with Rewards.   ADHD children have great difficulty working toward a long-term goal. They want brief, repeated payoffs rather than a single, long-term reward. In relation to the amount of delay we would expect from other children of a similar age, they want what they want immediately. Even with repeated rewards, ADHD children do not respond as well as other children to reward systems. These children tend to emphasize avoiding aversive or negative consequences (negative reinforcement) rather than earning positive consequences. Once a reward system and structure is removed, the ADHD child is more likely to regress to the negative trait.

DIAGNOSTIC CRITERIA

The Diagnostic and Statistical Manual of Mental Disorders of the American Psychiatric Association attempts to provide an operational definition of ADHD.[9] The onset of symptoms must begin before age seven, and a child must experience the disturbance for at least six months. Further, the child must not meet the criteria for a pervasive developmental disorder such as retardation, schizophrenia, or severe emotional or behavioral problems. Diagnostic criteria for ADHD are given in exhibit 2.1.

Exhibit 2.1

Diagnostic Criteria for
Attention-Deficit Hyperactivity Disorder.[10]

CRITERIA FOR ADHD

A criterion is met only if the behavior is considerably more frequent than that of most people of the same age.

A. A disturbance of at least six months during which at least eight of the following are present:
  1. Often fidgets with hands or feet or squirms in seat (in adolescents, may be limited to subjective feelings of restlessness)
  2. Has difficulty remaining seated when required to do so
  3. Is easily distracted by extraneous stimuli
  4. Has difficulty awaiting turn in games or group activities
  5. Often blurts out answers to questions before they have been completed
  6. Has difficulty following through on instructions from others (not due to oppositional behavior or failure of comprehension) (e.g., fails to finish chores)
  7. Has difficulty sustaining attention in task or play activities
  8. Often shifts from one uncompleted activity to another
  9. Has difficulty playing quietly
  10. Often talks excessively
  11. Often interrupts or intrudes on others (e.g., butts into other children's games)
  12. Often does not seem to listen to what is being said to him or her
  13. Often loses things necessary for tasks or activities at school or at home (e.g., toys, pencils, books, assignments)

14. Often engages in physically dangerous activities without considering possible consequences (not for the purpose of thrill-seeking) (e.g., runs into street without looking)

B. Onset before the age of seven

C. Does not meet the criteria for a pervasive developmental disorder.

CRITERIA FOR SEVERITY OF ATTENTION-DEFICIT HYPERACTIVITY DISORDER

Mild: Few, if any, symptoms in excess of those required to make the diagnosis and only minimal or no impairment in school and social functioning.

Moderate: Symptoms or functional impairment intermediate between "mild" and "severe."

Severe: Many symptoms in excess of those required to make the diagnosis and significant and pervasive impairment in functioning at home and school and with peers.

The manual does provide an adequate description of the behavioral problems faced by many ADHD children. However, these criteria are based solely on behavior observed by a clinician, parent, or teacher. This type of information can be subjectively reported without normative comparisons. We need as much objective data as possible to make reliable decisions about each child. Therefore, if used in isolation, the manual is inadequate for providing an accurate diagnosis. When this diagnostic criteria is the only factor used in assessment, the incidence of ADHD will tend to rise from 20 to 25 percent, making the incidence unreasonably high.[11] It is preferable to use these diagnostic criteria as part of a comprehensive evaluation, drawing on objective assessment instruments and observational data with age-appropriate norms.

Causes of ADHD

ADHD continues to be one of the most thoroughly researched conditions of childhood, yet the exact causes are still not known. There are probably multiple etiologies that contribute to ADHD and neurochemical abnormalities that might underlie this disorder are difficult to document. There is an increasing amount of data, however, pointing to a genetically endowed predisposition, along with a common neurological mechanism, for ADHD. Briefly, we will first consider some of the less productive research into the causes of ADHD.

One of the first factors thought to cause ADHD was *brain injury* resulting from infections, trauma or other injuries, or complications during pregnancy or delivery. However, the reviews of the evidence suggest that fewer than 5 percent of ADHD children have hard neurological findings indicative of actual brain damage.[12]

Birth injury has long been suspected to be a major cause of ADHD and other neurological problems of childhood. These suspicions led researchers to study 66,000 pregnancies in the Collaborative Perinatal Project. Detailed records of all aspects of pregnancy, labor, and delivery were recorded and psychological, neurological, and medical follow-up examinations were conducted during the child's development after birth. It was found that the Apgar score, a five-part rating system for the health of a newborn based on movement, tone, color, respiratory effort, and heart rate, did not correlate with the subsequent development of ADHD symptoms. These findings indicate that, on an individual basis, a history of difficulty with pregnancy or delivery is not a sufficient criterion to establish birth injury as the cause of ADHD.[13]

While certain types of trauma, infection, or disease of the central brain may contribute to the development of ADHD, these causes account for very few cases of ADHD children. Other researchers have speculated that ADHD may be due to some type of *delayed brain maturation*. This idea seems to have merit given the immature social behavior of ADHD children, frequent findings of neuromaturational delay in their neurological exams, and the similarity between their deficits in attention, impulse control, and self-regulation and those of younger normal children. At this time, there is no direct neurological evidence available to support this theory, so it remains hypothetical.[14]

Lead poisoning has also been examined as a possible contributing factor, but at this time there is sufficient evidence to indicate only that body lead levels can be minimally associated with hyperactivity and inattention in a general population. Furthermore, ADHD children generally show very little or no increase in their body lead indicators. Body lead may be a contributor to attention and learning problems in some children, but it is unlikely to be a major cause of ADHD.[15]

Food additives such as salicylates, food dyes, and preservatives were popularly believed to be causes of ADHD during the 1970s and early 1980s. Benjamin Feingold claimed that over half of all hyperactivity was caused by such substances. He then proposed a complex diet to eliminate these substances, and cited anecdotal evidence to support his theory.[16] However, substantial subsequent research was unable to support these claims. A few preschool children may have shown a slight increase in activity or inattentiveness when consuming these additives, but no evidence has been presented indicating that normal children can acquire ADHD symptoms by consuming such substances nor that they are detrimental to ADHD. Any improvements in behavior resulting from an altered diet were primarily a placebo effect. Most early formal studies did not show any clear evidence implicating artificial salicylates and food additives as a substantial cause of ADHD.[17]

In spite of insufficient results from early studies, recent studies have been more positive about diet and food intolerances. For example, investigators have eliminated multiple food offenders, instead of single foods, with some success. The authors of one study believe their diet had a stronger effect than previous ones studied because they eliminated many offending agents, rather than just one.[18]

Without doubt toxic influences are a significant factor in the lives of these children. In my own practice I have seen many children with ADHD and/or learning problems who suffer with a variety of allergies. In a study completed recently, 94 percent of ADHD children have had three or more ear infections, compared to a 50 percent incidence for normal children; and 69 percent of ADHD children have had ten or more ear infections compared to only 20 percent of normal children.[19] This strongly suggests some type of allergy relationship. Some ADHD children definitely have food intolerances, with dairy products being frequent offenders.

Yet it is not clear how all of these elements fit together. Additional rigorous scientific investigation is needed to provide further information about such possible relationships. Dr. C. K. Conners has recently completed work suggesting a link between *when* certain foods are eaten and resulting effects on behavior. For example, sugar and carbohydrates can cause problems if eaten alone, but can be tolerated if eaten with protein.[20] Perhaps this suggests that if you want to have a cinnamon roll for breakfast, you had better have a lean steak or beans along with it to avoid becoming a Fidgety Phil.

Refined sugar is commonly implicated with ADHD,[21] yet despite widespread propaganda among the general public about the negative effects of sugar, proponents such as Smith have provided no corroborating scientific studies to substantiate their reports. A number of controlled studies of sugar have been conducted over the years and have generally shown no negative outcomes across varied groups of children. Some individual children will, indeed, react with ADHD symptoms when ingesting refined sugar and/or other additives, but there have been no documented effects for significant numbers of children.

Medical illness can cause poor attention in many nonspecific ways. There is disagreement about whether attention problems that emerge from illness should even be called ADHD. Specific illnesses which have been linked to ADHD symptoms include iron deficiency, anemia, hyperthyroidism, pinworms, rheumatic chorea, hypoglycemia, and petit mal epilepsy. These are not common causes for ADHD, but should be considered in any complete medical evaluation.

Medications taken to treat other illnesses are known to trigger ADHD symptoms. For example, anticonvulsants such as Phenobarbital® and Dilantin® can reduce attentiveness and concentration.[22] However, it is unlikely that these medications are a major cause of ADHD. But it is a good idea for the clinician working with ADHD children who also have epilepsy to be cautious about the possibility of the anticonvulsants aggravating a pre-existing condition.[23]

HEREDITY AND NEUROLOGICAL FACTORS

Heredity is the single factor shown to be a common denominator among ADHD children. Children with ADHD are four times more likely to have siblings and parents with ADHD than are normal children.[24] Children with ADHD who are raised by an adoptive family are four times more likely to have natural parents with ADHD than are adopted children without ADHD.[25]

A fairly recent study evaluated the heritability of hyperactivity among a large group of identical and fraternal twins. Concordance for clinically diagnosed hyperactivity was 51 percent for the identical twins and 33 percent for the fraternal twins. Thus, if one identical twin develops ADHD, the other twin carries a significantly increased risk of developing ADHD. The authors estimate that the heritability for the traits of ADHD is 30 to 50 percent, indicating that genetic factors play a significant role in this disorder.[26]

Before proceeding further, let's briefly consider brain functions that relate to attention disorders. Thinking functions of the brain can be described in terms of localization within the cerebral hemisphere. When a person reads a question asking for the answer to a math problem, information is transmitted from the eyes through the visual pathways to the occipital lobes. It is then coordinated with the parietal lobe region. The meaning of the words and numbers is obtained upon transfer of the impulses to the parietal lobe where the answer is prepared. Information is then sent to the frontal region of the brain where the response is translated into a verbal or written response.[27]

There is no neurological marker presently understood for ADHD. As far as we know, there is no single part of the brain that is underdeveloped or injured. No single part of the brain, when removed, results in ADHD symptoms. Cognitive functioning can be identified with specific locations in the brain, but no such localization seems to exist for attention. This means that ADHD is more a system problem than a component dysfunction. It is analogous to the brake fluid in a car's braking system. Although the mechanical components of the brake system may work properly, if the fluid is absent or decomposed to the point that it can't send the message from the brake pedal to the wheels, then the wheels will not receive the information telling them to slow down. As a result, the car runs right through a stop sign, resulting in a collision or a ticket from a nearby policeman.

So what causes the ADHD brain system to fail? The brain stem centers contain cell bodies that produce necessary chemicals such as norepinephrine, serotonin, and dopamine. These chemicals are then sent through the axons to all areas of the brain. At this time, research suggests that the dysfunction of this dopamine system is an important contribution to ADHD. Comparative studies of cerebral spinal fluid in ADHD children and normal children indicate decreased brain dopamine in ADHD children.[27] Evidence from other studies using blood and urinary metabolies of brain neurotransmitters have yielded conflicting results. Some studies show that there is improvement in the metabolic changes of dopamine in the spinal fluid when ADHD is treated with medication. The evidence published so far seems to point to a selective deficiency in the availability of dopamine.[29]

Additional support for the dopamine hypothesis comes from the fact that the encephalitis epidemic of the early 1918s which produced Parkinsonism in adults also produced ADHD symptoms in children. Research has shown that Parkinsonism results from dysfunction of the dopamine system. This close association between ADHD and Parkinsonism suggests a common cause in the dysfunction of the dopamine pathways.[30]

Animal studies have also shown that increased activity and difficulty with certain kinds of learning are not produced by damage to a specific location of the brain. Rather, these ADHD-like symptoms are a result of damage to the nerve cell endings that deliver dopamine to strategic locations throughout the entire brain. When the nerve endings containing dopamine were destroyed in rats, thus thwarting the use of the dopamine system throughout the brain, the resulting symptoms were identical to ADHD in humans. Further, when the rats were given methlphenidate (Ritalin®), their behavior improved.[31]

Goldstein and Goldstein have proposed a brain-based model of ADHD with an attention center in the brain that utilizes dopamine. This center receives input from other areas of the brain, such as the frontal lobe, and in turn communicates with the rest of the brain to regulate the degree of attention and concentration. The center programs intense concentration such as the child would need in a classroom while trying to understand a complex concept. In addition, this center regulates the ebb and flow of dopamine to allow a child to be easily distracted as would be appropriate on the playground. With this model, ADHD is seen as a dysfunction of the brain stem attention center. Children who have ADHD are unable to utilize the normal brain stem attention center to adjust levels of attention and concentration in the manner available to normal children.

In summary, the current theory about ADHD is that what is transmitted genetically is a tendency toward dopamine depletion in the prefrontal-striatal-limbic regions and their rich interconnections. Research suggests that chemical pathways utilizing dopamine neurons that originate within brain stem nuclei help to modulate attention. The resultant cause for ADHD is a type of brain or organ dysfunction which produces a barrier resulting in behavioral disinhibition and diminished sensitivity to behavioral consequences or incentive learning. It seems that in a minority of cases, children without this genetic predisposition can develop ADHD through illness or injury. At this time, there is very little evidence that ADHD originates from social or environmental factors, such as family dysfunction, poverty, diet, toxins, or faulty parenting.

ASSESSMENT PROCEDURES FOR ADHD

GENERAL CONSIDERATIONS

Diagnosis of ADHD must include observations and data representing all aspects of a child's life. The counselor needs detailed information from the parents, including both a current description of the problem and developmental information about the child and family. Also needed are objective observations provided by the child's teacher(s) and a physician's medical evaluation. Once this information has been gathered, the counselor completes a clinical interview of the child and undertakes formal diagnostic testing.

Always remember the anxiety and concern a family brings to your office. You may have seen hundreds of children, but all the family is concerned about is how you are going to help them deal with *their* child. You need to be professional and objective in your efforts, letting the love of God radiate through you in the process. The family needs to be treated humanely, diplomatically, sensitively, and compassionately. Be patient and understanding of their pain. Give an overview of the process and tell them specifically what the evaluation will involve, how long it will last, and what it will cost. Keep them informed, and don't drag out the evaluation. Let the family know your faith is important in dealing with difficult assessments like ADHD, and don't be afraid to acknowledge the limits of your knowledge and that of the profession.

Cost Considerations

Comprehensive evaluations for ADHD and related learning problems can be quite expensive. The evaluator needs to be careful and prudent about using only those tests and procedures that are likely to yield relevant information that is not available through other resources.

Even if the family has insurance, a conscientious professional should be thorough, but not excessive. It does very little good to use up all of the family's mental health insurance benefits with evaluation and diagnostic costs and have no resources left for treatment.

A professional working in a setting outside the public schools is ethically obligated to inform the family of free evaluations through their local school district. Evaluations of intelligence, achievement, speech, language, and motor development are available under Public Law 94–142. Many parents may be unaware of this resource, and counselors need to be sufficiently aware of the procedures available in the local community to provide this referral service to the parents. Another way to assist parents with local resources would be to put them in contact with a support group such as Children with Attention Deficit Disorders (CHADD).

PARENT INFORMATION

The assessment process usually begins with an intake interview with one or both of the parents and should include an overall summary of the child's problem. This might lead to a discussion of the parents' history to determine if they experienced similar problems when they were young. Many other aspects of the developmental history, disciplinary methods, and prior professional contacts are needed.

Barkley has prepared a clinical interview form specifically for interviewing parents of child and adolescent ADHD patients. It is included in *Attention-Deficit Hyperactivity Disorder: A Clinical Workbook,* and can be reproduced for personal use.[32]

Another form that is helpful is the child history form developed by Goldstein and Goldstein.[33] It can be mailed to the parents for completion prior to the intake interview or given to them at the first session. Mailing the form to be completed prior to the first interview will save time and increase the accuracy of recall during your interview. Together, the detailed interview and the history form will give the counselor an accurate picture of the child's developmental patterns.

Observation of the parent-child interaction is always productive. This begins in the waiting room and can include formal observation sessions in the office or playroom. Sometimes the clinician may even want to make a home and/or school visit.

The parent interviews and background information forms need to be accompanied by objective parent report questionnaires. The most widely used and best researched forms are the Conners Parent's Rating Scale[34] and the Child Behavior Checklist.[35]

The Parent Rating Scale has been revised to forty-eight items. Each item is scored on a four-point scale, which includes rating categories of "Not at all," "Just a little," "Pretty much," and "Very much." Ten of the items are used to compute the hyperkinesis index, which includes descriptors of excitability, impulsivity, excessive crying, restlessness, failing to finish things, distractibility, inattention, being frustrated in efforts, disturbing other children, and wide or drastic mood changes. A cutoff point of approximately two standard deviations higher than the mean can be evidence of significant attention-related problems in the home setting.

The second form, the Child Behavior Checklist–parent form, was developed by Achenbach to record behavioral problems and competencies of children ages two through sixteen. The form contains 113 items in which the parent or caretaker rates behavioral descriptions, as on the following scale:

0—Not true, as far as you know
1—Somewhat or sometimes true
2—Very true or often true

The checklist also contains questions concerning the child's social activities and social interaction. Information from these items is used to calculate age- and sex-referenced social competence scales. The chief ADHD indicator is the hyperactivity factor for males aged six to sixteen and females aged four to sixteen. For males aged four to five, the immaturity and aggression scale is the primary indicator. For all children, the results should be at the 98th percentile on that particular scale to be significant.[36]

To assess the impact of the child's possible attention disorder on home and community situations, the Home Situation Questionnaire is recommended.[37] Developed by Barkley and revised by DuPaul, the questionnaire yields scores for the number of problem settings and the mean severity. Any child whose score is greater than 1.5 standard deviations above the mean (93rd percentile) for their age and sex is considered to be deviant on this scale. Norms are available for boys and girls ages six to twelve in Barkley's *Clinical Workbook*. Norms developed by Breen for boys and girls ages four through eleven are published in *Managing Attention Disorders in Children*, by Goldstein and Goldstein.

For adolescents, Robin and Foster have developed an Issues Checklist for parents and teen-agers.[38] The Issues Checklist assesses self-reports of specific disputes between parents and teen-agers. It consists of a list of forty-four issues that can lead to disagreements between parents and their teen-age children, such as chores, friends, and homework. Deviant scores are considered to be 1.5 to 2 standard deviations above the mean.

The Conflict Behavior Questionnaire, also developed by Robin and Foster, is another self-report inventory than can be used to assess perceived communication and conflict problems between parents and adolescents. The separate versions for each parent and child contain seventy-three and seventy-five true/false items that reflect general arguments, misunderstandings, the inability to resolve disputes, and specific verbal and nonverbal deficits.

The information from the issues checklist and the conflict behavior questionnaire can be helpful in tailoring a family therapy program, particularly in the areas of communication skills, problem solving, and conflict resolution. Repeated administration can be used to monitor progress and assess change. Copies of both forms, with norms, can be found in Barkley's *Clinical Workbook*.

TEACHER REPORTS AND SCHOOL FUNCTIONING

A careful and detailed school history is essential to obtain a clear diagnosis of ADHD. The clinician needs to understand any progression or continuance of concentration and attention problems. The parental history, early report cards, teacher comments, and periodic achievement tests, along with previous testing reports, need to be reviewed. It is essential to have data from the school that speaks to the child's behavior, work completion, achievement, academic potential, and social interaction.

Descriptions from various school situations and teachers are needed. Most ADHD children do not have equal behavioral difficulties in all school situations. An awareness of the child's areas of success, will aid the counselor in understanding the child's coping skills. This data not only helps confirm the ADHD diagnosis, but also provides options for a treatment plan.

The Conners Teacher's Rating Scale is the most widely used and researched questionnaire for teacher rating of attention disorder behaviors. The form contains twenty-eight items that yield three factors: conduct problems, hyperactivity, and inattentive-passive. The scale is also scored for a ten-item hyperkinesis index. The format is identical to the Conners Parent Rating Scale, described earlier. A cutoff point of approximately two standard deviations higher than the mean can be considered a significant indicator of attention problems in the classroom.

Another instrument that has been developed in response to statistical and definitional criticisms of the Conners scale is the ADD/-H Comprehensive Teacher Rating Scale (ACTeRS). The teacher completes each description of the child on a five-point scale where "almost never" equals one, and "almost always" equals five. Children falling at the 20th percentile or lower have attention problems. This scale is also reported to be quite sensitive to medication influences.[39]

The Child Behavior Checklist-Teacher Report Form, designed by Achenbach, is a parallel form to the Child Behavior Checklist-Parent version described earlier. It contains much of the same information as the parent form. In place of the social competence scale, an adaptive functioning scale has been developed, reflecting the child's work habits, level of academic performance, degree of teacher-child familiarity, and the general happiness of the child. Scales at or above the 98th percentile are significant.[40]

It is worth noting that the hyperactivity and aggression scales on this teacher report form look fairly similar for a population of attention-disordered children and a population of aggressive, conduct-disordered children. The clinician can discriminate between these populations on the basis of background and history. For example, aggressive children are likely to come from chaotic homes where physical punishment or abuse are present and aggression is modeled by the parent(s).

The School Situations Questionnaire is the equivalent version to the Home Situation Questionnaire. The teacher responds to eight school situations, indicating whether a child has problems paying attention or concentrating. If yes, then the teacher indicates the severity on a scale of one to nine. The useful scores are the number of problem settings and the mean severity. Norms are available for boys and girls ages six to twelve.[41]

A final rating scale that can be completed by the classroom teacher is the Academic Performance Rating Scale. This scale, developed by DuPaul, assesses a child's productivity and accuracy in completing school work. While this information can be inferred from report cards, this form also contains questions that deal with organization and attention skills which can shed light on the child's attention deficits and provide more clues about how the child approaches work. This can be particularly useful in implementing practical suggestions during the intervention phase of the procedures. Scores greater than 1.5 standard deviations from the mean are at the 93rd percentile and can be considered clinically significant. This rating scale can be found in the Barkley *Clinical Workbook*, along with norms for boys and girls from grades one through six.[42]

Remember that teachers are busy people and have twenty to forty other children to manage. Most of the forms described above are fairly short and take only a few minutes to complete. The counselor should be sensitive to demands on teachers' time when deciding which forms to send. Usually I have the parents deliver the forms to the child's teacher with instructions and a return envelope. This allows the teacher to complete the forms and send them directly to me. Frequently the teacher will be more candid in commenting if they know the parent will not see the forms.

CLINICAL ASSESSMENT OF THE ADHD CHILD

INITIAL OBSERVATIONS

The initial observation phase of the diagnostic process begins the moment you meet the child in the waiting room. As with any clinical impression, you will want to observe how the child relates to his or her parent(s). What is the child's appearance? The degree of alertness or attention? Other features to be monitored include eye contact, startle response, expression, anxiety, muscular tension, mannerisms, activity level, fidgetiness, motivation, distractibility, self-confidence, speech and language, comprehension, relationship and emotional response to examiner, orientation to testing, changes in behavior from beginning to end of session, and thought processes. Goldstein and Goldstein have prepared a one-page summary of many of these features in an observation checklist that may be useful if you have not developed your own system.[43]

Most formal evaluations last from one to four hours and may be conducted in one or two sessions. This gives the clinician quite a bit of time to make observations. Most ADHD children are on their best behavior in the beginning. Frequently their difficulties become evident in their responses only after an hour or so when their limits are tested with increasingly difficult items.

CLINICAL MEASURES OF ATTENTION DISORDER

Structured psychometric testing has the potential to provide the evaluator with standardized, norm-referenced data about the child. Both quantitative and qualitative data can result from well designed and carefully administered testing. However, in spite of the extensive research on ADHD, there is still no single test or battery of tests that can be designated the definitive test for diagnosis of attention disorders. The most common psychometric tests used for the attention deficit child include tasks that measure reflection, vigilance, and sustained attention. These are called continuous-performance tests (CPTs). None of these tests is a pure measure of attention ability, and frequently questions are raised about reliability and validity. But with caution and understanding, the competent evaluator can use some of these tests to obtain quantitative, objective data regarding the child's attention related skills. Also, important qualitative observations can be made about the process the child goes through while responding to the test items.

Exhibit 2.2, adapted from the Goldstein and Goldstein text, lists a variety of tests that have been used by researchers in the assessment of ADHD. Some have more direct relevance than others. Only a few would ever be used in any one case. Most of these tests need to be integrated into a total evaluation package. For example the Wechsler Intelligence Scale for Children (WISC) and other measures of academic achievement and personality are often needed to rule out other classifications or to determine concurrent problems.

Exhibit 2.2

Assessment Measures Sensitive to Attentional Skills[44]

VIGILANCE
Detroit Test of Auditory Attention for Unrelated Words
Detroit Test of Visual Attention for Objects
Wechsler Intelligence Scale for Children—III (WISC)
    Digit Span subtest
Seashore Rhythm Test
Speech-Sounds Perception Test
Gordon Diagnostic System—Vigilance Task

SUSTAINED ATTENTION
Rapidly Recurring Target Figures Test
WISC—III
    Coding subtest
Seashore Rhythm Test
Speech-Sounds Perception Test
Symbol Digit Modalities Test
Halstead Trail-Making Test
Illinois Test of Psycholinguistic Abilities (ITPA)
    Visual Closure subtest
Gardner Motor Steadiness Test

FOCUSED ATTENTION
Stroop Color Distraction Test
ITPA
    Visual Closure subtest
Halstead Trail-Making Test
Rapidly Recurring Target Figures Test

SELECTIVE ATTENTION
Rapidly Recurring Target Figures Test

DIVIDED ATTENTION
WISC
Arithmetic subtest
Digit Span subtest
Halstead Trail-Making Test

IMPULSIVITY
Matching Familiar Figures Test
WISC
   Mazes subtest
Gordon Diagnostic System—Delay Task
Halstead Trail-Making Test

Each of the tasks included in Exhibit 2.2 measures a component of attentional skill. None is considered a pure test of attention. But since attentional skills are a necessary precondition to success on any type of evaluative measure, attention can be inferred from the child's approach to the tests.

Several clinic-based tests of sustained attention and impulsivity have recently been standardized for use in evaluating symptoms of ADHD. One of the most widely studied laboratory measures of vigilance or attention span within the ADHD population are the continuous-performance tests.

One continuous-performance test that has been developed recently is the Gordon Diagnostic System.[45] This is a portable, solid-state, childproof, computerized device that administers a nine-minute vigilance task where the child must press a button each time a specified, randomly presented numerical sequence occurs (e.g., a 1 followed by a 9). The validity and reliability studies of this system are good; it enables the administrator to discriminate ADHD children from normal children, and is sensitive to stimulant medication.[46] No single score should be used as the sole determinant of a diagnosis of ADHD. There can be instances of both false-positives and false-negatives. About 2 percent of normal children can be classified as ADHD and roughly 15 to 35 percent of legitimate ADHD children can score normal on the test.[47] The Gordon Diagnostic System is rather expensive, so only clinicians who do many ADHD evaluations will be able to justify its purchase.

In spite of its expense, the Gordon system is one of the few measures of attention that has enough available evidence on its psychometric properties and sufficient normative data to be adopted for clinical practice. Like all rating scales, it provides one source of information to be integrated with the balance of data gathered by the evaluator.

The Stroop Word-Color Association Test is a timed test measuring the ability to suppress or inhibit automatic responses. The child is asked to read one hundred color words as quickly as possible, although the names are printed in a different-colored ink from the color specified in the name (e.g., the word "red" is printed with blue ink). The test has been shown to discriminate ADHD from normal children[48] and attention deficit disorder with hyperactivity (ADD/+H) from attention deficit disorder without hyperactivity (ADD/–H). Its sensitivity probably rests in its assessment of impulsivity.

The Hand Movements Test is a subtest of the Kaufman Assessment Battery for Children. It is a well-standardized and normed test for children based on a measure of frontal lobe function. Children are presented with the challenge of imitating progressively longer sequences of three hand movements. This test has also been a successful factor in discriminating ADHD from normal children, and hyperactive from non-hyperactive ADHD children.[49] Its sensitivity may come from the combination of difficulty with fine motor coordination and inattention.

Three subtests from the Wechsler Intelligence Scale for Children have been factor analyzed into a category called freedom from distractibility.[50] The subtests used are arithmetic, coding, and digit span. Data is conflicting on whether these subtests can discriminate ADHD from normal children. Goldstein and Goldstein recommend their usage, but Barkley does not. Since the WISC is often used in determining at least general intelligence, the data from these subtests will frequently be available. You can compare the results with the other data, follow the research literature on this issue, and make up your own mind about their utility.

DIRECT OBSERVATION

Systematic formal behavior observations in natural settings can be another useful component in the diagnosis and assessment of ADHD children. Barkley provides a detailed presentation of coding systems and procedures that can be used to obtain objective and reliable observation data. Direct observations are time consuming and often difficult to standardize, but Barkley believes that observational data, when combined with parent, child, and teacher interviews and rating scales, can add greater validity, integrity, and rigor to the clinical process.[51]

CHILD SELF-REPORT MEASURES

As part of the total evaluation for attention disorder, the practitioner needs to obtain at least a general overview of the ADHD child's self-awareness, emotional adjustment, and coping and problem-solving skills. Several self-report, interview, or test procedures are recommended.

Achenbach and Edelbrock have developed a parallel form of the revised Child Behavior Checklist designed to be filled out by children eleven through eighteen. This form provides two profiles for competence and behavior problems, and can discriminate referred from nonreferred adolescents, as well as ADHD youths from normal teen-agers.[52]

The Piers-Harris Self-Concept Scale was developed as a brief self-report measure to evaluate self-concept in children and adolescents. Subtitled "The Way I Feel about Myself," the eighty-item true-false questionnaire is designed to evaluate children's conscious feelings about themselves. It can be scored by hand or computer.[53]

Many other instruments may be used to measure the emotional features of a child. My preference is to give the Bender Gestalt, several types of sentence completion forms, and portions of the Education Apperception Test, Thematic Apperception Test, or Projective Story Telling Test. For cognitive and achievement assessment, I use portions of the revised Woodcock-Johnson Psychoeducational Assessment Battery.[54] The revised test is quite comprehensive. Cognitive skills similar to

WISC results can be obtained, along with reading, math, spelling, and writing achievement levels.

At face value, several short-term memory subtests or cluster scores from the cognitive battery appear to measure some aspect of attention, but we await further research to objectify any relationship. In the meantime, the clinician can compare Woodcock-Johnson scores to other known measures of vigilance or continuous performance.

MEDICAL EVALUATION

It is essential that children being considered for a diagnosis of ADHD have a complete pediatric physical examination. To be useful, however, the exam must be thorough enough to help achieve a diagnosis or identify other comorbid conditions. The physician's role includes directing the search for remediable medical causes of ADHD, participating in the multidisciplinary diagnostic evaluation and, when medication is indicated, supervising the medication intervention program. To these ends the components of a medical evaluation enumerated below should be included.

1. The physician tries to determine if there are any medically remediable causes for ADHD symptoms such as hyperthyroidism, pinworms, sleep apnea, iron-deficiency, anemia, or medications such as phenobarbital. While not remediable, interview and examination may explore related disorders arising out of perinatal factors, previous ear infections, brain injury or encephalitis, previous lead poisoning, and heredity. The major purpose here is to provide a differential diagnosis of ADHD from other medical conditions and to treat those problems appropriately.

2. The child's physician will also need to make a decision concerning the need for medical diagnostic testing. This can range from blood count to an MRI scan. Each test is helpful in excluding specific medical illnesses that can occasionally masquerade as ADHD. Neurological tests such as EEG, CAT scan, and PET scan are not nor-

mally needed, but may be useful if the child's neurological history is significant. These tests do not necessarily validate a diagnosis of ADHD, and should not be ordered unless specific indications of other disorders are present.

3. The doctor will conduct an appropriate physical and neurological examination. The research is confusing in regard to the usefulness of soft-signs and minor physical anomalies in the diagnosis of ADHD. Revisions in the examination for neurological abnormalities, now called "subtle signs," have been made and offer better discrimination potential.[55] Goldstein and Goldstein recommend assessment of eye movements, finger sequencing, tandem gait, and choreiform movements. Storm has recommended the pediatrician conduct a neurodevelopmental exam that includes minor neurologic indicators, fine-motor function, language screening, large-muscle skills, temporal/sequential organization, and visual processing.[56]

4. Finally, the physician conducts the baseline evaluation to determine if there are any contraindications to medication intervention and to serve as a comparison at future reevaluations. Gathering information on risks of possible medication intervention is part of the physician's initial evaluation.

MAKING THE ADHD DIAGNOSIS

WORKING DEFINITION

Goldstein and Goldstein have suggested a working definition that describes the types of multicomponent data necessary to make a diagnosis of ADHD. This approach also provides a guide for the integration of the assessment data. The components of this working definition are summarized here. These criteria should be considered when making the diagnosis of ADHD.

1. *Diagnostic criteria.*   The diagnostic criteria in the *Diagnostic and Statistic Manual of Mental Disorders* form the most

frequently used and best researched definition available at the present time. Therefore, the child should meet these criteria. The definition specifies the child should demonstrate at least eight of the criteria. Goldstein and Goldstein have suggested ten items should be present for a child five or under, with the behavior previously evident for twelve months. If a child is over twelve, six items occurring over a six month period is sufficient for inclusion, rather than eight. Also, for any age candidate the onset of these problems probably will be seen before the age of four rather than seven. (See exhibit 2.1)

2. *Elevated Rating Scales.*   The child must score at or beyond two standard deviations difference in comparison to the same chronological age and sex on at least one questionnaire sensitive to attention problems. The most commonly used scales are the Conner's questionnaires (both the parent and teacher versions),[57] the Achenbach Child Behavior Checklist,[58] and the ACTeRS.[59] The elevated rating scales criterion must be met by two independent raters, usually the child's parent and teacher.

3. *Objective measures.*   There is no single test that measures ADHD. However, there are a number of objective, norm-referenced measures which range from computer-based tests to paper and pencil tasks. The ADHD child should demonstrate difficulty with attentional skills such as reflection, vigilance, persistence, and poor visual concentration.

4. *Situational problems.*   The inclusion of situational data allows the evaluator to assess the impact of the child's attentional problems on daily living. Children with attention disorder often have problems across numerous situations. There is usually a consensus between parents and teachers concerning the severity and frequency of these problems. Should there be disagreement between the home and school reports, the clinician will need to consider carefully the reason for this disparity. The difference could result from rater disagreement or measurement errors, as well as from the fact that the child may be more problem free in one situation than the other. It certainly is true that the more pervasive the behavior the greater the need for comprehensive intervention.

Goldstein and Goldstein suggest the standard for this criterion is that there are problems in at least half of the situations screened on the home situations and school situations questionnaires developed by Barkley and DuPaul.

5. *Differential diagnosis.*   The clinician must gather sufficient historical, behavioral, and assessment data to rule out or minimize the contribution of medical problems, learning deficits, language disorders, auditory processing disabilities, specific intellectual deficits, and psychological problems of childhood that could contribute to attention-disordered symptoms.

6. *Attention disorders with and without hyperactivity.*   It is important to remember the above criteria are probably more true of the attention disordered child with hyperactivity. The child who experiences attention difficulties without hyperactivity may not present as many behavioral problems in school or at home. The ADD child without hyperactivity will have difficulties during individual seat work and in small group activities. Otherwise, he or she may not experience any problems. Overactive and aggressive behavior is easy to observe because of its disruptive nature. Nonhyperactive children may go unnoticed because they do not create turmoil or cause trouble.

Research paints two dramatically different pictures of attention disordered children. Children with hyperactivity exhibit aggressive conduct problems and bizarre behavior, appear guiltless or unpopular, and perform poorly at school. In contrast, those without hyperactivity are anxious, shy, socially withdrawn, moderately unpopular, and poor in sports and school performance. Both groups experience depression and low self-esteem.[60]

Barkley has looked at the research regarding the subtyping of ADHD with hyperactivity (ADD/+H) and ADHD without hyperactivity (ADD/–H) and concluded that we must begin considering ADD/+H and ADD/–H as separate and unique childhood psychiatric disorders and not as subtypes of an identical attention disturbance.[61] For now, Barkley views the ADD/–H group as having ADHD, following the *Diagnostic and Statistical Manual* guidelines. In contrast, he sees the ADD/–H group as having a focused attention disorder involving poor focus of attention/awareness and deficient speed of cognitive processing of information.

These dissimilar features highlight the confusion caused by using the word hyperactivity to cover all types of attention disorder problems. There are many children with problems of attention, but only some of them are truly hyperactive. Keep this in mind as you proceed through the diagnostic process. There are certainly treatment implications for these two very different profiles.

An illustration of this diagnostic process is included in a case study in Appendix II.

SUMMARY

ADHD affects three to five percent of the childhood population. Boys are six times more likely than girls to have the disorder. Children experiencing ADHD commonly have difficulties with inattention and distractibility, overarousal, impulsivity, and difficulty with rewards. The current theory about ADHD is that there is a transmitted genetic tendency toward dopamine depletion in the prefrontal-striatal-limbic regions and their rich interconnections. Research suggests that chemical pathways utilizing dopamine neurons that originate within brain stem nuclei help to modulate attention. The resultant cause for ADHD is a type of brain or organ dysfunction which causes a type of barrier that results in behavioral disinhibition and diminished sensitivity to behavioral consequences or incentive learning.

Children without this genetic predisposition can develop ADHD through illness or injury, but this seems to be a minority of cases. At this time there is very little evidence that ADHD can arise purely out of social or environmental factors such as family dysfunction, poverty, diet, toxins, or faulty parenting.

The assessment process includes parent interviews and background information, data from the school, medical evaluations, and clinical observations and formal testing of the child. Forms, scales, and tests useful in the diagnosis process are available.

In making the diagnosis of ADHD, criteria described in the American Psychiatric Association's *Diagnostic and Statistical Manual* should be considered, along with elevated rating scales, objective measures, situations problems, and differential diagnosis.

NOTES

1. See Sam Goldstein and Michael Goldstein, "The Multi-disciplinary Evaluation and Treatment of Children with Attention Deficit Disorders," 16th ed. (Seattle, Wash.: Neurology, Learning and Behavior Center. 1991); Russell A. Barkley, *Attention Deficit Hyperactivity Disorder. A Handbook for Diagnosis and Treatment* (New York: The Guilford Press, 1990); and the American Psychiatric Association's Diagnostic and Statisical Manual of Mental Disorders, 3rd ed. (Washington, D.C., 1987).

2. See P. Szatmari, D. R. Offord, and M. H. Boyle, "Ontario Child Health Study: Prevalence of Attention Deficit Disorder with Hyperactivity," *Journal of Child Psychology and Psychiatry*, 30 (1989): 219-230; and D. M. Ross and S. A. Ross, *Hyperactivity: Current Issues, Research, and Theory*, 2nd ed. (New York: Wiley, 1982).

3. George F. Still, "Some Abnormal Psychical Conditions in Children," *Lancet*, 1 (1902): 1008–1012, 1077–1082, 1163–1168.

4. See G. Weiss and L. Hechtman, "The Hyperactive Child Syndrome," *Science*, 205 (1979): 1348–1354; and D. M. Ross and S. A. Ross, *Hyperactivity: Research, Theory, and Action* (New York: Wiley, 1976).

5. Sam Goldstein and Michael Goldstein, *Managing Attention Disorders in Children* (New York: John Wiley & Sons, 1990).

7. V. I. Douglas, "The Response of ADD Children to Reinforcement: Theorectical and Clinical Implications," *Attention Deficit Disorder: Identification, Course and Rationale*, L. N. Bloomingdale, ed. (Jamaica, N.Y.: Spectrum, 1985).

8. Sam Goldstein and Michael Goldstein, *Parent's Guide: Attention-deficit Hyperactivity Disorder* (Salt Lake City: Neurology, Learning & Behavior Center, 1990).

9. American Psychiatric Association, *Diagnostic and Statistical Manual*, 52–53.

10. Ibid. 52–53.

11. Goldstein and Goldstein, "Multi-disciplinary Evaluation," 5–8.

12. H. B. Ferguson and J. L. Rapoport, "Nonsociological Issues and Biological Variation," *Developmental Neuropsychiatry*, M. Rutter, ed. (New York: Guilford Press, 1983) 369–384.

13. K. B. Nelson and J. H. Ellenburg, "Apgar Scores and Long-term Neurological Handicap," *Annals of Neurology* 6.1982 (1979): (Abstract).

14. Barkley, *Handbook*, 96–97.

15. E. A. Taylor, "Childhood Hyperactivity," *British Journal of Psychiatry*, 149 (1986):562–573.

16. Benjamin Feingold, *Why Your Child Is Hyperactive* (New York: Random House, 1975).

17. C. Keith Conners, *Food Additives and Hyperactive Children* (New York: Plenum, 1980).

18. B. J. Kaplan, et al., "Dietary Replacement in Preschool-aged Hyperactive Boys," *Pediatrics* 83 (1989): 7–17.

18. R. J. Hagerman and A. R. Falkenstein, "An Association Between

Recurrent Otitis Media in Infancy and Later Hyperactivity," *Clinical Pediatrics* 5 (1987): 253–257.

20. C. Keith Conners, "Food and Behavior," (presented at second annual CHADD conference, Washington, D.C., November 9, 1990); and C. K. Conners, *Feeding the Brain: How Foods Affect Children* (New York: Plenum Press, 1989).

21. Lendon H. Smith, *Your Child's Behavior Chemistry* (New York: Random House, 1975).

22. R. S. Milich and W. E. Pelham, "Effects of Sugar Ingestion on the Classroom and Playgroup Behavior of Attention Deficit Disordered Boys," *Journal of Consulting and Clinical Psychology* 54 (1986): 714–718.

23. M. Wolraich, et al., "Effects of Sucrose Ingestion on the Behavior of Hyperactive Boys," *Journal of Pediatrics* 106 (1985): 675–682.

24. J. Morrison and M. Stewart, "A Family Study of Hyperactive Child Syndrome," *Biological Psychiatry* 3 (1971): 189-195.

25. J. Morrison and M. Stewart, "The Psychiatric Status of Legal Families of Adopted Hyperactive Children," *Archives of General Psychiatry* 28 (1973):888–891.

26. R. Goodman and J. Stevenson, "A Twin Study of Hyperactivity: The Aetiological Role of Genes, Family Relationships, and Perinatal Adversity," *Journal of Child Psychology and Psychiatry* 7 (1989): 691–709.

27. Goldstein and Goldstein, "Multi-disciplinary evaluation," 19–23.

28. L. A. Raskin, et al., "Neurochemical Correlates of Attention Deficit Disorder," *Pediatric Clinics of North America* 31 (1984): 387-396.

29. Barkley, *Handbook*, 97.

30. Goldstein and Goldstein, "Multi-disciplinary Evaluation," 19–23.

31. S. E. Shaywitz, et al., "Psychopharmacology of Attention Deficit Disorder: Pharmacokinetic Neuroendocrine and Behavioral Measures Following Acute and Chronic Treatment with Methylphenidate," *Pediatrics* 69 (1982): 699–694.

32. Russell A. Barkley, *Attention-Deficit Hyperactivity Disorder: A Clinical Workbook*, (New York: The Guilford Press, 1991).

33. S. Goldstein and M. Goldstein, *Child History Form* (Salt Lake City: Neurology, Learning & Behavior Center, 1990).

34. C. Keith Conners, *Conners' Parent Rating Scale* (North Tonawanda, N.Y.: Multi-Health Systems, Inc., 1989).

35. Thomas M. Achenbach and Craig S. Edelbrock, *Manual for the Child Behavior Checklist and Revised Child Behavior Profile* (Burlington, Vt.: University of Vermont, 1983).

36. Goldstein and Goldstein, "Multi-disciplinary Evaluation," 57–60.

37. Barkley, *Workbook*, 58–60.

38. Arthur L. Robin and Sharon L. Foster, *Negotiating Parent-Adolescent Conflict: A Behavioral Family Systems Approach* (New York: Guilford Publications, 1989).

39. Rina K. Ullmann, Esther K. Sleator and Robert K. Sprague, "Introduction to the Use of ACTeRs," *Psychopharmacology Bulletin*, 21 (1985): 915–920;

and *ADD–H: Comprehensive Teacher's Rating Scale* (Champaign, Ill.: MetriTech, Inc., 1985).

40. Thomas M. Achenbach, *Manual for the Teacher's Report Form and the 1991 Child Behavior Profile* (Burlington, Vt.: University Associates in Psychiatry, 1991).

41. Barkley, *Workbook*, 58–60.

42. Barkley, *Workbook*, 63–67.

43. Goldstein and Goldstein, *Managing Attention Disorders*, 349.

44. Goldstein and Goldstein, ibid., 132.

45. M. Gordon, D. DiNiro, and B. B. Mettelman, "Observations of Test Behavior, Quantitative Scores, and Teacher Ratings," *Journal of Psychoeducational Assessment*, 7: (1989) 141–147; and M. Gordon, "Microprocessor-based Assessment of Attention Deficit Disorders," *Psychopharmacology Bulletin*, 22 (1986): 288–290. Information can be obtained from Gordon Systems, Inc., P.O. Box 746, DeWitt, NY 13214. Phone: (315)466–4849.

46. Michael Gordon, "The Assessment of Impulsivity and Mediating Behavior in Hyperactive and Nonhyperactive Boys," *Journal of Abnormal Child Psychology*, 7.3 (1979): 317–326.

48. G. Grodzinsky, "Assessing Frontal Lobe Functioning in 6 to 11 Year Old Boys with Attention Deficit Hyperactivity Disorder," (Unpublished doctoral dissertation, Boston College, 1990).

49. M. A. Mariani, "The Nature of Neuropsychological Functioning in Preschool-age Children with Attention-Deficit Hyperactivity Disorder," (Unpublished doctoral dissertation, Boston College, 1990).

50. A. S. Kaufman, "Factor Analysis of the WISC-R at Eleven Age Levels Between 6.5 and 16.5 Years," *Journal of Consulting and Clinical Psychology*, 43 (1975): 135–147.

52. Thomas M. Achenbach and Craig Edelbrock, *Manual for the Youth Self-Report and 1991 Profile* (Burlington, Vt.: University Associates in Psychiatry, 1991).

53. E. V. Piers and D. B. Harris, *Piers-Harris Children's Self-Concept Scale* (Los Angeles: Western Psychological Services, 1984).

54. R. W. Woodcock, *Woodcock-Johnson Psychoeducational Battery–Revised* (Allen, Tex.: Teaching Resources, 1989).

55. M. B. Denckla, "Revised Neurological Examination for Subtle Signs," *Psychopharmacology Bulletin*, 21 (1985): 773–789; and M. B. Denckla, et al., "Motor Proficiency in Dyslexic Children With and Without Attentional Disorders," *Archives of Neurology*, 3 (1985): 231–233.

56. G. Storm, "ADHD and the Developmental Pediatrician," *Medications for Attention Disorders and Related Medical Problems*, E. D. Copeland, ed. (Atlanta: SPI Press, 1991) 69–79.

57. C. Keith Conners, *Conners' Teacher Rating Scales* (North Tonawanda, N.Y.: Multi-Health Systems, Inc., 1989).

58. Thomas Achenbach and Craig Edelbrock, *Manual for the Child Behavior Checklist and Revised Behavior Profile*, (Barlington, Vt: University of Vermont, 1983).

59. Rina Ullman, Esther Sleator, and Robert Sprague, *Manual for the ADDH Comprehensive Teacher's Rating Scale*, (Champaign, Il.: Metritech, Inc. 1991).

60. B. B. Lahey, et al., "Attention Deficit Disorder With and Without Hyperactivity: Comparison of Behavioral Characteristics of Clinic-referred Children," *Journal of the American Academy of Child and Adolescent Child Psychiatry*, 26 (1987): 718–723.

61. Barkley, *Workbook*.

Chapter Three

Attention-Deficit Hyperactivity Disorder: Treatment

Aттentiоn-dеficit hyperactivity disorder is a disorder that is managed, not cured. To manage the disorder, all the data gathered during the assessment process is subsequently used to attend to each specific problem identified in the child and the family. The counselor must determine whether these problems are academic, social, emotional, or spiritual. Each must be identified and treated. Everyone involved with the child—mental health professional, teacher, and parent—must remember it is rare for only one type of intervention to be used in a total treatment plan. We must remind ourselves to be patient. This is a long and complex process.

This chapter summarizes treatment strategies in parent training and counseling, child training in self control and social skills, improvement of family skills in communication and problem solving, classroom management, medication, and spiritual issues. A list of specific resources is provided in Appendix I.

PARENT TRAINING AND COUNSELING

Researchers are beginning to view ADHD not as a skills deficit but as a performance deficit. This means ADHD may not be the result of a lack of cognitive skills, abilities, or strategies; rather, it may be an inability to apply what is known to the demands of a particular setting. ADHD is not a deficit in knowing what to do, but in doing what you know. If true, this accounts for the exasperating tendency of ADHD children to fail to use what they have been taught, even when it is in their best interests to do so.

This also implies that an ADHD child's problem may not be addressed successfully by interventions which emphasize skill development. If a major part of the child's problem is a relative insensitivity or "barrier" to social consequences, the child will be affected more by moment-to-moment events than by general rules or the prospect of future consequences.[1]

Given this view of ADHD, a permanent change in behavior will be brought about most effectively by the child's primary caretakers. On a daily basis, it is the parents and teachers who must manage the impulsive, disinhibited, inattentive, and poorly regulated behavior for which ADHD children are notorious. Thus, although self-control and social skills programs for ADHD children are an important part of the treatment, the most generalization and benefit will be gained by first teaching the parents how to better manage their child's behavior.

STEPS IN PARENT TRAINING

The first step for increasing parental competence is education. The goal is to assist parents in understanding the causes of the ADHD child's behavior. The parents need to learn to view the world through the eyes of their child; they need to comprehend why their child has so much difficulty meeting the demands of the environment. Pamphlets, books, video tapes, and support groups can be used to supplement the input from the counselor. Goldstein and Goldstein have several booklets and videos that can be used for this purpose,[2] and there are several support groups that can be helpful.[3]

A second step in helping the parents of an ADHD child is to assist them in making a distinction between behavior that results from incompetence and that which results from noncompliance. You wouldn't punish a four-year-old child because of an inability to read the newspaper. In the same way, the ADHD child's tendency to become overaroused, easily frustrated, impulsive, and restless are often unintentional. By successfully distinguishing between incompetent and noncompliant behavior, parents can reduce negative feedback and increase compliance and success. This will deter the development of a more intense oppositional behavior pattern.

The next step is to teach positive direction. Most ADHD children hear a lot of "Stop that," and "Don't do that." It is far more common to point out to a child what is wrong than to give direction on how to do it right. Rather than focus on what is to be stopped, the parents need to spend more time demonstrating what is to be started. The instruction to the parents should emphasize how to convey to the child ways of meeting expectations rather than punishing him or her for failure.

One strategy is to have the parents tell the child what they want instead of what they don't want. If a child has his feet on the coffee table, for example, the parent should tell the child to put his feet on the floor. This is more helpful than, "Don't put your feet on the table." Especially for the ADHD child, to be told, "Don't put your feet on the table," still leaves a whole range of inappropriate things for him to do with his feet. He might put them on the wall. And when his mother complains about that, he will respond with, "But I did what you said. I took them off of the table."

A better option would be for the mother to say, "Put your feet on the floor under the table." If the child does not comply within fifteen seconds, it has nothing to do with attention disorder; it is noncompliance. At this point positive or negative consequences will prove more beneficial, and compliance is more likely when parental direction is given.

The final step of the model suggested by Goldstein and Goldstein is to direct parents to make certain they end interactions successfully. ADHD children have long histories of failure. Frequently, a child who has failed to comply to a parent's expectation is punished, and that is the end of the matter. For example, a daughter may be reprimanded for leaving her toys outside and then sent to her room. With ADHD children, when punishment is given for noncompliance, it is essential that the child return to the situation and comply. The parents must learn to be unwaiveringly consistent about enforcing the principle that regardless of how long it takes, the child will eventually comply with parental requests. Of course, this assumes appropriate and realistic expectations by the parent.

Within these steps, specific management techniques need to be taught and practiced. The techniques include the use of time-outs, differential attention or ignoring, and overcorrection or positive practice. Other strategies that help include the use of response-cost, negative reinforcement, cognitive self-monitoring, and adjusting the size of punishment.

Once these foundation issues are covered, other family factors dictate subsequent steps in treatment. Couples with serious marital problems are directed to marriage counseling; parents of an oppositional child can be referred to an intense parenting program designed to place parents back in charge; parents of a depressed child are encouraged to seek therapy for the child and receive instruction on how to cope with the child's depression. Depending on the success of other interventions, some parents do not need any further training until their child reaches another developmental crisis.[4]

SELF-CONTROL AND SOCIAL SKILLS TRAINING

Stimulant medication is by far the most commonly employed treatment strategy in the clinical management of ADHD children. But there are problems and limitations in using medication as the singular intervention. For example, as many as 20 or 30 percent of ADHD children do not respond favorably to medication. Either there is no improvement, or there are significant negative side effects that rule out continued usage. Another reason for using other forms of intervention is the need for both the parents and child to learn new and improved methods of handling their interactions. Even if medication is helpful, the child is going to have times of noncompliance. Years of negative experience have undoubtedly left all family members with bad habits that need to be altered.

Also, during times when medication is not taken, the child and parents need to rely on other means of handling behavioral difficulties. Evenings, weekends, and vacation periods are often designated as drug-free holidays and can be times of major emotional and behavioral setbacks if improved management and behavioral changes are not in place. Another area of concern is the social arena of the ADHD child's life. Usually the child has experienced problems making and keeping friends, getting along with teachers, and being isolated socially. The child needs help in learning the self-control and socialization skills that have been missing to this point. For these reasons a program to encourage these skills and behaviors is strongly recommended.

Self-control is thought to develop in three stages. In the first stage a child's behavior is controlled and mediated by outside events, primarily determined by the parents. In the second stage, the child learns to control personal behavior to some degree but requires some type of self-generated external direction (self-talk) as a means of initiating and following through with appropriate behavior. In the third stage, the child develops the ability to internalize these strategies. In this stage the child is no longer dependent on outside sources to direct proper behavior. As a result, his or her behavior is more self-controlled through a covert, unobserved process. If this developmental process does not take place, the child may have problems such as those found in ADHD children.

A basic premise of skills training is that children's behavior can be altered by teaching them to think differently. Cognitive therapy emphasizes that the way we think about ourselves and the world around us affects the way we feel and behave. In many situations, ADHD children have developed cognitive distortions or errors in thinking which color their perception of reality. They may take a little bit of information and overgeneralize or jump to conclusions. They may engage in all-or-nothing thinking by interpreting circumstances in black-or-white terms. When children or parents repeatedly engage in these and other kinds of thinking errors, maladaptive behavior patterns may develop. By learning how to think differently, the child is able to gain self-control and modify behavior as he or she interacts with family and peers.

SELF-CONTROL

A program teaching self-control should include material that teaches children to (1) inhibit responding, (2) repeat the problem or instruction, (3) describe the nature of the problem, (4) describe possible alternative approaches to the problem, (5) evaluate the possible outcomes or consequences of each, (6) undertake the problem solution while engaging in self-instructed guidance, and (7) evaluate their own performance.[7]

Self-control strategies used to facilitate learning these behaviors include external cueing, self-recording, self-evaluation, self-instruction, modeling, role playing, self-attribution, self-reinforcement, and self-punishment.[8]

Kirby and Grimley have organized an eight-step verbal self-instruction training program that can focus on a specific skill deficit. The practitioner first models the task for the child and provides an overt verbal description while engaging in the task. The instructor verbalizes the definition of the task and possible approaches for solving the task. The student is also shown a method for selecting a strategy and applying it. Methods of self-monitoring, self-evaluation, self-reward, and selecting an alternative approach if the strategy proves unsuccessful, are also modeled. The instructor then guides the child through the task and assists the child in developing verbal mediational strategies for self-guidance. The instructor whispers self-instructions and teaches the child how to do this. Eventually, the overt verbal instructions are faded out, and the task is completed with only covert instruction.[9]

Questions have been raised about the effectiveness of self-control training and children's abilities to generalize the skill to other situations.[10] Most authors encourage self-control training for ADHD children but suggest renewed efforts to increase the use of these skills outside the instructional setting. To address these and other concerns, practitioners such as Braswell and Bloomquist, as well as Goldstein and Goldstein, have revised and refined their procedures with enhanced generalization in mind.[11]

The integrated cognitive-behavioral model of teaching self-control skills proposed by Goldstein and Goldstein includes eight components.

1. *Define behavior.* Defining behavior requires the practitioner to operationally define the behavior to be changed. It is then essential for the ADHD child to demonstrate an accurate understanding of the definition.

2. *Teach self-recording and self-evaluation.* The initial goal of self-recording is to help the child become a better observer of his or her behavior. It is important for the student to have a common-sense understanding of the possible reasons for his or her behavior and to develop the ability to observe and monitor that behavior accurately.

    Self-evaluation allows the child to begin making judgments about the behavior. In a nonthreatening way, parents, teachers, and the counselor provide feedback in an effort to increase the child's accuracy in self-evaluation and self-recording.

3. *Provide externally administered contingencies.* If the child's self-evaluation reports are inaccurate, it may be beneficial to provide reinforcements when the child's reports closely match the instructor's observations. Once a criterion is met, rewards can be provided based on the child's improvements in behavior. Positive reinforcement is the best choice for a consequence. Response-cost can also be used.

4. *Teach self-instruction and attributional techniques.* As the child's behavior changes, it is important to begin providing the child with cognitive strategies to modify his behavior. At the same time, it is necessary to provide attributional training to reduce helplessness and to develop an internal locus of control.

5. *Transfer control of contingencies to child.* Once the child has demonstrated consistent change with externally provided contingencies, has developed cognitive strategies, and has demonstrated the use of the strategies, he should be given the opportunity to judge, evaluate, and reinforce his own behavior. The use of self-chosen positive reinforcement

is recommended as the initial intervention. Sometimes it can be beneficial to allow the child to choose and administer his own punishment for inappropriate behavior.

6. *Provide opportunities for generalization.* This step is essential. It is important to provide supervised opportunities for the child to demonstrate and use these skills outside of the instructional setting. This is usually done before fading out the consequence system. Specific planning for time, setting, and response generalization must be done.

7. *Fade contingencies.* At this point, the child has probably begun to reinforce himself internally. The use of external rewards or punishments will be less necessary. While some type of consequences will be necessary indefinitely, the more immediate and tangible reinforcements can be faded gradually.

8. *Intermittently monitor and provide maintenance contingencies.* Beginning with one week intervals and extending to one month, a brief refresher contact should be made. Instruction and feedback about appropriate behavior, encouragement for positive changes, and further direction are given. Longer term rewards may be provided for the child's continued improvement.

Resources for self-control training are provided in Appendix I.

SOCIAL SKILLS TRAINING

The majority of ADHD children experience either social incompetence or aggression, or both. While medication has been shown to be effective in reducing aggressive behavior, a component of social skills training is essential for the ADHD child having problems in these areas. Two of the major goals of social skills training are that the ADHD child will become more knowledgeable about appropriate and inappropriate social behavior, and that they will learn the specific social skills targeted and identified during the assessment process.

There is quite a bit of overlap between social skills, or prosocial skill training, and the self-control training described earlier. Many of the programs described in the self-control section are also useful in the social skills curriculum.

To be successful, a social skills training program needs to be customized to the specific needs of each child. An individualized set of target behaviors should be itemized for the student at the beginning of the intervention phase. This guarantees that the needs of the child are being addressed (as opposed to using a standardized, boilerplate program for all children). Also, individual objectives allow for better evaluation of the success of the training efforts.

Most programs seem to focus on four major skill areas: (1) social entry, (2) conversational skills, (3) conflict resolution and problem solving, and (4) anger management.[12]

Twenty-one skills are taught in the program outlined by Goldstein and Pollock in *Social Skills Training for Attention Deficit Children*. These skills include listening; meeting new people; introducing others; participating in conversations; ending conversations; rewarding self; asking a question, asking for help, or asking a favor; asking for help with a problem; following instructions; sharing; interpreting body language; playing a game; suggesting an activity; working cooperatively; offering to help; saying thank you; giving a compliment; accepting a compliment; apologizing; understanding the impact your behavior has on others; and demonstrating the ability to understand the behavior of others.[13]

Providing training in skills alone will not be sufficient to help the child overcome years of bad habits and a negative reputation among his peers. A successful program must also give attention to generalization programming and strategic peer involvement.

Generalization programming strategies can be divided into two categories: within-training strategies and environmental support. Within-training strategies are procedures and practices conducted to increase the chance a skill will be over-learned and the child will use the skill outside the training context. Barkley has described six strategies to promote generalization. These are (1) increasing training length, (2) using real-life scenarios, (3) using multiple exemplars and diverse training experiences, (4) incorporating self-monitoring homework exercises, (5) focusing on relevant and pivotal skills, and (6) having booster sessions.[14]

Environmental support is accomplished by (1) increasing appropriate skills through various prompts such as posters, signs, and cue cards in various settings that remind the child of rules and desirable behaviors; (2) developing programs to directly reinforce appropriate skills in the natural environment and to decelerate inappropriate social behavior through the use of sanctions and punishment; and (3) teaching children to self-recruit reinforcement for their own encouragement and maintenance.

Strategic peer involvement is the other component of a successful social skills endeavor. A child who was previously rejected by peers may make new and skillful efforts to engage in positive interactions, but have them rebuffed because of the child's prior negative reputation. This can cause the child to become very discouraged and can even contribute to a relapse. Four strategies for addressing peer involvement that can be used to minimize these unfortunate effects are (1) peer involvement in training, (2) improved general classroom behavior, (3) use of peer tutors, and (4) home-based friendships.[15]

For ADHD children, the root of self-control programs and social skill training efforts is the need for active and comprehensive parental involvement. The content of either of these programs will have little effect unless the clinician makes special efforts to enlist and involve the natural change-agents in the child's life—the people closest to the child. These people are usually the child's parents, close relatives, teachers, and classmates.

Resources for teaching social skills can be found in Appendix I.

PARENT-ADOLESCENT INTERVENTION

By the time the typical ADHD child reaches adolescence, problems with attention span, impulsivity, and tendency to emotionality have often improved since childhood. But at least to some degree these problems remain and are often expressed relative to current issues such as the teen-ager's acceptance of responsibility (chores, homework, school performance), disagreements over rights and privileges, and choices about friends and activities. The struggle for independence, which is typical for adolescents, is often intensified and heightened by ADHD characteristics.

Teen-agers often resist some of the behavioral management procedures that work for younger children. To help the family, the counselor can give advice on contingency management methods that are appropriate for adolescents. Strong consequences are needed. Grounding, losing the use of the car, garnishing allowances, and performing community service are a few that can be suggested. Parents should make consequences short-lived so the teen-ager is not boxed in forever. The student needs to see light at the end of the tunnel. A teen-ager's time-binding capacity is not very good at best, let alone when he or she has ADHD. It may be necessary to reinforce the parent's authority with external authority from the juvenile justice system or local police.

The counselor can encourage the parents to establish a core set of "bottom line" rules for living in the family. These rules are not negotiable, and should include serious consequences for violation.

COMPONENTS OF INTERVENTION WITH ADOLESCENTS

One of the major needs of ADHD families is to receive help in resolving conflicts. Various programs are designed for this purpose, which (1) train the parents and adolescent in a set of problem-solving steps that can be used with each area of conflict, (2) teach the parents and adolescent a behavioral style for approaching the process of conflict resolution, and (3) address the irrational beliefs that may be held by the family members that may influence and contaminate their interactions.[16]

For the family with an ADHD adolescent, there are four major factors that influence the degree of trouble they may have as the teen-ager tries to individuate from his or her parents. These dimensions are (1) deficits in problem-solving and communication skills, (2) cognitive distortions, (3) family structure problems, and (4) the biologically determined characteristics of ADHD, including inattention, impulsivity, and hyperactivity.[17] An intervention effort must evaluate the severity and nature of these issues for each family.

In *Negotiating Parent-Adolescent Conflict*, Robin uses several phases of intervention for ADHD adolescents. They can be summarized as (1) engaging family in ADHD education, (2) addressing medication issues, (3) restoring parental control, (4) improving behavioral study skills for improving school performance, (5) teaching problem-solving and communication skills, (6) addressing beliefs and attributions (cognitive restructuring), (7) providing individual therapy to the teen, and (8) disengagement/termination.

Of course, the counselor should keep in mind the major developmental differences between adolescents and younger children. ADHD teen-agers, like all teen-agers, think they have all of the answers and, typically, do not want any help. Experience suggests that most of these situations are best approached with a democratically oriented, problem-solving style of intervention. The counselor will want to develop a collaborative relationship with the adolescent. Generally the more directive approach found useful with younger ADHD children does not work as well with teen-agers.

RESOURCES FOR PARENT-ADOLESCENT TRAINING

Several programs described in Appendix I are appropriate for adolescents. One program specifically aimed at ADHD teen-agers and their families has been developed by Robin and Foster. This program, discussed in *Negotiating Parent/Adolescent Conflict*, is designed to teach family members methods of effective communication, approaches to resolve conflicts and disputes, ways of restructuring inappropriate attitudes, and effective skills to help family members relate in an adult-to-adult manner rather than an adult-to-child manner. The program presents material dealing with problem solving, communication training, cognitive restructuring, and approaches to generalization.

EDUCATIONAL AND CLASSROOM INTERVENTION

It's no wonder the ADHD student has problems in school. Successful school performance depends on the ability to persist and maintain concentration for long periods of time in situations where the student must inhibit body movement and maintain an appropriate level of arousal, and where gratification is delayed until report cards are issued. As our educational system demands increasingly more of these skills, and at an earlier age, the ADHD child can be expected to experience increased frustration and failure. Not surprisingly, referrals for an ADHD evaluation frequently originate in the classroom.

The efforts of the counselor in the school context resemble those undertaken with the parents. First, the teacher must be enlightened about the cause and nature af attention disorders. The teacher needs to understand the developmental perspective of the attention-related impairment. It is necessary for educators to make the same distinction between noncompliance and incompetence as the parents. The differential effects of various consequences must be understood because an ADHD student may not respond to the same arrangement of rewards and punishments as other students. The potential impact of this in classroom management must be conveyed to the teacher in practical and nonthreatening ways.

The second major step in the teacher counseling process is to pinpoint the most problematic areas of concern. Because an ADHD child can have so many inappropriate classroom behaviors, it is necessary to identify and define those that need immediate attention. This is much like a triage decision in emergency medicine. Problems must be prioritized and specific intervention procedures developed for each area of concern. Usually, there will be two types of interventions: (1) self-management procedures aimed at helping the child take control of his or her own behavior, and (2) interventions that alter the school environment in order to help the child function more effectively.

Background resources for teachers can be found in Appendix I.

IDEAS FOR CLASSROOM MANAGEMENT

While the references provided in Appendix I detail procedures and suggestions for working with teachers and ADHD students, it would be appropriate to include here some of the more important principles or guidelines for increasing the success of the ADHD child.

Student-centered interventions. In the classroom, there are several things teachers can do to help the ADHD child. These interventions focus on student actions.

- Provide simple, single directions, seek feedback from the child, and repeat directions as needed.
- Ask the student to state classroom rules out loud.
- Encourage self-directed speech where the child stops, considers what he is going to do, and listens to himself talk about the problem and possible solutions.
- Allow the child to provide a personal schedule and define the pacing for work completion (rather than imposing a timetable).
- Provide external visual or auditory cues to promote continued attention and task completion.

Teacher-centered interventions. Some interventions are more strongly focused on the teacher.

- Maintain close contact with parents.
- ADHD children move more easily from formal to informal, focused to unfocused, and structured to unstructured settings, rather than the reverse.
- Match academic tasks to the child's abilities.
- Pace the amount of assignments or seat work to fit current ability of child to complete successfully. Several shortened work periods will be more productive.
- Place child in least distractible part of classroom, usually near the teacher.
- Provide a constant setting and routine, but within that routine use variable tasks and intermittent reinforcers.
- Increase novelty and interest level of tasks through use of increased stimulation (e.g., color, shape, texture, sound).
- Vary presentation format and task material. Utilize different modalities. Intersperse low and high interest tasks.
- Supplement classroom instruction with direct-instruction, drill of important academic skills, or computer-assisted instructional programs. Schedule most important academic subject during morning hours.
- Allow and tolerate some movement and restlessness, as long as child is completing work.

- Provide as much immediate feedback and teacher attention as possible.
- Use positive reinforcement freely and often. Make sure the reward is meaningful to the student and the requirements are within the child's ability to succeed.
- Learn to use negative reinforcement (the child responds appropriately to escape or avoid a negative consequence such as the teacher's admonishment) more effectively through differential attention and reinforcement.
- Be positive. Tell the student what you want to have happen rather than what you do not want to have happen.
- Use multiple reinforcers for hierarchies of desired behavior and ask student his or her opinion about favorite reinforcers.
- Use response cost system where student loses previously established rewards when he or she exhibits inappropriate behavior.
- Encourage use of cognitive self-control interventions where student learns to think differently and modify behavior.
- End interactions with the student successfully. Have student try again, succeed, and be praised. This needs to happen often.
- Prepare the student for changes in routine by forecasting and announcement.
- Success in the child will come as much from adjustments in the expectations of the teacher as from other interventions.
- Help other teachers anticipate potential problems and develop preventive strategies. This includes educating new teachers at the beginning of the school year.

Parent-centered interventions. As stated earlier, all successful programs need the active and comprehensive involvement of parents. Some of the more important parent actions include the following.

- Maintain close contact with classroom teacher.
- Regarding homework:
  - Have student check materials before leaving school.

  - Use a written assignment sheet and organized system of keeping track of work.
  - Review assignment sheet daily.
  - Use calendar for long-term projects.
  - Have quiet place and regular homework time.
  - Monitor homework completion.
  - Make privileges contingent upon homework completion.
  - Check materials before leaving home for school.
  - Implement procedures to encourage self-management of above ideas.

• Help child get organized. The need is for structure, structure, structure.

• The student's approach to study should match the type of test questions.

• Implement home/school report card system on daily or weekly basis to monitor progress.

Resources for helping the student build study skills are given in Appendix I.

ALTERNATIVE CLASSROOM PLACEMENT

The preferred practice in most schools is to keep ADHD students in the regular classroom, often referred to as "mainstreaming." This "least restrictive environment" principle directs schools to establish programs that allow handicapped children to interact with nonhandicapped peers as much as possible. Most school districts, then, will err in the direction of not segregating special-needs children. Of course, this is also the least expensive option.

But if the ADHD child has significant emotional, behavioral, or learning problems, placement in special education classes or resource rooms may be necessary. For a number of years ADHD students could not qualify for special education services under Public Law 94–142 unless they had other problems, such as learning disabilities or emotional disturbance. As a result, parent groups became very active in encouraging Congress to allow ADHD children to qualify for services.

In the fall of 1991, the U.S. Education Department sent a letter to state school superintendents advising them of their responsibility to service ADHD students. The letter outlined three ways students with ADHD could receive assistance through special education programs. First, students diagnosed with ADHD in addition to other disabilities, such as mental retardation or learning disabilities, may receive federally funded special education by virtue of those other diagnoses. This represents no change.

Second, children who have only ADHD, but whose alertness is chronically or acutely impaired by the disorder may receive services under the category of "other health impaired." Before this letter there was confusion over whether this catch-all category applied to ADHD children. As of this writing, it now applies.

The third way students may qualify is under section 504 of the Rehabilitation Act of 1973. Schools do not receive any federal funding for students classified under section 504, but the law does obligate schools to modify classroom practices for any student whose physical or mental impairments substantially limit their learning abilities. This section of the Education Department letter encouraged interventions for the regular classroom, such as tailoring homework assignments, repeating and simplifying instructions, and using computer-aided instruction.[18]

There is still mixed opinion about providing services to ADHD children. The guidelines are likely to change, so counselors are advised to keep abreast of the developments in local school districts. The saying, "You are only as good as your Rolodex," is very true when it comes to helping families find educational resources. Counselors may be able to refer families to the local chapter of CHADD, which usually keeps parents posted on the regulations and procedures for working with the schools. Parent support organizations, plus your own network, will be very important in locating the public or private schools, tutors, camps, enrichment resources, etc., that are necessary when raising an ADHD child.

MEDICAL INTERVENTION

Psychostimulant medication is the most common treatment for children with ADHD. More children receive medication to manage ADHD than for any other childhood disorder. And more research has been conducted on the effects of stimulant medications on the functioning of children with ADHD than any other treatment modality for any childhood disorder. The majority of these studies show medication intervention to be a significant help to ADHD children.[19]

Despite the widespread use of stimulant medications and numerous studies about the topic, there is still controversy over their use. And all too frequently medications are improperly prescribed and monitored.

The most important concept to emerge from the vast amounts of research into ADHD is that no treatment approach is successful alone. Neither medical, behavioral, psychological, nor educational intervention is adequate by itself. The whole child must be treated. Successful intervention makes a difference in both the short term and the long term. We want to implement changes that will develop confidence, competence, organization, discipline, and character to last a lifetime. The teacher may complain the child won't sit still in the classroom while the parents are unhappy that their child can't remember directions. As counselors, we must help the family deal with these immediate concerns. At the same time, we must consider the future needs of the child. Giving the child 10 mg of Ritalin may help the child sit in his seat and remember directions, but it may not be sufficient to help him make friends.

Several studies have shown that multidisciplinary approaches to the treatment of ADHD work better, in the long term, than medication alone.[20] Possibly one of the greatest benefits of including stimulant therapy is that, when used in combination with other techniques, it maximizes the effects of those concurrently applied treatments.

HISTORY OF STIMULANT MEDICATION USAGE

The history of stimulant drug use dates to the discovery by Bradley, in 1937, of the therapeutic effects of Benzedrine® on behaviorally disturbed children. In 1948 Dexadrine® was introduced with the advantage of having equal efficacy at half the dose. Ritalin® was released in 1954 with the hope it would have fewer side effects and less abuse potential. Today, Ritalin is used in over 90 percent of the ADHD cases where some type of stimulant medication is prescribed.

In 1957, Laufer described the "hyperkinetic impulse disorder," which he believed was caused by a maturational lag in the development of the central nervous system. He asserted that stimulant drugs were the treatment of choice for this disorder and postulated that they acted by stimulating the midbrain, placing it in a more syhchronous balance with the outer cerebral cortex. This was an oversimplification, but the exact mechanism of action of these drugs is still unknown.[21]

It is postulated that stimulant drugs act by affecting the catecholamine neurotransmitters (especially dopamine) in the brain. Some believe ADHD develops from a dopamine deficiency, which can be corrected by stimulant drug treatment. At one time it was felt stimulant drugs created a paradoxical reaction in ADHD youngsters. This is no longer believed to be the case, since the response to stimulant drugs is neither paradoxical nor specific.

Attention deficit can be viewed as a result of the malfunction of the attention system. This system allows the brain to discriminate situations where focused, deliberate behavior is appropriate from situations where quick, impulsive actions are needed. ADHD children are not able to control their attentional skills. They may be intently concentrating when they should be aware of their surroundings. Or they may be easily distracted and ready to run off when they should be focused. Medication works to enhance the functioning of the attentional system so that children can choose when to be sensitive to outside distractions and when to focus their attention. The attention center is stimulated by these medications, and the child has improved control.[22]

The decision to proceed with medication intervention must be based on the comparison of the risks, benefits, and alternative treatments available. We will look at these considerations individually.

SHORT-TERM SIDE EFFECTS

After reviewing 110 studies involving more than 4200 hyperactive children, Barkley concluded that the primary side effects noted were insomnia, anorexia or loss of appetite, weight loss, and irritability. These and other side effects were reported to be transitory and to disappear with a reduction in drug dosage.[23]

Other mild but less common side effects included sadness, depression, fearfulness, social withdrawal, sleepiness, headaches, nail biting, and stomach upset. These were also reported to resolve spontaneously with a decrease in dosage, or they were considered acceptable side effects in light of clinical improvement. These side effects are mild, but they occur in 20 to 50 percent of children treated with stimulant medication.[24]

Toxic psychosis and seizures have occurred in a very few cases, and the symptoms resolved when the medication was discontinued. Children with a family history of epilepsy may be at greater risk, and the physician should consider this when evaluating the possibility of stimulant medication treatment.

One serious side effect of stimulant medications is a possible increase in nervous tics. A number of irreversible instances of Tourette's disorder have also been reported as secondary to stimulant treatment. Tourette's disorder is a neurological condition composed of multiple, persistent motor tics and compulsive vocalizations.[25] The combination of motor and vocal tics is considered diagnostic, but they need not occur at the same time.

Perhaps fewer than one percent of ADHD children treated with stimulants develop a tic disorder, but in 13 percent of the cases, stimulants may exacerbate preexisting tics. Therefore, it is prudent to screen children with ADHD for a personal or family history of tics or Tourette's disorder prior to initiating stimulant therapy.

Another side effect that has been reported is a "behavioral rebound" phenomenon. Typically, this is described as a deterioration in behavior that occurs in the late afternoon and evening following daytime administrations of medication. Research has suggested this seldom happens, but when it does, adjustments in dosage and scheduling usually resolve the problem.

The consensus is that side effects of medical stimulants do occur, but in the majority of cases, either they cease after one or two weeks of continued treatment or they are alleviated by adjusting the dosage. Alternatively, different stimulant medications can be tried. It has been estimated that one to three percent of children with ADHD cannot tolerate any dose of stimulant medication.[26]

LONG-TERM SIDE EFFECTS

To date, there are no reported cases of addiction or serious drug dependence with these medications. Studies have examined the question of whether children on these drugs are more likely to abuse other substances as teen-agers, and the results suggest there is no increase in the likelihood of drug abuse.[27] More research is needed on this topic, but the risk of future drug abuse appears to be quite low.

Another possible long-term side effect is the suppression of height and weight gain. Presently, it is believed that suppression in growth is a relatively transient side effect of the first year or so of treatment and has no significant effect on eventual adult height and weight. Furthermore, there is evidence to suggest that if medication is discontinued at various points in the year a growth rebound will occur. Nevertheless, it is wise for the physician to monitor growth in children receiving stimulant medications.[28]

With what we now know about stimulant medication, contraindications include known hypersensitivity or allergic reaction to the drug, seizure history, glaucoma, hypertension, history of tics, hyperthyroidism, and pregnancy.

BENEFITS OF MEDICATION

Between 70 and 80 percent of children appear to exhibit a positive response to stimulant medication, and for about 20 to 30 percent of the children, medication brings about a dramatic improvement. The effect is both immediate and obvious. Often within the first hour after treatment a perceptible change in handwriting, talking, motility, attending, planfulness, and perception is observed. Classroom teachers may notice improvement in deportment and academic productivity after a single dose. Parents will report a marked reduction in troublesome sibling interactions, inappropriate activity, and noncompliance. Even peers can identify the calmer, more organizing, cooperative behavior of these stimulant-treated children.[29]

In summary, the primary benefits are the improvement of attention span and the reduction of disruptive, inappropriate, and impulsive behavior. Compliance with authority figures' commands is increased, and children's peer relations also may improve, primarily through reduction in aggression. In addition, if carefully titrated, the medication can enhance academic performance.[30]

Although these medications are certainly helpful in the day-to-day management of ADHD, they have not been demonstrated to lead to enduring positive changes after their cessation. Research has been very clear that stimulant medications are not a panacea for ADHD and should not be the sole treatment employed in most cases. The numerous skill deficits these children have still need attention and remediation.

PRESCRIBING PROCEDURES

Ritalin® (methylphenidate) is available in 5, 10, and 20 mg tablets. This is a short-acting tablet that most commonly lasts four hours. Ritalin-SR® is a sustained-release product with effects lasting six to eight hours. The usual initial dosage of standard Ritalin for children under eight is a single 5 mg tablet in the morning; for children over eight it is a single 10 mg tablet in the morning. Each week the daily dosage can be increased by 5 mg and 10 mg a day, respectively. Usually tablets are taken at breakfast and lunch. Occasionally an after-school dose is necessary. The total maximum dosage should not exceed 60 mg, although under extreme situations 80 mg/day dosages are prescribed.[31]

The amphetamines are quite similar in their pharmacologic makeup. Dexedrine (d-amphetamine) comes in 5, 10, and 15 mg tablets and capsules; in a liquid elixir preparation with 5 mg per teaspoon; and in slow-release capsules of 5, 10, and 15 mg. The dosage is approximately half that of Ritalin.

Benzedrine is available in 5, 10, and 15 mg tablets and in a 15 mg sustained-release capsule. The dosage range is similar to Dexedrine (5–60 mg/day).

Desoxyn® is available in 2.5 and 5 mg tablets and in 5, 10, and 15 mg sustained-release capsules. Pharmacological actions are similar to those of Dexedrine and Benzedrine.

Cylert® (pemoline) is given once a day, which gives it an advantage over the shorter-acting preparations. It has a gradual onset of action. Significant clinical benefits may not be evident until the third or fourth week of treatment, possibly as late as the sixth week. The drug is available in 18.75, 37.5 and 75 mg tablets and in 37.5 mg chewable tablets. The recommended starting dose is 37.5 mg/day, and the dosage is increased in daily increments of 18.75 mg per week until the desired clinical effects are reached. The effective daily dose for most patients ranges between 56.25 and 75 mg. The maximum daily dose is 112.5 mg. Periodic liver function tests are required.[32]

Tricyclic antidepressants including Tofranil® (imipramine) and Norpramine® (desiprimine) have also been prescribed for the treatment of ADHD. The bulk of the literature suggests that, overall, psychostimulants tend to be superior to the tricyclics in managing ADHD symptoms.[33] However, there may be a subgroup of children, particularly those who show signs of anxiety, depression, or sleep problems, or who have tics or psychosis, who may respond better to the tricyclics.

Clonidine® (catapres) is an antihypertensive medication that has recently been used to treat ADHD symptoms. Its frequency of side effects in ADHD children has not yet clearly been demonstrated. It is available in transdermal skin patches which allow the release of medicine evenly throughout the day. Since Clonidine is also used for treatment of Tourette's syndrome, it may prove useful in ADHD children who have tics or who have developed tics on methylphenidate.

Prozac® (fluoxetine), the nation's most-prescribed antidepressant, has recently been used with ADHD children. While a number of physicians have used Prozac with ADHD children, at this time there is very little research to document its usefulness with this population.

Regardless which medication is employed, some common principles should apply.

1. The dose should be the lowest possible and be given only as many times per day as necessary to achieve adequate management of the child's behavior.

2. In most cases, medication should be discontinued on holidays or summer vacations, unless absolutely necessary.

3. Titration should be based on objective assessment of the child's resulting behavior and should start with the lowest possible increment.

4. Sufficient time (e.g., five to seven days) should be allowed for evaluation of the efficacy of each dosage.

5. Parents should never be given permission to adjust the dosage of medication without consulting the physician. (Often overmedication occurs, since parents may increase the dosage every time the child misbehaves.)

6. Never force medication on a family or child, particularly an adolescent.

7. Provide accurate information to the family about all aspects of the medication.

WHEN TO USE MEDICATION

One of the most difficult decisions to make in clinical practice is when to use medication. The fact a child has been diagnosed as ADHD does not imply an automatic recommendation of drug treatment. Barkley has summarized the following guidelines as aids in making the medication decision.[34]

1. Has the child had adequate physical and psychological evaluations? Medications should never be prescribed if the child has not been directly examined in a thorough manner.

2. How old is the child? Pharmacotherapy is often less effective or leads to more severe side effects among children under the age of four. It is, therefore, not usually recommended in such cases.

3. Have other therapies been used? If this is the family's initial contact with the professional, prescription of

medication should perhaps be postponed until other interventions have been attempted. Alternatively, when the child's behavior presents a severe problem and the family cannot participate in child management training, medication may be the most practical initial treatment.

4. How severe is the child's current misbehavior? In some cases, the child's behavior is so unmanageable or distressing to the family that medication may prove the fastest and most effective manner of dealing with the crisis until other forms of treatment can commence. Once progress is made with other therapies, some effort can be made to reduce or terminate the medication, though this is not always possible.

5. Can the family afford the medication and associated costs? Long-term compliance rates are typically poor and may be especially problematic among families of low socioeconomic status. Of course, the ability to afford and comply with alternative treatments would also be suspect.

6. Are the parents sufficiently intelligent to supervise the use of the medications and guard against their abuse?

7. What are the parents' attitudes toward pharmacotherapy? Some parents are simply "antidrug" and should not be coerced into agreeing to this treatment.

8. Is there a delinquent sibling or drug-abusing parent in the household? In this case, psychostimulant medication should not be prescribed since there is a high risk of its illicit use or sale.

9. Does the child have any history of tics, psychosis, or thought disorder? If so, the stimulants are contraindicated, as they may exacerbate such difficulties.

10. Is the child highly anxious, fearful, or more likely to complain of psychosomatic disturbances? Such a child is less likely to respond positively to stimulant medications and may exhibit a better response to antidepressant medications.

11. Does the physician have the time to monitor medication effects properly? In addition to an initial assessment of drug efficacy and establishment of the optimal dosage, periodic reassessment of drug response and effects on height and weight should be conducted throughout the year.

12. How does the child feel about medication and its alternatives? With older children and adolescents, it is important that the use of medication be discussed with them and its rationale fully explained. In cases where children are "antidrug" or oppositional, they may sabotage efforts to use it. Sometimes the metaphor of wearing glasses for a visual handicap can help explain medication without a stigma.

EVALUATION OF MEDICAL INTERVENTION

Since the response of each child to medications is different, it is important to collect object data regarding changes in the child's behavior across several doses. The best approach is to determine the child's optimal dose in the context of a double-blind, placebo-controlled assessment paradigm that includes multiple measures collected from the home, school, and clinic.[35] The use of a placebo reduces the effects of positive biases that can show up on rating scales when the rater knows the child is taking a medication.

Often the resources are not available to complete a placebo-controlled medication evaluation, but the clinician should make sure some types of objective measures are obtained. The Revised Conner's Teacher and Parent Rating Scales (CPRS/CTRS), the ADD Comprehensive Teacher Rating Scale (ACTeRs), the Home Situations Questionnaire (HSQ), and the School Situations Questionnaire (SSQ) can be used successfully for this purpose. These were all described in the previous chapter on assessment procedures. Barkley also recommends the ADHD Rating Scale, the Academic Performance Rating Scale, and the Stimulant Drug Side Effects Rating Scale. They can be found in his *Clinical Workbook*.

When giving these tests, it is important to recognize that there is often a practice effect, particularly between the first and second administration of rating scales, that can result in a significant decline in scores. It is recommended that the scales be given twice before using them in drug trials and to use the second administration as the baseline against which to measure changes.

There are many other considerations in implementing and monitoring medication intervention. The material by Goldstein and Goldstein, Barkley, and Copeland are very helpful and complete.[36]

OTHER MEDICAL INTERVENTIONS

Any concurrent illnesses, such as allergies, should be treated as effectively as possible. Research has not validated concerns about food additives, sugar, or diet with ADHD children in general, though there may be a correlation in a particular child. Encourage your clients to follow valid standard medical, nutritional, and psychological practices, but listen to the descriptions of their child. Many parents have a good sense of how different environmental factors influence their son or daughter. Remember to alter only one thing at a time. If the parents' descriptions seem to have merit, help them systematically explore changes in diet or environment that might be affecting their child. Dr. Conners' book, *Feeding the Brain: How Foods Affect Children* (Plenum, 1989), might be a helpful resource here.

SPIRITUAL INTERVENTION

GENERAL SPIRITUAL GUIDELINES

As we conclude our discussion of treatment of the ADHD child, we need to fulfill the commitment to treat the whole person by addressing some relevant spiritual issues. Christian parents will come to a Christian counselor because of their common faith. They expect the counselor to understand the causes, diagnosis, and treatment of ADHD, but beyond that, the Christian parents depend on the counselor's faith and trust in God as an added resource in discerning what to do for their child. This section provides a brief sample of some of the ideas and principles I have used in counseling with parents of ADHD children.

In addition to clinical intervention procedures, parents may ask how Scripture relates to these child management procedures. I often tell parents that their mandate for Christian parenting is first found in Deuteronomy.

> Hear, O Israel: The LORD our God, the LORD is one. Love the LORD your God with all your heart and with all your soul and with all your strength. These commandments that I give you today are to be upon your hearts. Impress them on your children. Talk about them when you sit at home and when you walk along the road, when you lie down and when you get up. Tie them as symbols on your hands and bind them on your foreheads. Write them on the doorframes of your houses and on your gates.(Deut. 6:4–9 NIV)

The whole basis of Christian parenting is predicated on our faith in God. Nothing else matters unless we first love God with our whole being. The rest of the injunctions follow from that requirement. This passage suggests that parents have four methods of influencing or guiding their child.

The first form of influence is by the example set by each of the parents. We are to "impress" our children on both matters of faith and of life. We do this by action, as well as by word (see 1 Kings 9:4; 2 Chron. 17:3; and 2 Tim. 1:5). The old saying, "Do as I say, not as I do," simply does not carry any weight. You can expect the child to follow the model that is seen every day much more readily than the occasional lecture. Of course, this starts the first day of life. If a teen-ager has experienced fifteen years of negative communication from his or her parents, changes in behavior and thought processes are not going to happen overnight.

The second form of influence is the instruction or teaching provided by the parents. We are to "talk" about our love of God, our beliefs and values, and why they are important (Prov. 22:6; Col. 3:16; 2 Tim. 3:15). Deuteronomy 4:9 instructs us,

". . . Teach them to your children and to their children after them."(NIV) This can be informal as well as formal. It can occur during the chat that takes place while taking the garbage out, in the stories told at dinner time, as well as in the instruction given during devotions or at family meetings. It's true. Sometimes the message appears to be going in one ear and out the other, but the values, attitudes, opinions, and beliefs of the child are guided by parental instruction. The choice of schools and extracurricular activities also fall into this category, and should be undertaken with care and thoughtfulness.

The next form of parental impact takes place through consequences. The "commandments" mentioned in Deuteronomy 6:6 included the consequences of God's discipline. Likewise, parents are to exercise loving authority with their children (Prov. 19:18; 23:13, 14; 29:15, 17).

The final injunction to parents is to present our children to God in prayer (Gen. 17:18; 2 Sam. 12:16). The Bible speaks of several New Testament parents who petitioned Christ for the benefit of their children (Matt. 17:15; Mark 7:26). We are to pray continually for our children, petitioning God for their spiritual and physical well-being. Encourage parents to make prayer and spiritual warfare a high and ongoing priority.

The ADHD child needs consistent structure, as all children do; it's just that the ADHD child needs more of it, and for a longer periods of time. The Scriptures identify basic principles of structure that ADHD children need. I share these with parents.

The first principle is *clarity* (Matt. 5:37). Because these parents are competing with a distractible and inattentive nature, they need to make their instructions clear and simple. When parents say "no," they should act accordingly. It only makes the problem worse if an ADHD child learns that Mom will eventually give in if badgered long enough. The parent should make the rule and stick to it unless there is clear evidence to change. The rules and consequences for violating those rules should be spelled out clearly. Rewards for success should be equally clear.

The second principle is *consistency*. Psalm 15:4 talks about a man keeping his word. Two types of consistency affect an

ADHD child. First is the need for both parents to enforce the same expectations, to the same degree, from day to day, week after week. This is consistency over time. No one does this perfectly, but the goal is to be as reliable as possible.

A second aspect is consistency between parents. Dad should enforce the rules to the same degree that Mother enforces the rules. An ADHD child cannot handle a wide variation between the disciplinary styles of the parents. The parents need to work for as much uniformity as possible.

Constancy is the third principle we see in Scripture that applies to the ADHD child (2 Tim. 1:5). Just as Timothy saw sincere faith in three generations of women, parents are to be diligent, persistent, and constant. ADHD children are demanding. Patience will run out and cross words will be spoken but grace needs to be extended to the child again and again. This is what the child needs. The parents need to tell the child they love him or her, and they need to show it on a regular and continuing basis.

Another principle seen in Scripture is the importance of *enforceability* (Eccles. 8:11). Parents should not make idle threats. If parents do not intend to or cannot carry out a threat, they should not make it (Prov. 29:20). Hasty comments are harmful. ADHD children have trouble using rules and abstract values to control their behavior. They are governed by the immediate, so parents need to enforce rules immediately. None of this, "Wait until your father gets home." By that time the child will have forgotten what the consequence was all about, and its effect will be lost.

Finally, we see the principle of *fairness* (Gen. 25:28, 37:3). These Old Testament references show that resentment develops when children perceive they are not being treated fairly. Granted, children often confuse equality with fairness, but parents need to discuss their mutual expectations for their ADHD child. These expectations should correspond with both developmental considerations and known ADHD features. Fairness occurs when their expectations match the abilities of their child.

Parents should further consider carefully the differences between noncompliance and incompetence. It is unfair to reprimand or punish a child for doing something that is out of his or her control. With ADHD children, it is certainly not easy to make that distinction, but that is where experience and prayerful discernment come into action—to help parents know when to "lower the boom" and when to back off.

Being a Christian parent does not take the hard work out of raising an ADHD child, but it does give us the spiritual resources to cope with the frustrations.[37]

<h3 style="text-align:center">SUMMARY</h3>

ADHD is a condition that is managed, not cured. Each of the child's problems must be identified and treated. It is rare for only one type of intervention to be used in a total treatment plan.

The first component of the treatment plan discussed in this chapter was parent training and counseling. The steps for increasing parental competence are education, distinguishing incompetence from noncompliance in the child, teaching positive direction, and learning to end interactions successfully.

The second component is self-control and social skills training. A basic premise of skills training is that children's behavior can be altered by teaching them to think differently. Most social skills programs focus on four major skill areas: (1) social entry, (2) conversational skills, (3) conflict resolution and problem solving, and (4) anger management. A variety of programs is available to teach parenting skills as well as self-control and social skills.

The next component in a treatment plan is parent-adolescent intervention. Families with ADHD children need help in resolving conflicts. Programs are available to help with this. They can be used to (1) train the parents and adolescent in a set of problem-solving steps that can be used with each area of conflict; (2) teach the parents and adolescent a behavioral style for approaching the process of conflict resolution; (3) address any irrational beliefs held by the family members that may influence and contaminate their interactions.

There are numerous ideas to facilitate educational intervention, including ideas for training teachers as well as specific procedures for classroom management.

Psychostimulant medication is the most common treatment for children with ADHD. The significant benefits of medication are evident in 70 to 80 percent of the children to whom it is given. Various prescribing procedures were discussed. Evaluation of effects is very important, and there are short-term and long-term side effects, which necessitate a variety of instruments and methods for monitoring medication.

NOTES

1. Russel A. Barkley, *Cognitive-Behavioral Therapy with ADHD Children*, L. Braswell and M. L. Bloomquist, ed. (New York: The Guilford Press, 1991) vii–xi.

2. Sam Goldstein and Michael Goldstein, *Parent's Guide: Attention-deficit Hyperactivity Disorder*, (Salt Lake City: Neurology, Learning & Behavior Center, 1990); and S. Goldstein, *Why Won't my Child Pay Attention? A Video Guide for Parents* (Salt Lake City: Neurology, Learning and Behavior Center, 1989).

3. Helpful support groups are (1) ADDA, 4300 West Park Blvd., Plano, TX 75093; (2) "A Newsletter on Attention-Deficit Hyperactivity Disorder," from Challenge, P.O. Box 2001, West Newbury, MA 01985, (508) 462–0495; and CHADD, National Headquarters, Suite 185, 1859 North Pine Island Road, Plantation FL 33322, (305) 587–3700.

4. Sam Goldstein and Michael Goldstein, *Managing Attention Disorders in Children*, (New York: John Wiley & Sons, 1990).

5. Sam Goldstein and Michael Goldstein, *The Multi-disciplinary Evaluation and Treatment of Children With Attention Deficit Disorders*, 16th ed. (Seattle, Wash.: Neurology, Learning and Behavior Center, 1991).

6. Russel A. Barkley, *Attention Deficit Hyperactivity Disorder. A Handbook for Diagnosis and Treatment*, (New York: The Guilford Press, 1990).

7. Philip C. Kendall and Lauren Braswell, *Cognitive-Behavioral Therapy for Impulsive Children*, (New York: The Guilford Press, 1985).

8. Goldstein and Goldstein, *Managing Attention Disorders*, 270–282.

9. Edward A. Kirby and Liam K. Grimley, *Understanding and Treating Attention Deficit Behavior*, (New York: Pergamon Press, 1986).

10. D. M. Ross and S. A. Ross, *Hyperactivity: Current Issues, Research, and Theory*, 2nd ed. (New York: John Wiley & Sons, 1982).

11. Lauren Braswell and Michael L. Bloomquist, *Cognitive-Behavioral Therapy with ADHD Children* (New York: The Guilford Press, 1991).

12. Barkley, *Handbook*. 550

13. Sam Goldstein and E. Pollock, *Social Skills Training for Attention Deficit Children*, (Salt Lake City, Ut.: Neurology, Learning and Behavior Center, 1988).

14. Barkley, *Handbook*. 565–569

15. Ibid. 569–571

16. Arthur L. Robin and Sharon L. Foster, *Negotiating Parent-Adolescent Conflict: A Behavioral Family Systems Approach* (New York: Guilford Publications, 1989).

17. Arthur L. Robin, "Training Families with ADHD Adolescents," *Attention Deficit Hyperactivity Disorder*, Russel A. Barkley, ed. (New York: The Guilford Press, 1990) 462–497.

18. S. Moses, "Letter on ADD Kids Gets Mixed Reactions," *The APA Monitor*, 22.12 (1991): 36–37.

19. Russell A. Barkley, *Attention-Deficit Hyperactivity Disorder: A Clinical Workbook* (New York: The Guilford Press, 1991).

20. J. M. Swanson, "Learning Disabilities: Proceedings of the National Conference (1987)" (Parkton, Md.: York Press, 1988), 532–546; and D. P. Cantwell, "Hyperactive Children Have Grown Up," *Archives of General Psychiatry*, 42 (1985): 1026–1028.

21. Barkley, *Handbook*.

22. Goldstein and Goldstein, *Managing Attention Disorders*. 256–258

23. Russell A. Barkley, "A Review of Stimulant Drug Research with Hyperactive Children," *Journal of Child Psychology and Psychiatry*, 18 (1977): 137–165.

24. Ross and Ross, *Hyperactivity: Current Issues*; and R. A. Barkley, "Predicting the Response of Hyperkinetic Children to Stimulant Drugs: A Review," *Journal of Abnormal Child Psychology*, 4 (1976): 327–348.

25. Russell A. Barkley, "Tic Disorders and Tourette's Syndrome," *Behavioral Assessment of Childhood Disorders*, 2nd ed., E. Marsh and L. Terdal, ed. (New York: The Guilford Press, 1988) 69–104.

26. Ibid. 69–104.

27. K. D. Gadow, "Prevalence of Drug Treatment for Hyperactivity and Other Childhood Behavior Disorders," *Psychosocial Aspects of Drug Treatment for Hyperactivity*, K. D. Gadow and J. Loney, ed. (Boulder, Colo.: Westview Press, 1981) 13–70.

28. Barkley, *Handbook*. 589–90.

29. C. K. Conners and K. C. Wells, *Hyperkinetic Children: A Neuropsychological Approach* (Beverly Hills, Calif.: Sage, 1986).

30. Barkley, *Handbook*. 594–97.

31. Barkley, *Clinical Workbook*. 94–96.

32. Ibid. 94–96.

33. S. R. Pliszka, "Tricyclic Antidepressants in the Treatment of Children with Attention Deficit Disorder," *Journal of the American Academy of Child and Adolescent Psychiatry*, 26 (1987): 127–132.

34. Russell A. Barkley, *Handbook*.

35. Russell A. Barkley, et al., "Development of a Multi-method Clinical Protocol for Assessing Stimulant Drug Responses in ADHD Children," *Journal of Clinical Child Psychology*, 17 (1988): 14–24.

36. Edna D. Copeland, *Medications for Attention Disorders (ADHD/ADD) and Related Medical Problems* (Atlanta: SPI Press, 1991).

37. More discussion about these kinds of issues is included in my book, *The Hyperactive Child* (Wheaton, Ill.: Victor Books, 1992), which is written directly to Christian parents of ADHD children. A discussion is included of how the greater church community can be involved in interventions for the ADHD child.

Chapter Four

The Sexually Abused Child: Identification and Treatment

A SIX-YEAR-OLD BOY WHOSE PARENTS are divorcing was brought in by his mother with allegations that his father had sexually abused him. A young girl would not sleep by herself, had panic attacks, and wouldn't allow her mother out of her sight. Later disclosures alleged sexual abuse by a relative. A mother had been beaten by her drunken husband, and now her four-year-old daughter was making references to, "Daddy touched me in my private spot."

These cases represent a significant portion of the children I see at CRISTA Counseling Service where I conduct my practice. Almost all of my clients come from some type of church background, and they come to CRISTA because they desire a Christian focus to their counseling. The tragic implication of my own experience, and that of Christian counselors around the country, is that the incidence and severity of child sexual abuse is every bit as high in the church community as in the secular population.[1]

Approximately 250,000 new cases of sexual abuse are thought to occur every year. Perhaps one out of every three girls will be abused by the time she is eighteen. The incidence of sexual abuse among boys is likely to be greatly under-disclosed, but even so, one out of every six or eight boys is reported to have been abused. The number of alleged incidents of sexual abuse has risen tremendously over the past fifteen years, causing most experts to deduce that this reflects an actual increase in incidents. More reports are being filed because more children are being abused. In spite of the amount of public information about the subject, child sexual abuse continues to be epidemic.[2]

Without exception, any counselor who works with children is going to have to deal with some aspect of the identification, validation, and treatment of child sexual abuse.

Definition

Child sexual abuse is the sexual exploitation of a child who is not developmentally capable of understanding or resisting the contact or who is psychologically and socially dependent on the offender. A wide spectrum of sexual activities may be considered abusive. These activities follow a continuum from exposing genitals, kissing, fondling, masturbation, and oral-genital contact, to penetration of the vagina or rectum by a finger, penis, or object. Contact can range from nonviolent and nontouching behavior to physical violence and touching.

The two criteria that establish child sexual abuse as a form of violence are the lack of consent and resultant injury to the victim. Because the child is immature, uninformed, and often dependent on the perpetrator, he or she cannot give or withhold consent. The child lacks any real power to resist or make choices. Injury, the second criterion, can be physical or emotional. The sexual abuse of a child flagrantly disregards the child's best interests. It is a case of an older, stronger person using a child for sexual gratification. In addition to possible physical injury or disease, the child experiences a host of harmful consequences.

THE IMPACT OF SEXUAL ABUSE

Sexual abuse is a profoundly disruptive, disorienting, and destructive experience; the long-term aftermath can last a lifetime. There are also immediate and devastating events that follow the disclosure of the abuse. The victim has experienced a degree of physical and emotional stimulation beyond a child's capacity to understand. The confusion about feelings, boundaries, trust, and identity interfere with the child's accomplishment of normal developmental tasks. This further compounds the problem and places the child in jeopardy to experience more negative events. For example, the child may get teased because he or she doesn't fit in with peers.

The victim is frustrated by the contradictions surrounding the abusive relationship. The child looked to the caretaker or parent for love and safety, and instead was victimized. He or she is burdened with a secret that cannot be shared. This leads to feelings of alienation and separation from the rest of the family. The child may also harbor guilt over feelings of enjoyment during the sexual contact or of the "preferred status" the perpetrator gives the child within the family structure.

The victim usually experiences feelings of remorse and sorrow, along with blame and responsibility for what has happened. At some level the child feels used. He or she has been treated as an object rather than a person and is depreciated in value, which may cause the child to feel dirty or damaged—physically and emotionally.

David Finkelhor, a major researcher in the area of child sexual abuse, analyzed the empirical data on short-term effects of sexual abuse. He concluded that abused children often show symptoms, including fear or anxiety, depression, difficulties in school, anger or hostility, inappropriate sexualized behavior, and running away or delinquency.[3]

The long-term effects of child sexual abuse include depression, self-destructive behavior, anxiety, feelings of isolation and stigma, poor self-esteem, difficulty in trusting others, a tendency toward revictimization, substance abuse, identity conflicts, body image disturbances, and sexual maladjustment.[4]

EVALUATING THE EFFECTS OF SEXUAL ABUSE

Careful attention to mediating factors can help the counselor understand how devastating the experience has been to the child. Remember, all trauma must be interpreted in terms of the eye of the beholder. What is important here is how the child reacts to the victimizing circumstances. One child may see a teen-ager exposing himself in the park and run home to tell her parents. She is angry, but thinks it's no big deal. Another child may experience the same thing and be terribly upset for days.

The features that seem to have the most impact are:

- *The relationship of the molester to the victim.* The more closely related or highly trusted the molester, the more damage to the child.[5]

- *The use of force or violence.* The more force or violence, the greater the damage, especially if serious physical injuries result.[6]

- *The degree of nonviolent coercion.* The greater the amount of fear and guilt used in controlling the victim, the more serious the damage.

- *The severity of abuse.* Intercourse is more emotionally harmful than genital exposure or other noncontact forms of abuse. However, extensive and long-term fondling has been found in some instances to rival the damage caused by intercourse.[7]

- *The duration of abuse.* Sexual abuse that takes place over a long period of time is most harmful. The child has greater opportunity to utilize and refine defense mechanisms, such as dissociation. This can become more problematic as the child gets older.[8]

- *The frequency of incidents.* The more chronic and frequent the incident, the greater the emotional damage. The child experiences a greater sense of helplessness and vulnerability.[9]

- *The age and developmental status of the victim.* Some discrepancy exists in this research. There is a trend toward viewing the younger child as more vulnerable to damage. The reasoning is that because the child has fewer coping strategies, the damage will likely be greater.[10]

- *The emotional climate of the child's family.* Dysfunctional families with characteristics such as family discord, mental health problems, divorce, drug and alcohol dependence, spouse abuse, social isolation, and insufficient income, can add to the emotional damage an abused child experiences. This can be harmful, separate, and distinct from the abuse.[11]

- *The reactions of significant adults to the report of abuse.* The less emotional support the victim receives from his or her family members and the community, the greater the degree of damage.[12]

- *The guilt the child feels.* The greater the amount of guilt a child feels for having felt pleasure, for causing the abuse, or for the disruption following disclosure, the greater the impact.[13]

The chart in exhibit 5.3, will help the counselor estimate the degree of damage to a sexually abused child. This chart, along with other features of traumatization can assist the counselor in devloping a treatment plan.

SYMPTOMS OF SEXUAL ABUSE

The process of identifying an abused child begins with a careful look at any outward behavior that has been linked by clinical experience and research with the presence of abuse. The following sections provide a comprehensive presentation of the symptoms that may be displayed by a child who has been sexually abused.

BEHAVIORAL INDICATORS

A trauma such as child sexual abuse is certain to result in some type of symptoms. Usually there are not clear physical signs of abuse, so the child is the best, and sometimes, only source of warning signals. These behavioral signs vary according to the age of the child.

- Indirect hints or open statements about abuse
- Difficulty in peer relationships, i.e., violence against younger children

- Withdrawn, less verbal, depressed, or apathetic
- Abrupt and drastic personality changes
- Self-mutilation
- Preoccupation with death, guilt, heaven or hell
- Retreat to fantasy world, dissociative reactions—loss of memory, imaginary playmates, child uses more than one name
- Unexplained acquisition of toys, money, or clothes
- Fear, clinging to parent, requires reassurance
- Unwillingness to participate in physical/recreational activities
- Refusal to undress for P.E. class at school
- Sudden increase in modesty
- Fear of bathrooms and showers
- Self-conscious about use of bathroom, severe reaction if intruded upon
- Anger, acting out, disobedience
- Refusal to be left with potential offender or caretaker
- Becoming uncomfortable around formerly trusted person[s]
- Lack of trust
- Active hostility and anger toward formerly trusted person
- Runaway behavior
- Refusal to go home or stated desire to live elsewhere
- Extreme fear or repulsion when touched by an adult of either sex
- Touching to either extreme
- Inappropriate dress, use of clothing to reverse roles—child looks like sophisticated adult, mother like teen-ager
- Onset of poor personal hygiene, attempts to make self appear unattractive
- Sophisticated sexual knowledge
- Precocious, provocative sexual behavior
- Seductive, indiscriminate display of affection
- Pseudo-maturity, acts like small parent
- Regression to earlier, infant behavior—bed wetting, thumb sucking
- Sleep disturbances, nightmares
- Sleep habits change, stays up late, or seems constantly tired
- Continual, unexplained fear, anxiety, or panic
- Onset of eating disorders—anorexia, bulimia, compulsive eating

- Inability to concentrate in school, hyperactive
- Sudden drop in school performance
- Overly compliant or almost compulsive in action
- Arriving early at school and leaving late with few, if any, absences
- Excessive masturbation
- Combination of violence and sexuality in artwork, written schoolwork, language and play
- Hysterical seizures
- Attempts to establish boundaries, such as wearing clothing to bed
- Total denial of problem with total lack of expression or feeling

PHYSICAL AND MEDICAL INDICATORS

Some of these signs of abuse can only be evaluated by a physician. Others can be observed by a parent or caretaker who has fairly close contact with the child. And a few symptoms can be observed by concerned persons such as the child's teachers. While sexual abuse often leaves no physical signs, the existence of symptoms appears to represent some of the most conclusive evidence of abuse.

- Passive during pelvic examination. A nonabused child is more agitated during first pelvic; a raped child will yell and scream, while a repeatedly abused child will quietly spread legs.
- Bruises and hickeys or both in the face or neck area or around the groin, buttocks and inner thighs
- Torn, stained, or bloody underclothing
- Bleeding from external genitalia, vagina, or anal regions
- Swollen or red cervix, vulva, or perineum
- Positive tests for gonococcus or spermatozoa
- Pain or itching in genital areas
- Difficulty in walking or sitting
- Venereal disease or gonorrhea infections
- Pregnancy
- Unusual and/or offensive body odors
- Abrasions and erythema of the vulva area, laceration of posterior fourchette

- Small perihymenal scars and scarring of posterior fourchette
- Abrasions and laceration of hymen with tearing between three o'clock and nine o'clock
- Scarred and thickened transected hymen and rounded redundant hymenal remnants with adhesions sometimes binding hymen laterally and distorting the opening
- Complete or partial loss of sphincter control
- Fan-shaped scarring extending out from anus in six o'clock position
- Pain on urination
- Penile swelling and penile discharge
- Vaginal discharge and urethral or lymph gland inflammation[14]

FAMILIAL INDICATORS

The following symptoms are taken from research on families where child sexual abuse has been found to occur. Not all abused children have families with these particular features. But if a number of these signs are observed, the children should be considered at some level of risk.

Sibling behavior. The following behaviors are often present in cases where sexual abuse is perpetrated by a sibling.

- A brother and sister behave like a girlfriend and boyfriend
- Child fears being left alone with sibling
- Children appear to be embarrassed when found alone together
- Child is teased or antagonized by sibling but does not retaliate
- Siblings report another child is favored by parent

Parent behavior. The presence of the following familial features could indicate the child is at risk for sexual abuse.

- Stepfather present in home
- Parent, particularly the natural mother, absent from home by death, divorce, long-term work, or military
- Emotionally distant or sexually punitive mother
- Mother does not have high school education

- Little or no appropriate physical affection from father
- Strained marital relationship
- Dysfunctional family system, blurring of generational lines
- Parent often alone with one child; work or school schedules which cause one parent or caretaker, particularly the father or male family member, to spend great deal of time with a child
- Favoritism by parent toward one child or an overly protective or jealous parent
- Reversal of roles between mother and daughter
- Parent severely restricts child's outside contacts with peers
- Mother chronically ill or disabled
- Questionable sleeping arrangements, often sleeping with one parent or exposure to parental sexual behavior
- Domineering, inflexible father won't allow wife to drive or interact with outsiders
- Father who either directs all family activities or seldom participates in any family/social functions
- Strong parental reaction to sex education activities at church or school
- Parent or other family member has been sexually abused
- Social, physical, and geographic isolation of family
- Overcrowding or substandard living conditions
- Alcohol or substance abuse in family

GOALS OF EVALUATION

When beginning the interview process with a case of suspected child sexual abuse, it is important to have clear goals. If the referral is made based on circumstances and symptoms that strongly suggest abuse, disclosure becomes the initial goal. Once a clear disclosure is made by the child, enough additional information must be obtained to ensure safety for the child and other possible victims. Also, diagnostic details are needed to identify the child's needs so treatment plans can be made.

An interview can also be investigative in its focus. In this case the purpose is to determine the validity of the allegations or disclosures made by the child or family member. The specifics of who, what, when, and where need to be identified clearly. Of course, this must be done in a manner that does not "lead" the child; the investigation must follow proper procedure for discovery and prosecution.

In other cases, you may work with an abused child after someone else has obtained the disclosure and determined the initial facts of the case. The therapeutic goal in these cases is to provide the child an opportunity to deal with his or her feelings. These feelings include anger, embarrassment, guilt, ambivalence, shame, and remorse. Here the focus is on the child's feelings rather than the facts of the abuse. Corroboration of earlier details may be obtained in the process, but it is not the primary goal.

Part of the diagnostic process requires identifying the nature and extent of the emotional damages from the abuse. The question is, How deeply and in what way has the child been affected? This information is needed for treatment, but it might also be required by the court in determining the sentence for the perpetrator. Civil damages also might be affected by this type of description.

If the legal process is already underway, treatment may be your primary area of concentration. The type of trauma and its effects on the child, the child's symptoms, and the nature of the child's support system will help guide treatment at this stage.

Another type of sexual abuse case involves incest. Within treatment of the incest victim, the question of contact with the offender often arises. The purpose of sessions at this point is to determine the child's readiness for visitation or contact with the father or other relative. Once contact is established there is the need to monitor the child's reactions to determine the helpful or harmful effects. Recommendations regarding continued visits are made based on these observations.

A similar goal arises in evaluation for parenting plan or custody arrangements when allegations of sexual abuse emerge. First, there is the need for validation of the allegations. Then, based on whether the allegations are founded or unfounded, the recommendations for the parenting plan can be made.[15] (See chapters 10 and 11 for more details on this process.)

EVALUATION PROCEDURES

DEVELOPMENTAL LEVEL OF CHILD

The cognitive, emotional, and social level of the child will determine many interpretations and conclusions in a case of suspected abuse. The counselor needs a sense of the intellec-tual level of the child. This helps the counselor gauge the words and concepts used with the child. The counselor also needs to know what kinds of ideas and phrases are likely to originate with a child and what might be more unnatural and thus spoken through coaching or mimicking.

Counselors must have a sense of the normal developmental sequence for sexual knowledge, vocabulary, and interest patterns of children. With this information, the counselor can estimate whether the child is relaying ideas and vocabulary that are unusual or inappropriate for his or her age. For example, when asked, "How do people get babies?" a child of three or four is likely to answer in terms of geography. A typical answer might be, "You go to the baby store and buy one," or "Babies come from tummies," or "From God's place." The four- and five-year-old child will answer the same question in ways that suggest babies are manufactured. They know babies have not always existed. Typically, children of this age believe babies are built at the baby factory, hospital, or store.

Between the ages of five and eight there is a transition in understanding. Procreation and conception are described with a mixture of physiology and technology. The child may know that love and marriage, sexual intercourse, and a union of sperm and egg are necessary, but cannot put these factors into a coherent whole. By eight, most children can give an explanation in terms of concrete physiology. After age eight, the answers show much more sophistication, depending on the instruction provided to the child.[16]

The counselor must take into account the unique thinking patterns of young children during the interviews. Here are some general examples that apply to the preschool-age child. They are quite literal and concrete in their thinking. Children three to five years old tend to answer "yes" to please adults. Thus, it is important to go beyond closed-ended questions in the evaluation. The thinking and speech of preschoolers is not logically organized. They tend to say what enters their minds without the usual inhibitions of older children and adults. The counselor must sort through the spontaneous reference to splotches of Play Doh® or finger paint on the floor while questioning the child about the mechanics of the abuse. The child can shift from thinking about the stuff that came from the abuser's penis to the paint on the floor in an instant.

This happened to me while interviewing a four-year-old. I asked a question about penile discharge to elicit the details of abuse by the father. The boy told me that the "stuff was blue." In court, the defense attorney could have taken this as evidence of the child's overactive imagination (which he had) if I had not cycled back to the question in several different ways.

The preschool child learns from direct personal experience and makes very few inferences or generalizations. When you hear a child say, "Because Dad hurt me on my birthday, I knew I couldn't trust him anymore," you are probably getting someone else's words. This is not the usual thinking pattern for that age.

The preschool child's understanding of space, distance, and time is illogical and nonlinear. When asking a child "when" something happened, use reference points like birthdays, holidays, meals, or bedtime—not calendar or time references.

The attention span of a young child is limited. Avoid long interviews. Also be ready for short bursts of information following by unrelated conversation or play. Many times while playing with a child he or she will tell me a few details, and then go flying around the room like an airplane. After a short interval of play, another question may elicit a brief relevant comment before the child goes off on another play tangent.

DECEPTION

Children do lie. They will lie in order to avoid or escape punishment. This behavior is maintained through negative reinforcement and is a basic law of behavior. If a child is told not to tell about the abuse because his or her dog will be killed, there is a very good chance the child will lie and keep the secret. Children also lie to impress adults, get approval, and obey parents. One researcher cited a number of studies where adolescents later acknowledged they had lied in order to leave a conflicted but nonabusive setting. Other children from divorcing families have lied during their struggle to get acceptance within the family—the child tried to report what one parent or the other wanted to hear. Children may also lie to keep their family intact by recanting their story.[17]

If a young child is told on numerous occasions that his mother hurt him because she was sick and didn't love him, the child may repeat the statement. But children cannot manufacture stories based on information or experiences they have not learned. They do know the difference between fact and fantasy. The counselor will have to ask and listen carefully to comprehend the child's understanding.

For example, a child may tell you he "has a great big black dog at home whose name is Chex." Further discussion might reveal that the child has wanted a pet dog or that a neighbor has a dog like that. This can also happen with elements of disclosure. While asking about where the abuse happened, the child might see a Mickey Mouse puppet in the playroom and say it happened when she and Dad went to Disneyland. You need to confirm, when possible, that they did go on that trip. Also, ask the child for more details. When the details are not forthcoming, it may be because that trip was not part of the child's actual experience.

DIAGNOSTIC SIGNS

A change of behavior while talking or playing can have diagnostic value; however, there must be a baseline of reference for each child. An attention deficit disordered child may be continually changing toys or topics of conversation. If you ask this type of child a question about some aspect of the abuse and he or she changes the subject, this behavior should not automatically be viewed as avoidance of a painful subject.

The mother of a three-year-old girl was concerned about possible sexual abuse by the estranged father. Ordinarily the girl would play with one toy for quite a while. As we were playing with the doll house and family figures, I asked her some general questions about the father figure in the family, and she suddenly started moving around the area in an agitated state, muttering phrases that I couldn't understand. There was no question this was a dramatic change of behavior from her usual play activity. I viewed this behavior as significant. Further inquiry during that session revealed initial disclosures about the suspected incident.

Agitated behavior is not something that can be easily coached in a three-year-old. If coached at that age, a child would tend to share the information at the beginning of a session. If her mother had told her to tell Dr. Martin about the time Daddy touched her bottom, she will fulfill her assignment at the first opportunity. She will share this information in the first few minutes of the interview, without the customary accompanying, frightened behavior.

The basic elements of inquiry are who, what, when, and where? Always try to ask open-ended questions that do not lead the child by making suggestions. "Tell me what happened," "What did the man do?" and "Where did he touch you?" are examples of initial inquiry questions. Explore whether there was a progression of sexual activity from grooming (dressing and combing hair) to intimate, physical contact. Remember to use the terms and language suggested by the child. Do not correct the child's terms for anatomical parts or sexual activity. The slang terms they use may well have come from the perpetrator and you need to hear them.

USE OF ANATOMICALLY CORRECT DOLLS

Anatomical drawings or dolls may be used after initial disclosure is made. These tools can be helpful in obtaining elaboration or additional details; however, they should not be used for the beginning part of the inquiry. The courts have sometimes ruled that anatomically correct dolls are suggestive and lead the child to make statements that are not valid. Some evaluators have recommended against the use of anatomical dolls unless other approaches prove fruitless.[18] Therefore, care should be taken in the use of this tool. If anatomical dolls are necessary, the following guidelines are suggested:

- Do not use them during rapport building or to obtain initial description.

- Use when the child has indicated abuse and is having trouble describing exactly what happened.
- Let the child know before showing that these are "special" and different dolls.
- Give the child time to explore the dolls. Exploratory behavior does not necessarily indicate sexual abuse.
- Listen. You may hear details as the child explores.
- Do a body parts inventory to determine the names the child uses for various parts of the doll's body. Start with public parts and then ask about the private parts. Avoid suggesting names. Do not correct the child. Use these terms in subsequent conversation.
- Ask who taught the child the names for the body parts.
- Do not ask which is male or female. The child may not see the dolls as having a specific sex. You can have the child identify who each doll is.
- Have the child pick a doll to represent himself and a doll to represent the person identified as the abuser.
- Ask the child to show you what happened. Do not use the word "pretend." Encourage the child to verbalize what is being demonstrated.
- Use active feedback to confirm the child's story.[19]

FURTHER METHODS FOR OBTAINING DETAILS

While interviewing the child, be sure to note nonverbal signals such as rhythmic body movement. Also look for explicit reenactment or dissociative states where the child shows glazed-over eyes, suggestive, or repetitive body movement, or animal-like sounds. Asking a child to "show me" can sometimes overcome reluctance if there was ever a promise made not to "tell." Using toy telephones or puppets to do the telling can also be helpful. Sometimes the child will need to whisper or hide under a blanket, table, pillow, or tent when telling. Large sunglasses can also give the child a feeling of anonymity or disguise that will allow more freedom to disclose hard-to-tell details.

During the interview it is helpful to ask about bathing and bedtime routines since these are frequently the times that sexual abuse occurs. In regard to bathing, ask questions such as: Who starts the bath? Who undresses you? Who was in the bathroom with you? What was the person wearing? Where are the places that he or she touched? Bedtime questions could include: What do you wear to bed? Who kisses you goodnight? Where is the kiss placed? Does anyone come into your room after the lights are out? Who?

The disclosure details regarding when the incident occurred will continue as you try to elicit information about the general time of day or night, day of the week, or time of the year. In children under six, the concept of time is unreliable. Familiar events such as birthdays, holidays, bedtime, or TV programs can sometimes be used to clarify the time. Multiple instances of abuse will blur the child's recall of separate incidents. Try to be sensitive to a child who has an otherwise good memory but can't isolate abusive episodes.

Validation details are an important part of the investigative process with a child. If the child is able to recall other verifiable aspects of his or her life at the time of the abuse, there is reason to believe the abuse disclosures will also be true. To this end, ask the child questions such as: Where did you live when this happened? What color was the house? Was it a house or an apartment? Who lived close to you? What school did you attend? What was your teacher's name and what grade were you in? Who lived with you when this happened? What was the name of your pet?

CREDIBILITY

Determining the validity of a child's disclosure is mostly a matter of belief. Seldom is there physical corroboration, a witness, or confession of the abuse. There is tremendous pressure on the child to recant or deny the story. This pressure is often brought on by nonsupportive family, perpetrator denial, or judicial delay. Therefore, it is important to obtain reliable, accurate impressions about the child's credibility. Experience and research have suggested the primary components in evaluating a child's story.

- Reports of multiple incidents over time
- A progression from less intimate to more intimate sexual activity

- Revelation of direct or implied understanding between the child and offender that the activity should be kept secret, or the presence of elements of pressure and coercion
- Explicit details of sexual behavior
- Peripheral details such as place of residence, or time of year

Important aspects of qualifying a child as a witness in court include: the ability to receive and relay information accurately, the ability to tell the difference between truth and a lie, and the ability to know the importance of telling the truth in court. The counselor should have a clear understanding of the child's ability to meet these conditions and be ready to assist the court in determining the child's qualifications.

One system of assessing allegations of child sexual abuse is the *Statement Validity Analysis*. It is adapted from European research by Raskin, Steller, and Rogers, and may have much to offer in assessing the credibility of victims, witnesses, and the alleged perpetrator. The method uses a criteria-based content analysis and a statement validity assessment of interviews and testimony. It is based on the Undeutsch hypothesis that the report of actual events must differ from fabricated reports in a qualitative manner.[20] Rogers has summarized some comparative characteristics of actual versus fictitious statements made by victims in sex abuse cases. Those comparisons are adapted and presented in Exhibit 4.1.

Exhibit 4.1

Characteristics of Victim Statements in Intrafamilial Sex Abuse[21]

Actual Sexual Abuse	Unreliable/fictitious allegations
1. Statements internally and logically consistent, large numbers of unique details, flowing narrative, pieces eventually all fitting together	1. Statements become increasingly inconsistent over time, show diminished number of unique details, stereotypic in pattern; does

Actual Sexual Abuse	Unreliable/fictitious allegations
where minor peripheral details may be added or drop out, but no major reversals; consistent with external data where such is available; includes non-self-serving details.	not fit together into a cohesive fabric, contains major reversals, details tend to be self-serving, may not be consistent with external data where such is available; no flowing narrative may have been given; major details have been formed through interview technique of leading, pressuring, shaping.
2. Statements are rarely dramatic, rarely seeking to make the perpetrator appear in a totally negative light, but more ambivalent in tone; statements about details consistent with what is known about similar crimes, e.g., perpetrator takes usual self-protective steps against being discovered, follows expected patterns seen in chronic incest.	2. Statements are often dramatic, claims of being forced drugs or alcohol, alleged multiple victims, and/ or multiple perpetrators, orgies, describes situations in which alleged perpetrator has not taken ordinary steps against discovery of molestation.
3. Rarely is force alleged, but usually verbal manipulation, bribes, claims "we will both get in trouble if you tell." The less adept perpetrator is more likely to threaten or coerce the victim. In rare cases where physical force is used in intrafamilial situations, it is usually within the context of generalized family violence, where threat of force is the most common mode of handling conflict or	3. Statements almost invariably progress from relatively innocuous behaviors to increasingly intrusive, abusive, aggressive activities ultimately with threats to harm or kill child or significant others if victim discloses; in some young children allegations of torture, killings are made of animals and or humans.

Actual Sexual Abuse	Unreliable/fictitious allegations
disputes between family members.	
4. Details provided are usually consistent with what is known about sexual physiology and response cycles.	4. Details may not be consistent with what is known about sexual physiology, response cycles except in areas where child has been questioned extensively so that the right answers are learned.
5. Described changes in social and sexual relationship across time are consistent with what is known about perpetrator/victim long-term relationship patterns.	5. Details provided are not consistent with what is known about perpetrator/victim relationship patterns unless this is superimposed by interviewers who are aware of what these patterns are; victim may progressively claim intrusive/advanced assault patterns occurred at younger and younger ages.
6. Rarely does the victim make issue of memory. There may be instances of not remembering known incidents, or not remembering particular details at the height of stress. In the usual memory loss, the report will be consistent with what is known about memory processes, e.g. recency effects, fading, loss of peripheral details first rather than loss of the major events; memory can usually be recalled by providing non-leading cues.	6. Typically will not admit memory problems, but may claim not to remember when caught in contradictions, or when feeling guilty about making untrue statements; alleged memory losses do not fit what is known about memory processes; may later absolutely deny statements which were insisted upon earlier.

Actual Sexual Abuse	Unreliable/fictitious allegations
7. Recantation may occur for the entire incident or all alleged incidents when pressure is applied within the family situation to relieve the legal/economic ramifications of the accusation. Often the mother pushes for recantation overtly or covertly. This pattern is seen in initially intact family units who are now separated due to the legal case.	7. Classical recantation is unlikely; mother usually supports if not promotes the allegations; family pattern is typically two family units following a prior separation or divorce.
8. Supportive parent has not participated in one or more formal interviews of the child in regard to the allegations, nor observed the child interviews.	8. Supportive parent often highly involved in the emergence of the allegations, has usually participated in child protective services or law-enforcement interviews; parent makes allegations that child resists confirming, followed by repeating part of what parent said later.
9. Child may appear pseudomature, responsible, self-blaming, embarrassed and while reluctant to disclose, the statements are consistent across time. One or both parents may comment on age-inappropriate sexual interests or behavior preceding or following the allegations coming to light.	9. Child is often immature, dependent, manipulative, enmeshed with mother, seen by both parents as naive about sexual matters.

A more detailed knowledge of the statement validity analysis process is necessary to evaluate an actual transcript. But the characteristics described in exhibit 4.1 should be useful to any counselor trying to assess the credibility of sex abuse allegations within an incestuous context.

The method of dealing with allegations of child sexual abuse has undergone several changes in emphasis in recent years. Three or four decades ago the incidence of abuse was thought to be as low as one in hundreds of thousands. During the 1970s and 1980s, the survey research brought home the overwhelming fact that as many as one out of three females was abused and perhaps one out of six males. There was also the initial assumption that children seldom lied about sexual abuse. But in recent years, particularly within custody conflicts, the possibility of false allegations has been found to be very high. Therefore, the clinician must be extremely careful not to assume automatically that all statements made by a child are valid. With the prevalence of detailed information about abuse and sexuality available today, it is easier for a child to recount sexual descriptions. This same information has also made it easier for a hostile or vengeful spouse to construct false allegations.

Exhibit 4.2 summarizes an adaptation of Richard Gardner's list of the more differentiating characteristics found is cases of founded allegations of child sexual abuse.[22] While exhibit 4.1 alluded primarily to the statements made by the victim in intrafamilial sexual abuse, exhibit 4.2 includes the child, as well as the nonoffending parent and the perpetrator.

Exhibit 4.2

Fabricated vs. Bona Fide Allegations of Abuse[23]

CHARACTERISTICS OF CHILD

FABRICATED	BONA FIDE
1. Welcomes chance to talk about abuse.	1. Hesitant, fearful to talk. Disclosure requires several interviews.

FABRICATED	BONA FIDE
2. Contradictions and inconsistencies in description.	2. Less variation because real experience exists.
3. Presence of child custody dispute.	3. No parental dispute.
4. Other evidence of Parental Alienation Syndrome (PAR).	4. No manifestation of PAR.
5. Can't describe as many details because there is no actual experience.	5. Can give exact details because reality exists.
6. Describes unlikely details or events.	6. Situation, description is probable.
7. Simplistic, absurd, naive description.	7. Realistic and appropriate description.
8. No guilt, even hostility. Seems glad to report perpetrator.	8. Guilt, reluctant to tell, no vengeance. Guilt over participation. Guilt over problems allegations cause to abuser.
9. Doesn't feel genitals have been damaged.	9. Worries genitals have been damaged. Social as well as sexual damage.
10. Seems to enjoy the attention.	10. Does not enjoy attention. Has been programmed for secrecy and shame.
11. No preoccupation with sex other than fabricated incident.	11. Preoccupation with sexual behavior. Will give litany and then go play. Searching for gratification. Has been sexually excited.
12. No generalized fear of adults same sex as perpetrator. No fear of alleged abuser.	12. Morbid fear of abuser, as well as of other same-sex adults.
13. No fear of home. No desire to spend excess time away from home. Willing to go to home of abuser.	13. Extremely fearful of being alone. Stays away from home. Won't go to offender's house.

FABRICATED	BONA FIDE
14. Not compliant in interview.	14. Compliant.
15. Not withdrawn. Outgoing and verbal.	15. Withdrawn, nonverbal; may have fantasy world.
16. Not depressed.	16. Depressed, even suicidal.
17. Sexual information comes from fabricating adult, school, TV, or peers.	17. Information comes from real experience with abuser.
18. Not prone to psychosomatic illness. No regressive behavior.	18. Prone to psychosomatic and regressive behaviors and problems.
19. Has a litany. Routine description.	19. No litany at outset. Although may occur after several repetitions.
20. No reenactment of abuse in play.	20. Reenactment of trauma in play is likely. Need for desensitization.
21. Not likely to make physical contact with therapist.	21. Likely to be seductive and physical with examiner.
22. Uses adult terminology.	22. Uses terms used in home or by abuser.
23. No sleep disturbances.	23. Sleep disturbances, particularly if abuse occurred in bed or at night.
24. Reports only one or two events.	24. Often reports long history and progression of abuse.
25. In joint interview with abuser, not likely to act seductive or fearful.	25. Likely to act seductively to abuser, or show high level of fear.
26. If retraction is made, shows guilt over problems caused.	26. If retraction is made, shows fear. Result of threats made by abuser.

CHARACTERISTICS OF ACCUSING MOTHER

FABRICATED	BONA FIDE
1. Advertises to world. Not afraid of public disclosure	1. Ashamed, withdraws, tends to minimize.
2. Expands, exaggerates, fans every spark.	2. Would rather it be less, not more.
3. Wants hired gun evaluator against abuser.	3. Receptive to impartial evaluation and therapy to lessen future risk.
4. In joint session with child, child is often checking with mother.	4. In joint session with child, child does not check with mother.
5. Does not appreciate legal process trauma.	5. Tries to avoid trauma.
6. Does not acknowledge importance of father/child relationship. Does not want father to see child ever.	6. More open to eventual contact with father.
7. Not likely to have been abused as child.	7. Likely to have been abused.
8. Not passive: more aggressive, outspoken.	8. Passive, disabled, absent.
9. Presence of child custody dispute.	9. No dispute.
10. Inconsistencies in describing events other than alleged abuse.	10. Lack of duplicity or inconsistencies.

CHARACTERISTICS OF ALLEGED ABUSER—FATHER

FABRICATED	BONA FIDE
1. No instances of gifts, bribery by abuser.	1. Gifts are common.
2. No threats involved in scenario.	2. Threats common.

FABRICATED	BONA FIDE
3. Father is indignant, willing to take lie detector test.	3. False indignation, passive silence, ambivalent about taking lie detector.
4. Child is angry at father in mother's presence, but out of mother's presence, child is not as hostile to father.	4. Child is not as affected by mother's presence.
5. Father is not likely to have been abused as child.	5. Likely to have been abused.
6. No associated sexual deviations.	6. Presence of sexual deviations. Sexual addiction symptoms.
7. History of good equal, heterosexual relationships. Adequate self-esteem. Can handle female rejection.	7. Negative past relationships. Poor self-esteem. Welcomes passive, compliant, participation of child.
8. Not prone to regression in situations of stress.	8. Regression when stressed.
9. Less likely to abuse drugs and alcohol.	9. Abusive of alcohol and drugs.
10. Not likely to be social isolate.	10. Isolated, few friends. Can be controlling in home.
11. No special career choice relative to family contact.	11. Chooses work opportunities that bring him into contact with children.
12. No difference in probability between father and stepfather.	12. Stepfather more likely to be abuser.
13. Not rigid, moralistic, or legalistic.	13. Tends to be rigid, controlling, etc.
14. Presence of custody dispute.	14. No dispute.
15. Inconsistencies in details of events other than abuse.	15. No inconsistencies.

TREATMENT ISSUES

Treatment of the sexually abused child can be divided into three phases: crisis intervention, short-term therapy, and long-term therapy. Within each phase, the goals are to empower the child by improving his or her self-esteem, and by defining and establishing personal boundaries. Other goals include learning to trust others, as well as beginning to feel more secure and confident. The victim also needs assistance to learn how to make choices within an environment that allows such decisions to be made. The process can be difficult, but these general goals are very appropriate for any abused child.

CRISIS INTERVENTION

Obvious symptoms of abuse or disclosure of sexual abuse throw the family system out of balance. The usual forms of coping are tested and sometimes found to be lacking. The counselor needs to offer immediate support to the child and parents by providing emotional, spiritual, and practical assistance. This includes help for the victim and family coping with the investigative process, medical examinations, and interviews with caseworkers and law enforcement officers. There may be sessions with attorneys and prosecutors, and possible court appearances. The family will need help dealing with the fallout among family, friends, and the community following public disclosure of the abusive events. Each of these events can be traumatic to the family. The counselor can help by forecasting many of the procedures that will be needed and by providing referrals to qualified professionals, as well as by giving encouragement.

During this traumatic period, safety and circumstance factors parallel the investigative process. The counselor needs to be careful about dual roles. It is possible to provide crisis intervention support through practical guidance and reassurance, and by combining a stabilizing voice of reason with one of compassion. But the counselor may also be responsible for investigating data surrounding either symptomatic behavior or partial disclosure.

The validation of the abuse should be made by another professional if the claims are made prior to the counselor's initial involvement. If the disclosure arises within the evaluation process, the counselor may need to continue gathering as much information as possible.

The same dilemma may occur outside custody evaluations. The key consideration is the safety and well-being of the child. If the counselor can provide supportive crisis intervention help while performing a thorough and objective investigation, the dual roles can coexist. The needs of the child should be the guide. Your ability to respond to these needs will depend on your skills and experience, along with the demands of the family.

Let me give an example. Suppose a child discloses elements of abuse involving the stepfather. As the family comes to you for assistance, it becomes evident they have minimal coping skills. Further, the incident brings to the mother's memory long forgotten details of her own childhood sexual abuse. You could very well have an overwhelmed family that takes so much of your time that the child's freedom to give further details is compromised. The message sent to the child by all the family uproar says, "See what you have done. Our lives are falling apart and it is all the doctor can do to help us survive." The child may pick up on all the urgent phone calls and emergency counseling sessions with the parent(s) and conclude that his own story is too dangerous to tell.

It is definitely unwise to try to work with the perpetrator in addition to the child. Issues of trust are preeminent here. The child is less likely to form a therapeutic bond with the counselor if the therapist is also working with the perpetrator. Always refer the offending person to another professional who has expertise in dealing with sex offenders.

During the crisis period, one of the most important tasks is to prevent the suppressive forces of the family, community, or legal system from harming the child. The counselor needs to establish a relationship of trust with the victim. The trusting relationship is built on a knowledge of the dynamics of abuse. The counselor will do everything possible to prevent threats, recrimination, badgering, and retaliatory measures which would have a crippling effect on the victim. If the child does recant previous allegations, the counselor needs to move quickly to determine why the story was changed. Most likely someone has frightened or pressured the child into changing the story. Another possibility is that the economic and legal implications of the disclosure have become more obvious to the child. As a result, the victim retracts the details from fear that it will impact the status quo. The child must be given enough support and data to outweigh the pressure from other sources or help get to the source of the pressure and assist in its removal.

Sometimes the stages following disclosure are accompanied by a supportive family, minimal disruptions, and a lack of observable symptoms in the victim. Even so, molested children need a minimum checkup of three to six appointments to assess for disruption and dysfunction. Using criteria such as those outlined in exhibits 4.1 and 4.2, the counselor can make a determination about the severity of the abuse, the existence of traumagenic states, and possible treatment options. Depending on the diagnosis, it is often necessary to carry out at least some short-term therapy.

SHORT-TERM THERAPY

The short-term therapy phase of treatment follows the crisis intervention period and usually lasts from one to six months. The extent of the damage factors described earlier in this chapter will have some degree of impact on the victim. Factors that play a part in evaluating the child's reaction to the traumatic events include the degree of force used; how closely related or trusted the perpetrator is; and the extent, duration, and frequency of the abuse. Therapy will more likely be short-term if the abuse was by someone outside of the family and consisted of minimal physical contact. Factors affecting the success of short-term therapy include a supportive family reaction, the child's abilty to adapt, and the absence of overt threats.

The issues of damaged goods, guilt, fear, depression, low self-esteem, and poor social skills are topics usually covered during this phase of treatment. A number of aspects crucial to the treatment of traumatized children and described by Beverly James in *Treating Traumatized Children*[25] are summarized below.

The child needs to acknowledge and explore his or her pain while in therapy, in order to integrate his or her experience. Helping children acknowledge and accept the realities of painful events in their lives is an essential part of treatment. If reality is not accepted, children will continue to put enormous energy into avoiding the source of their fears. They may be afraid to play, fantasize, or dream because suppressed feelings and memories might take over. We know that a surgeon or dentist must apply restorative techniques which can result in short-term pain. So, too, the counselor must guide and assist the child through the difficult process of uncovering the pain. The child needs help to understand and accept what happened, and then needs help to put that experience away. The tendency is to shield the child from more pain. However, the counselor must understand that healing pain is necessary for the child's long-term recovery.

A serialized course of treatment is often indicated, rather than one uninterrupted period of therapy. The treatment is sequenced over time so that it is responsive to developmental vulnerabilities that arise from trauma over time. Sequenced treatment is necessary because past traumatic events have different or additional meaning as the child matures.

This continuing influence can impair the child's development. For example, a sexually abused child initially may have felt some physical excitement and heightened stature as a result of the secretive behavior with an adult. Later, the emerging adolescent may struggle with thoughts of being gay or perverted. Yet, while working with the child at age six, a symptom cannot be treated if it has not emerged developmentally. Therefore, the counselor's role becomes much like that of the family physician, providing an ongoing relationship with the child and family as needed. This means that during the initial treatment sessions the counselor prepares a foundation for future treatment. The treatment program establishes short-term objectives and works toward resolving those issues. But termination of short-term treatment is an open door, allowing and encouraging the child and parents to return for checkups or additional clinical help. In the initial sessions the counselor helps the child and parents be aware of future indicators that a clinical "booster" is needed.

The needs of the child usually cannot be met effectively by a clinician working alone. There must be support from others involved with the child. The caregivers must be considered part of the treatment team, and their active participation is needed. Rarely is a weekly therapy session sufficient to meet all of the child's needs. Directed parental involvement will enhance the effects of the counseling sessions. The involvement of others lessens the child's feelings of shame and promotes self-acceptance. As the child experiences acceptance by other adults in dealing with the trauma, the child is also more able to accept it. Further, involved parents understand the process better, can support the counselor's suggestions more readily, and will not be as likely to terminate treatment prematurely.

A direct, active treatment approach is needed to elicit material from the child that is unlikely to emerge spontaneously. The direct, active approach also demonstrates that the issues need not be shameful and can be dealt with directly by the child. Children usually cannot initiate discussion of events and feelings that have overwhelmed them. Activities such as guided play, direct discussion, and an open and active approach assist children in acknowledging and integrating their traumatizing events. A clear, straightforward approach also helps demystify the process and empowers the parent and child to deal more competently with the issues.

Children need direct intervention to help them deal with the external realities and limitations of situations. The counselor can help the child deal with changes such as divorce or an injury. The child needs to know who he or she is, a unique person who is apart from external events. The counselor helps convey to the child that his or her place in the Kingdom of God is more than the external reality of a facial scar or an absent father.

A direct and open style of therapy also helps to avoid the contamination of secrets possibly held between the child and perpetrator. During the abuse, the child may have learned that the special alone time with the trusted adult was arranged for purposes other than nurturing the child. And it was a secret. The child is less likely to maintain a suspicious and non-disclosive attitude if the counselor is direct and open. Secrets should never be a part of the counselor's initiative.

Positive clinical messages have to be intense to be heard and felt through the child's defenses. Traumatized children are usually well defended, emotionally. But locked inside them are powerful and terrifying beliefs that they are helpless, evil, and totally to blame. The messages the child receives from therapy must match the intensity of these faulty beliefs in order to be heard, felt, and believed. The genesis and passage of messages must be fun for both the child and the treatment team. This helps to balance the hard work being accomplished. It is the fun that keeps the child emotionally receptive so that the intense positive messages can slip through the defenses. When the therapist is playful, the child gets the message that he or she is fun to be with. The child also learns appropriate play, cooperation, sharing, and direction-following skills that are often missing from their repertoire.

The clinical course must include attention to the physical, cognitive, emotional, and spiritual parts of the child, since the damage usually affects all these areas. Treatment strategies must be focused on each of these dimensions. As an example, a victim may reach some rational understanding that the abuse was not her fault. She may have had a chance to express feelings of anger about the incident and outcomes. But the child will also need to work through her feelings about a loving God who was supposed to protect her and didn't. Perhaps the child was abused by an uncle who claimed to be a Christian and was a youth leader in the church. The feelings of anger and beliefs of doubt and distrust need to be verbalized without condemnation.

These dimensions can be accessed through a variety of activities. Physical mastery can be achieved through skill development in activities such as ballet, gymnastics, martial arts, or sports. Cognitive mastery can come about through direct instruction, storytelling, use of metaphors or word pictures, and direct discussion of reality. TV programs, books, video tapes, and small group discussion can also be arenas for this area of development.

Emotional mastery comes from any experience that allows the child to feel safe enough to explore and express feelings that were once unaccessible and overwhelming. Art, creative expression, poetry, songs, creative writing, and play-therapy help uncover and delineate these feelings.

The spiritual impact, often neglected in secular counseling, is a special area of expertise for the Christian counselor. It is vital that the counselor be honest and accepting of the child's anger and distrust of God. Storytelling, parables, Bible reading, prayer, spiritual rituals, personal testimony, and discussion of the pain and suffering of Christ are a few of the activities that can assist in accessing the spiritual dimension.[25]

Many children engage in behaviors that are secret and dysfunctional, and that continue long after the traumatic incident itself. Dissociation and deviant sexual behaviors often develop after traumatizing events. These are not likely to be uncovered unless a determined effort is made to discover them by a knowledgeable clinician. Hidden trauma-reactive behaviors need to be identified by detailed, skillful probing within the context of a trusting, safe relationship. These behaviors must be dealt with to prevent the child's feelings of guilt and alienation from increasing.

Dissociative disorders may occur in children with a genetic predisposition to dissociate under stress. Added factors are exposure to ongoing life-threatening trauma, and an inadequate amount of adult support and protection. Under these conditions, the child's reaction to the initial trauma and the recall, or to a reminder of that trauma, may be a dissociative state. Counselors must be aware of the indicators of dissociative behavior and include an assessment for its presence in the diagnostic process. This possibility should be given attention throughout treatment. A child will not achieve recovery if he or she has isolated certain parts of his or her personality from awareness and from treatment. Dissociative disorders are a complex and relatively unknown aspect of treating sexually abused children.

Working with traumatized children means dealing sometimes with horrible situations. These situations may have a strong personal impact on the therapist, and this impact may interfere with treatment. Working with abused children who have been severely traumatized can be very disturbing to the counselor. Overwhelming feelings of disgust and horror may emerge when we hear the details of sodomy or of cult members urinating on a child. We can react to these horrors much like the child. Denial, avoidance, and fear can channel us into safer activities, like parent training, when we should be focusing on the child's experiences of bondage and terror. We need to be careful not to project our own feelings onto the child and say he or she isn't ready to work on those issues when, in fact, it may be the counselor who isn't ready. If you're in this field solely to feel good and receive continual positive feedback from your clients, this kind of work may not be for you. This work is emotionally, physically, and spiritually exhausting.[26]

Another issue that must be addressed is the therapist's anger toward the perpetrator or unprotective parent. An abused child can readily read the counselor's feelings and can misinterpret the therapist's anger as being directed toward the child. The child usually still has ambivalent feelings toward the trusted caregiver who violated that trust. If the child realizes the anger of the counselor is directed toward the abuser, feelings of shame, remorse, and sorrow can emerge as the child judges himself or herself guilty of wrongdoing. This can create distance in the therapeutic relationship.

As counselors with professional and Christian values and ethical standards, we must be brave enough to acknowledge and process our own emotional liabilities. If we ask this of the children with whom we work, we must be equal to the task. There is a parallel with this concept and the issue of self-control in an adult perpetrator. An offending teacher, for example, may try to excuse the molestation of a student by saying, "The student came on to me," or "She acted in such a seductive manner I couldn't resist." This type of excuse is without merit because the adult is expected to have the resources and maturity to exercise self-control. The same injunction applies to the child's therapist. It is a continued form of abuse to try to work with a child when the counselor's own views or attitudes prevent the child from getting the very best help possible. No counselor is perfect. We will never have all of the answers. But we should be in constant touch with our strengths and weaknesses as they relate to the quality of care we give our clients. For this reason, clinical supervision and consultation are often needed as support for the counselor.

LONG-TERM TREATMENT

According to Beverly James, the goal in working with traumatized children is to reach a point where they can say, "Yes, that happened to me. That's how I felt and how I behaved when it happened. This is how I understand it all now. I won't really forget it happened, but I don't always have to think about it either."[27]

Victims who have experienced significant trauma from the sexual abuse probably will be candidates for therapy lasting up to two years or longer. Factors contributing to the trauma include a variety of family relationships. On a continuum, the smaller the base of support for the child, the more dysfunctional the family system, and the more significant the offender, the longer the expected treatment period.

Repressed anger and hostility, an inability to trust, blurred boundaries, and role confusion are crucial issues in treatment. Other significant themes found in victims are pseudomaturity, the failure to complete developmental tasks, and a lack of self-mastery and control. Sgroi, MacFarland, Gil, and James all describe detailed methods, procedures and techniques for working on these issues.[28]

Exhibit 4.3, adapted from books by Edwards and Gil, as well as Suzanne Sgroi, summarizes the major issues found in abused children. Treatment suggestions are included under each topic.

Exhibit 4.3

Treatment of Sexual Abuse[29]

Damaged goods syndrome: The child feels physically, emotionally, and socially damaged.

- Refer child for a physical exam to determine if there are any physical injuries that require medical attention.
- Reassure child that physical injuries have been (or will be) treated.
- Help child understand that he or she is not damaged physically or emotionally.
- Help family members overcome distorted perceptions of the child and respond to the child in an appropriate manner.

Guilt: The child feels guilty about the sexual activity, about disclosing, and/or about any family disruption that followed disclosure.

- Help the child express guilty feelings.
- Help child and family members realize the child is not responsible for the sexual abuse.
- Reassure the child he or she is not responsible for any disruption in the family that followed disclosure.
- Reassure the child that he or she has a right to expect protection from the perpetrator.
- Reinforce the child's decision to disclose.
- Help the child (if sufficiently mature) identify elements of his/her behavior for which he or she should be responsible (e.g., use of manipulative behaviors).

Fear: The child is fearful of the consequences of his or her participation in the sexual activity and disclosure.

- Help the child identify and express his or her fears.
- Reinforce the child's decision to disclose.
- Refer to God's protection, but remember victim's experience to this point has been contrary.
- Facilitate practical measures to keep child safe.

Depression: The child is depressed following the disclosure.

- Observe the child for signs of depression or suicidal intent.
- Help the child ventilate his or her feelings.
- Believe, support, and love the child unconditionally.
- Sometimes recommend hospitalization and/or medication.
- If mother closely allied with offender, work toward reducing conflicting allegiances.

Low self-esteem: The child feels unwanted and undeserving and describes himself or herself in derogatory terms.

- Help child identify and express positive feelings about himself or herself.

- Provide opportunities to develop a "claim to fame." Needs areas of success.
- Affirm identity as a Child of God and a unique creation.
- Communicate God's unconditional love.
- Use Christ's suffering and anguish as a bridge for feelings of victim. Don't rush too quickly to Christ the victor; give child time to identify with Christ the victim.
- Emphasize God's grace.

Poor social skills: Child has inadequate social skills as result of parent's pressure to limit outside relationships.

- Provide child with opportunities to develop social skills (e.g., group therapy, anger management, self-control materials).
- Work with school personnel to facilitate social growth.

Anger and hostility: Although sometimes outwardly passive, the child is inwardly hostile and angry.

- Help child identify and ventilate angry and hostile feelings. Affirm that it is okay to be angry.
- Help child learn to express anger in assertive but non-destructive ways.
- Provide opportunities to express anger in a safe environment such as a group.

Inability to trust: The child is distrustful as a result of being abused by a trusted person.

- Provide opportunities to develop satisfying, trusting relationships (e.g., with therapist, "Big Brother").
- Encourage child to try new relationships, but work to ensure they are safe.

Role confusion: The sexual relationship with an adult has blurred boundaries and roles.

- Help child and family members resolve role confusion. It is important to have family member confirm counselor's statements about appropriate boundaries.

- Modify communication patterns among family members so they are consistent with appropriate roles.
- Work toward having perpetrator explain to the child that abuser is responsible for what happened, that the sexual activity was inappropriate, and that it will not happen again.
- Approach topic of forgiveness between offender and victim, but not too soon.
- If working toward reuniting family, work out detailed agreement on respect for boundaries.

Failure to complete developmental tasks: Preoccupation with sexual activity has interfered with child's accomplishment of normal developmental tasks.

- Help child assume more appropriate child role. Encourage child play.
- Obtain family's cooperation in helping child relinquish his or her inappropriate responsibilities. Entire system must change.

Lack of self-mastery and control: Child feels helpless as a result of the violation of his or her body and privacy.

- Help child understand that he or she has a right to self-determination and privacy.
- Provide opportunities for child to test his or her capacity for self-mastery and control (e.g., role-playing, learning about accountability).
- Teach family members how to reinforce the child's appropriate independent and responsible behaviors.

Ambivalent feeling toward the perpetrator: The child has negative and positive feelings toward the perpetrator.

- Help child sort out and express his or her negative and positive feelings.
- Reassure the child that it is acceptable to have both types of feelings.
- Teach the difference between physical contact and love.

Ambivalent feelings toward the nonoffending parent: The child has negative and positive feelings toward the nonabusive parent.

- Help child sort out and express negative and positive feelings.
- Reassure child that it is acceptable to have both types of feelings.

Fears concerning the reaction of others: Child is concerned about the responses of siblings, friends, etc.

- Identify how the child perceives the feelings and reactions of others.
- Help the child express his or her disappointments, fears, and anger.
- Help siblings identify and express their feelings about the abuse.
- Provide child with opportunities to develop healthy relationships.

Inappropriate boy-girl relationships: The child mistrusts others of the same sex as the perpetrator, displays inappropriate sexualized behaviors, etc.

- Provide child with opportunities to develop positive relationships with individuals of the same sex as the perpetrator.
- Provide instruction regarding appropriate behavior.
- Provide information regarding appropriate boy-girl or dating behavior.

Negative effects of the legal system: The child has a negative response to the court system.

- Prepare child for court proceedings by providing emotional support and information about the court process.
- Reinforce child's decision to disclose.
- Lack of information about sex: The child's knowledge about sex and birth control is limited and tainted.
- Provide child with age-appropriate sex education.
- Work with family to reinforce values as well as knowledge information.

CASE STUDY

A case study of the treatment of a sexually abused child is included in Appendix II. This case covered a two-year time span. Not all the details of clinical interventions are described, but a general flow of the treatment process is given.

SUMMARY

One out of every three females and one out of six or eight males have been sexually abused. Child sexual abuse is defined as the sexual exploitation of a child who is not developmentally capable of understanding or resisting the contact or who is psychologically and socially dependent on the offender.

Sexual abuse is a profoundly disruptive, disorienting, and destructive experience with both short-term and long-term effects. Factors which mediate the impact of sexual abuse on a child include the relationship of child to the molester; the use and degree of force, severity, duration, and frequency of the abuse; the age and developmental status of child; the degree of emotional support provided for victim; and the degree of guilt felt by child.

A variety of symptoms often appear as the result of sexual abuse. It is crucial to know the developmental level of the child before making final interpretations and conclusions about each case.

The issue of credibility and differentiating true from false allegations is an increasingly important, but difficult task for the counselor, but there are a number of characteristics to help in this process.

There are three phases of treatment: crisis intervention, short-term therapy, and long-term therapy. The case study presented in Appendix II illustrates some of the procedures and phases of treatment.

NOTES

1. Grant L. Martin, *Counseling for Family Violence and Abuse* (Dallas: Word, 1987). 147–152

2. See R. I. Witchel, "College Student Survivors of Incest and Other Child Sexual Abuse," *New Directions for Student Services* 54 Summer (1991): 63–76; Eliana Gil, *The Healing Power of Play* (New York: The Guilford Press, 1991);

David Finkelhor, *A Sourcebook on Child Sexual Abuse* (Newbury Park, Calif.: Sage, 1986); Kee MacFarlane and Jill Waterman, *Sexual Abuse of Young Children* (New York: The Guilford Press, 1986); and Diana Russell, *The Secret Trauma: Incest in the Lives of Girls and Women* (New York: Basic Books, 1986).

3. A. Browne and D. Finkelhor, "Impact of Child Sexual Abuse: A Review of the Research," *Psychological Bulletin* 99.1 (1986): 66–77 and J. A. Hunter, "A Comparison of the Psychosocial Maladjustment of Adult Males and Females Sexually Molested as Children," *Journal of Interpersonal Violence* 6.2 (1991): 205–217.

4. Browne and Finkelhor, "Review of the Research," 66–77.

5. C. Adams-Tucker, "Proximate Effects of Sexual Abuse in Childhood: A Report on 28 Children," *American Journal of Psychiatry* 139 (1982): 1252–1256.

6. L. O. Ruch and S. M. Chandler, "The Crisis Impact of Sexual Assault on Three Victim Groups: Adult Rape Victims, Child Rape Victims and Incest Victims," *Journal of Social Service Research* 5 (1982): 83–100.

7. David Finkelhor, "Early and Long-term Effects of Child Sexual Abuse: An Update," *Psychological Bulletin*, 99.1 (1986): 66–77 and Adams-Tucker, "Proximate Effects of Sexual Abuse," 1252–56.

8. Gil, *Healing Power*, 3–6.

9. Ibid., 3–6.

10. B. A. van der Kolk, *Psychological Trauma* (Washington, D.C.: American Psychiatric Press, 1987).

11. S. T. Azar and D. A. Wolfe, "Child Abuse and Neglect," *Treatment of Childhood Disorders*, eds. E. J. Mash and R. A. Barkley (New York: The Guilford Press, 1989) 451–489.

12. *"Sexually Exploited Children: Service and Research Project (Final report for the Office of Juvenile Justice and Delinquency Prevention),"* Tufts New England Medical Center, D. O. C. P. 1984.

13. K. MacFarlane and J. Korbin, "Confronting the Incest Secret Long After the Fact: A Family Study of Multiple Victimization with Strategies for Intervention," *Child Abuse and Neglect* 7 (1983): 225–240.

14. A. Heger, "Pediatrician Describes Examination for Abuse," *American Medical News* March 22 (1985): 14.

15. Comments in this section deal only with those procedures which currently raise the most questions in working with abused children. For additional details of the procedure for working with cases of suspected sexual abuse, consult G. L. Martin, *Counseling for Family Violence and Abuse.*

16. A. Bernstein, "How Children Learn About Sex and Birth," *Psychology Today* January (1976): 31–35, 66.

17. K. M. Quinn, "Children and Deception," *Clinical Assessment of Malingering and Deception*, ed. R. Rogers (New York: The Guilford Press, 1988) 104–122.

18. Richard A. Gardner, "Differentiating Between Bona Fide and Fabricated Allegations of Sexual Abuse of Children," *Journal of the American Academy of Matrimonial Lawyers* 5 (1989): 1–25; and B. W. Boat and M. D. Everson, "Research and Issues in Using Anatomical Dolls," *Annals of Sex Research* 1.2 (1988): 191–204.

19. Virginia M. Friedmann and Marcia K. Morgan, *Interviewing Sexual Abuse Victims Using Anatomical Dolls* (Eugene, Ore.: Migima Designs, Inc., 1985).

20. See M. L. Rogers, "Coping with Alleged False Sexual Molestation: Examination and Statement Analysis Procedures," *Issues in Child Abuse Accusations* 2.2 (1990): 57–68; "Review of the Current Status of the Use of Statement Validity Analysis Procedures in Sex Abuse Cases in the United States," *Issues in Child Abuse Accusations* 22 (1990): 69–75; D. C. Raskin and J. C. Yuille, "Problems in Evaluating Interviews of Children in Sexual Abuse Cases," *New Perspectives on the Child Witness*, ed. S. J. Ceci, M. P. Toglia, and D. F. Ross (New York: Springer-Verlag, 1989) 184–207; D. C. Raskin, ed., *Psychological Methods in Criminal Investigation and Evidence* (New York: Springer, 1989); M. Steller and G. Koehnken, "Criteria-based Statement Analysis," *Psychological Methods in Criminal Investigation and Evidence*, ed. D. C. Raskin (New York: Springer, 1989); and D. C. Raskin and M. Steller, "Assessing Credibility of Allegations of Child Sexual Abuse: Polygraph Examinations and Statement Analysis," *Advances in Legal Psychology: Psychological Research in the Criminal Justice System*, eds. F. Loesel, J. Haisch, and H. Wegener (New York: Springer-Verlag, 1988) 290–302.

21. Martha L. Rogers, "Coping With Alleged False Sexual Molestation," 57–68.

22. Richard A. Gardner, "Differentiating Between Fabricated and Bona Fide Sex Abuse Allegations of Children," Cassette recording. (Cresskill, N.J.: Creative Therapeutics, 1987).

23. Ibid.

24. Beverly James, *Treating Traumatized Children* (Lexington, Mass.: Lexington Books, 1989).

25. L. Heitritter and J. Vought, *Helping Victims of Sexual Abuse: A Sensitive, Biblical Guide for Counselors, Victims, and Families* (Minneapolis: Bethany House Publishers, 1989) and M. Hancock and K. Mains, *Child Sexual Abuse: A Hope for Healing*, (Wheaton, Ill.: Harold Shaw, 1987).

26. James, *Traumatized Children*, 3–4.

27. Ibid., 49.

28. Beverly James and Maria Nasjleti, *Treating Sexually Abused Children and Their Families* (Palo Alto, Calif.: Consulting Psychologists Press, Inc., 1983); and Suzanne M. Sgroi, *Handbook of Clinical Intervention in Child Sexual Abuse* (Lexington, Mass.: D. C. Heath and Co., 1982).

29. Dayan L. Edwards and Eliana Gil, *Breaking the Cycle: Assessment and Treatment of Child Abuse and Neglect* (Los Angeles: Association for Advanced Training, 1986), 161–164 and Suzanne M. Sgroi, *Handbook*, 112–145.

Chapter Five

Childhood Trauma, Dissociative States, and Ritual Abuse

Lisa has difficulty concentrating or paying attention. She is obsessed with things like blood, garbage, fire, earthquakes, and bombs. She is restive and highly dependent on her mother. Lisa also cries often, particularly when her mother is not present. She, has a strong fear of wolves, dogs, bugs, bears, church, doctors, and dinosaurs. Yet, dinosaurs used to be one of her favorite toys. She expresses fears that she has done something bad, is a perfectionist, and seems accident prone. Lisa occasionally talks about hearing voices from a "spirit friend" and acts impulsively.

What has happened to Lisa? Is she suffering from an overactive imagination? Perhaps she has been programmed by an overconcerned mother to parrot these fears and obsessions.

TRAUMA IN CHILDREN

The following discussion of trauma and its effect on children refers specifically to cases of child sexual abuse. However,

137

the general principles for helping a child cope with the trauma of sexual abuse apply as well to other forms of trauma.

Trauma refers to overwhelming and uncontrollable experiences that physically and psychologically impact a child by creating in them feelings of helplessness, vulnerability, loss of safety and loss of control.[1] The concept of the traumagenic states of childhood allows the counselor to examine the specific dynamics of a child's situation, assess the degree of psychological impact, and look for behavioral symptoms.

Several authors have described the idea of traumagenic states as an aid in assessing and treating traumatized children. Finkelhor and Browne identified four categories of traumatic states: sexualization, betrayal, stigmatization, and powerlessness.[2] James has expanded the number of categories to eight.[3] Exhibit 5.1 is an adapted summarization of these categories. Each of these categories of emotional conditions has its own characteristic dynamics, psychological impact, and behavioral manifestations. The therapist can use these categories to compare the child's experiences and presenting problems, though we cannot adopt generic formulas for diagnosis and treatment. Each child experiences trauma in a unique manner. An event may be traumatic for one particular child and not another. Or it may be traumatizing at one stage of a child's development and not at another.

Exhibit 5.1

Traumagenic States in Children[4]

Traumagenic Category	Dynamics	Psychological Impact	Behavioral Manifestations
Self-Blame	Child blames self because: • Good adult did something bad • Trauma was thrilling • Child experienced some type of reward • Child did not actively resist • If child all to blame can continue to love aggressor	• Guilt • Shame • Belief that self is bad	• Isolation • Attempts to rectify • Self-punishing acts • Self-mutilation • Suicide • Substance abuse • Sabotaging achievements

Traumagenic Category	Dynamics	Psychological Impact	Behavioral Manifestations
Self-Blame (cont'd.)	• Child has taken caretaker role • Child has identified with aggressor • Child associates something he/she did with onset of traumatizing event • Child creates illusion he or she can stop traumatizing event when he chooses • Child is told by others he or she is to blame		
Powerlessness	• Helpless; nothing protected the child • Fear • Isolation • Repeated violation of boundaries • Others did not believe	• Anxiety • Fear • Depression • Lowered sense of efficacy • Perception of self as victim • Need to control • Identification with aggressor • Experiencing part of self as being split off	• Nightmares • Phobias • Toileting problems • Delinquency • Pseudomaturation • Eating/sleeping disorders • Agitation • Withdrawal • Retreat to fantasy world • Running away • School problems • Vulnerability to subsequent victimization • Obsessive and age-inappropriate caretaking of others • Aggressiveness, bullying • Suicidal ideation and gestures
Loss and Betrayal	• Violation of trust • Exploitation by others • Physical and/or emotional loss	• Numbing of emotions • Denial • Suppressed longing • Guilt • Rage • Distrust of self and others	• Somatic reactions • Recurrent anxiety dreams • Regressive behaviors • Withdrawal • Inability to attend, distractible • Emotional disconnecting • Avoidance of intimacy • Elective mutism

Traumagenic Category	Dynamics	Psychological Impact	Behavioral Manifestations
Loss and Betrayal (cont'd.)			• Apathy • Indiscriminate clinging • Hoarding • Explosive aggression
Stigmatization	• Child is blamed, denigrated, humiliated • Family and community respond with horror • Child pressured not to tell • Child treated as if permanently damaged	• Guilt • Shame • Lowered self-esteem • Feels different from peers • Self-loathing	• Isolation • Avoidance of success • Compulsive drive to achieve, but never experiences self as good enough • Substance abuse • Self-destructive behavior
Eroticization	• Child rewarded for inappropriate sexual behavior • Child gives false information about sexual behavior and morality • Learns she has power and value as sex object • Physical parts given inordinate attention by adults • Conditioning of sexual activity with negative emotions and memories	• Preoccupation with sexual issues • Confusion about sexual identity • Confusion about sexual norms • Confusion of sex with love and caregiving or caregetting • Negative association to sexual activities and sensations • Positive association to exploitative sexual activities	• Sexualization of affection • Sexual preoccupation • Compulsive aggressive or sadistic sexual behavior • Precocious sexual activity • Sexual victimization of self or others • Responds to neutral touching as a sexual approach
Destructiveness	• Believes this behavior is necessary for survival • Identifies with aggressor and imitates destructive acts • Believes punishment is deserved and acts in ways to bring on hurt • Is attempting to understand and cope with experiences	• Reinforces self-blame, guilt, shame • Frightening loss of impulse-control • Confusion regarding self-concept • Confusion regarding values, morals • Addictive cycle: destructive acts relieve tensions caused by earlier abusive acts	• Engages in destructive, violent or sexualized behavior • Withdrawal • Preoccupation with revenge fantasies • Dangerous risk-taking • Ritualistic reenactment of all or part of traumatic events • Compulsive secret play • Elicits abuse from others

Traumagenic Category	Dynamics	Psychological Impact	Behavioral Manifestations
Destructiveness (cont'd.)	• Wants revenge for those who brought on trauma		
Dissociative Disorder	• Biopsychological predisposition to dissociate • Child lacks internal or external resources to cope with experience • Child experiences overwhelming terror • Child sees dissociative responses modeled in family • Dissociative splitting provides relief from pain • Thought of physical or emotional pain overwhelms child with fear • Child is blocked from processing feelings by secrecy and/or not being allowed to express anger, fear, neediness, etc.	• Fragmentation of personality • Inconsistent and distorted development • Depersonalization • Feels alienated from others • Encapsulates intense emotions	• Spontaneous trance states, sometimes associated with eye-roll • Dual identity: uses more than one name, refers to self as "we," uses third-person form of address • Denies witnessed behavior • Peculiar forgetfulness patterns • Odd variations in skills, schoolwork inconsistent • Sudden mood and behavioral shifts • Self-destructive
Attachment Disorder	• Caregiver unable or unwilling to form emotional attachment to child • Multiple generic caregivers • Child's increased anxiety from unmet needs leads to driven negative expression of need and conflict.	• Cannot trust needs will be met • Cannot find comfort or security in relationships • Isolated, lonely • Depressed • Low self-esteem • Lacks secure base from which to explore the universe • Unable to develop a sense of mastery	• Clingy • Rage reactions • Learning difficulties • Overcontrolling with peers and adults • Emotional detachment • Lack of emotional reciprocity • Engages in social interacions that block and avoid emotional vulnerability • Engages in relentless demands for caregiver attention while not

Traumagenic Category	Dynamics	Psychological Impact	Behavioral Manifestations
Attachment Disorder (cont'd.)	Caregivers respond punitively and child's anxiety increases • Child distances self from attempts to give emotional closeness out of distrust • Caretaking is unpredictable • Child's needs for human connection are not met • Reciprocity does not occur, so child does not experience self as being lovable • No pleasure is found in relationships, so child does not try to give or seek nurturance		experiencing satisfaction from interactions • Nonresponsive to affectionate caring • Lack of spontaneity, rigid • Rejects adult's efforts to soothe • Suppresses emotional responses and imitates behaviors of others • Sabotages potentially gratifying situations

TREATMENT

The traumagenic states detailed in exhibit 5.1 can be used to structure a description of the impact of a traumatizing event on the child as well as to develop a specific, detailed treatment plan. By using these possible traumagenic states when evaluating a child, the therapist can determine, for example, that the child has some feelings of powerlessness, loss, and betrayal, along with a great deal of self-blame. In addition, the evaluation might conclude that there is no dissociative disorder or destructive behavior, but rather, the child has a significant attachment impairment. This profile can then become the basis of the treatment plan.

James summarizes the basic process for treating traumatized children in four major categories.

1. *Communication:* the child learns how to delineate and express complex feelings

2. *Sorting out:* the child explores his or her understanding of what happened
3. *Education:* the child learns to understand the specific elements of the traumatizing experience
4. *Perspective:* the child's experience is accepted as something that has happened to him or her, without the need for exaggeration or minimization of its impact.[5]

This basic process is then applied to each of the traumagenic states described in exhibit 5.1.

CHILDHOOD TRAUMA AND DISSOCIATION

Let's briefly trace the development of dissociation in a traumatized child. First, a child is left in the care of a trusted person such as an older brother. Over a period of several months the brother begins a series of games. These "let's pretend" activities lead to sexual abuse. The child is increasingly exposed to sexual activity that leaves her frightened, confused, remorseful, agitated, and physically injured. During these times of abuse the child's nervous system goes into a fight or flight arousal stage. The child tries everything possible, physically and emotionally, to avoid being injured. But the efforts prove fruitless. The child is told not to tell and is threatened with bodily harm if the secret is shared. The abuse continues over weeks and months with no escape.

During the time of trauma the sympathetic nervous system is evoked. But since the fight or flight mechanism is not successful, something has to give. The parasympathetic nervous system kicks in to reverse the arousal, and the child begins to enter a state of shock. In effect, the child becomes numb. Confusion, disorientation, and loss of perception can take place. The child is not able to think clearly and is confronted with an inability to stop the pain. To live with this fear and dread, the child learns to distance or dissociate from the actual traumatic event. He or she also separates from the memories and feelings associated with the trauma. This dissociation is done to preserve the child's ability to function outside of the traumatic situation. In many ways, it is a very understandable and useful method of coping.

Traumatizing events such as sexual abuse have been identified as a significant predisposing factor in the formation of dissociative disorders in children. One study found 95 percent of the children had been exposed to sexual or physical abuse, or both, over a protracted period. In the majority of cases this begins at an early age, such as four or five, and continues for as long as ten years.[6]

One form of dissociation, multiple personality disorder (MPD), has been diagnosed with increasing frequency over the past decade. MPD was once thought to be very rare, but is now emerging from the shadowy realm of psychological curiosities. It has become a more definitive and recognized emotional disorder. Exact statistics are unknown at this time due to infrequent and faulty diagnosis.[7]

DEFINITION

Dissociation is a complex psychophysiological process with psychodynamic triggers that produces an alteration in the person's consciousness. During this process thoughts, feelings, and experiences are not integrated into the child's memory or awareness in the normal way. This segregation or separation of the mental processes results in the loss of their normal meaningful relationship to the rest of the child's personality.[8]

Two features are found in most dissociative reactions. The first is a disturbance in the child's sense of self-identity. This can include the loss of self-referential memory, the sudden inability to recall important personal information too extensive to be explained by ordinary forgetfulness. The phenomenon is called *psychogenic amnesia*. A variation of this characteristic is the lack of awareness of the existence of several alternating identities, as found in MPD. The second feature is a loss of memory for past events or complex acts that involved the child.[9]

Dissociative phenomena can be viewed as following a continuum that starts with normal behavior such as daydreaming and then moves to dissociative disorder, depersonalization, post-traumatic disorder, and finally, MPD. This relationship is shown in the diagram on the following page.

Continuum of Dissociative Phenomena

Daydreaming	Dissociation	Depersonalization	Post-traumatic Disorder	MPD

MULTIPLE PERSONALITY DISORDER

Multiple personality disorder, or MPD, can be understood as a chronic or persistent dissociative reaction. The diagnosis requires two or more distinct personalities, each of which is dominant at the time. The personality that is dominant at the time determines the child's behavior. Although usually not diagnosed until adulthood, these distinct personalities begin forming in childhood and eventually become complex and integrated personalities. Each personality has its own unique behavior patterns and social relationships.[10]

Kluft has proposed a four-factor theory for understanding the source of MPD. The first factor is the biological capacity to dissociate. As many as 25 percent of all children may be born with the ability to dissociate if the need arises. Factor two is the life experience of severe trauma. About 95 percent of MPD clients have suffered serious and continuing abuse at an early age. The dissociation was used to cope with the abuse. The third factor is the intrapsychic organization or structure possessed by the child. A high level of ability to fantasize and a high level of creativity are examples. The fourth factor is the interpersonal environment, which includes continuing abuse and a lack of nurturance. The child is not provided with supportive caretakers; the abuse continues but there is nobody available to stop it. The child must keep using dissociation to deal with the continuing trauma.

Identifying dissociative disorders in children can be difficult. Even normal children can display some of these symptoms, either through normal development or as a temporary response to situational stress. Further, dissociative behaviors may occur only in private or outside the child's awareness. As a result, they or their caretakers cannot report the symptoms to the clinician.

SYMPTOMS OF MPD IN CHILDREN

There are some symptoms that are fairly specific to dissociatively disordered children. The clinician should be careful to rule out other causative conditions such as allergic reactions to food or chemicals, organic disorders, drug usage, and other psychic disorders that resemble dissociative conditions. Some diagnostic signs include:

- Spontaneous trance states, when the child "spaces out" or stares off into space
- Use of another name
- A claim not be be himself or herself or a claim of dual identity
- Referring to self as "we"
- Change in ability to perform tasks
- Denial of behavior that has been observed by others
- Changes in vision, handwriting, style of dress
- Drastic changes in behavior, unexplained outbursts, disorientation
- Hearing voices
- Loss of time
- Drawing self as multiple persons
- Describing self as "unreal" at times, feels like an alien (a mild form of this is not uncommon in typical adolescent experience)
- Describing surroundings as becoming altered, feels remote from environment
- Getting lost coming home from school or from friend's house[11]

Ritual Child Abuse

Unfortunately, in my practice the need to assess and treat abused children has expanded to include extreme forms of physical, sexual, and emotional abuse. Stories from children strongly suggest the presence of abuse with ritualistic components. Before continuing with this discussion, I need to give a word of caution. We need to be careful about jumping to conclusions when a few elements of bizarre activity emerge from a child's disclosure. A few indicators do not guarantee the child has been a victim of ritualistic or satanic ritualistic abuse.

The concrete data showing clear evidence of satanic or ritualistic abuse is quite limited. Some investigators, such as Robert

Hicks, have concluded there may be very little, if any, basis for such accusations.[12] Hicks has gone to exhaustive lengths to determine whether there is a factual basis to allegations of satanic-inspired criminal activity. He accurately points out many instances of faulty investigative techniques, bad judgment, inconsistent testimony, erroneous logic, and observational bias. However, his philosophical presumptions and world view suggest he may be as biased in his perspective as those he criticizes. Even though his agnostic world view has filtered his research, Hicks is very correct when he argues for restraint, critical analysis, clear thinking, and exhaustive procedures in documenting allegations of satanic ritualistic abuse. A careful and discerning reading of authors such as Hicks can help us become better investigators. As Christians, we do believe in an active and motivated Satan. However, we should not allow ourselves to be guided by hysterical and unfounded allegations. Several investigators have addressed the problem of victim credibility and reliability, and should be consulted before trying to discern truth from fabrication.[13]

DEFINITION

Ritual abuse is a brutal form of trauma that consists of physical, sexual, and psychological abuse and involves the use of rituals. This type of abuse takes place in a context that is linked to symbols or group activities that have religious, magical, or supernatural connotations. These symbols or activities are repeated over and over, often in the presence of numerous perpetrators. Ritual abuse does not have to involve satanic rituals; however, most survivors report that they were ritually abused as part of satanic worship for the purpose of indoctrinating them into satanic beliefs and practices. This type of abuse rarely consists of a single event. Victims report repeated abuse over an extended period of time.[14]

The spectrum of activities ranges from participation and filming in child-child and adult-child sexual relations, to games, to forced participation in religious rituals with people in black robes, to being given drugs and taught prayers to the Devil. At the more extreme end of the spectrum are alleged reports of ceremonial sexual abuse, sophisticated brainwashing techniques, ritualized use of blood, urine, and feces, and the sacrificial killing of animals and other children.[15]

Victims report extreme efforts are made to create and maintain fear. For example, victims may be told their parents will be killed or their house burned down. Abusers will wear police uniforms during the abuse and the child will be told all policemen are members of the cult. Or the child will wake up after a drug-induced sleep and be told that a bomb or monster has been placed inside them. Blood will be found over the child's body as evidence of such "magical surgery."

Ritual abuse is more than sexual abuse. The terrorization, indoctrination, and bizarre nature of the abuse may often be the source of most of the trauma. Another facet is the fact that children are alleged to have been forced to become the victimizer. The child is made to terrorize or harm another child and thus experiences guilt and shame for the acts he has performed on others as well as fear and terror for the atrocities done to him.[16]

Exhibit 5.2 lists symptoms of ritualistic child abuse. As with any such list, the counselor should approach these symptoms with caution. Some odd or unusual behavior is a part of normal development. A fascination with "passing gas," for example, does not mean a child has been abused. Neither does the presence of even one or two extreme behaviors indicate the absolute reality of ritual abuse. The counselor must remain objective, follow proper investigative procedures, and not get caught up in narrow, biased thinking that precludes alternate explanations for these symptom.

Exhibit 5.2

Signs and Symptoms in Ritualistic Child Abuse[17]

1. *Sexual behavior and beliefs:* preoccupation with sexual topics, age-inappropriate knowledge about sex and/or sexualized behavior; compulsive masturbation; references to sexual activities between others or between self and others; pain in the genital area and fear of having their genital washed
2. *Toileting and the bathroom:* avoidance of using the bathroom; acting out inappropriate toileting behavior; preoccupation with urine and feces; discussion of urine and feces at mealtime; uses words for bodily

wastes which are not used in the home; drawing pictures of self or others urinating or defecating

3. *The supernatural, rituals, occult symbols, religion:* fear of ghosts, devils, monsters, vampires, evil spirits and occult symbols; singing odd songs or chants, performing ritualized dances; writing the number 666; drawing pentagrams, inverted crosses and other occult symbols, prays to the devil or performs magic

4. *Small spaces or being tied up:* fear of closets or other small spaces and being locked in same; fear of being tied up; trying to confine or tie up others; fear of being hung upside down

5. *Death:* fear of death or the death of family members or friends

6. *The doctor's office:* fear or mistrust of doctors; extreme fearfulness of shots, blood or blood tests; fear of death from shots, blood, or blood tests; sexual behavior on the examining table (e.g., appears to expect sexual contact with the doctor)

7. *Certain colors:* fear or strong dislike of black or red (sometimes orange, brown, purple); stating that black is their favorite color; referring to ritual use of the colors that are inconsistent with what has been experienced in family religious practices

8. *Eating:* eating disorders, refusal to eat foods, because they are red or brown; fear that food is poisoned; stating that they were forced to ingest blood, urine, feces, or human or animal body parts

9. *Emotional problems:* (including speech, sleep, and learning); rapid mood swings, resisting authority; agitation; hyperactivity; flat affect; poor attention span; learning problems; fearful clingy behavior; regression (including speech); accident proneness; sleep disturbance, etc.

10. *Family relationships:* fear that parents will die; fear of abandonment; fears of being kidnapped; fear that parents want to kill them; seems distant to parent, avoids close physical contact; attacks or initiates sexual contact with others; puts excrement on a sibling, parent or pet

11. *Play or peer relations:* destroying toys; hurting other children; acting out themes of death, mutilation, occultism, sexual perversion, excretion, cannibalism, and burial; play involves themes of drugging, threats, humiliation, torture, bondage, magic

12. *Other fears, disclosures, or strange beliefs:* fear of being put in jail or having the house broken into, robbed, or burned down; fear of robbers, bad people, strangers, and police; discusses drugs, pills and drug-like effects; discusses unusual places like cemeteries, mortuaries, church basements; believes that something foreign has been put inside their body such as a bomb, Satan's heart, a monster; alludes to having nude pictures taken of them, strikes provocative poses

Older children and adolescents may demonstrate a preoccupation with ideas and symbols of Satanism and the occult.

This may come out in their conversations and written material or in their drawings and doodles. These symbols may also be used on their body, such as tattoos, or on notebooks, book covers, lockers, and other personal possessions. Their clothing, jewelry, and adornments may take on the signs and symbols of the occult. But keep in mind teen-agers can pick up on the unusual or bizarre out of motivations other than involvement in the occult.

Withdrawal from family and long-established friendships and sudden disinterest in church and Christian values can be a normal part of the teen-age emancipation and rebellion. But this behavior can also accompany participation or victimization from the dark side.

Interest in the literature of the occult is probably quite suggestive. Written material about the occult, along with journal entries, coded messages, rituals, and chants can be symptomatic. The teen-ager's consumption of magazines, articles, poetry, or pictures that focus on death and violence, along with increased preferences for movies or TV that dwell on the occult would also be a concern.

Occult-related paraphernalia such as knives, candles, incense, bones, skulls, animal parts, artwork, jewelry, or ornamentation that portray satanic symbols could be used by the teen to set up altars or carry out rituals. Various books and organizations exist which can provide detailed descriptions and illustrations of many satanic signs, symbols, and significant celebrations or "holy days" during the year. Careful and selective examination of these materials can prove helpful. Just be cautious in your commitment to an objective, yet spiritually-aware approach to this subject.[18]

Dramatic methods of attempting suicide, such as self-immolation or cutting their own throats have been identified in adolescents involved in satanism and cult activity. Fantasies of killing their parents or others in some gruesome manner can be present; drug usage and anti-establishment, and anti-Christian sentiment may also be expressed.

Following a survey of pre-Inquisition historical documents describing satanism and satanic practices, Hill and Goodwin compiled a list of eleven elements of satanic rituals. These elements are: (1) secret nocturnal feasting around a special table or altar; (2) ritual orgiastic sex involving incest, homosexuality, and anal intercourse; (3) imitations and reversals of the Christian mass; (4) ritual use of blood, semen, urine, or excrement; (5) sacrifice of embryos and infants often using knives, often followed by cooking them in a cauldron and/or ritual cannibalism; (6) ritual use of animals; (7) ritual use of torches, candles, and darkness; (8) chanting, especially of names of demons; (9) drinking a drug or potion; (10) dancing backward in a circle or other ritual use of the circle; and (11) dismemberment of corpses and extraction of the heart.[19]

This historical evidence does not make contemporary victims' reports of ritual abuse true, but it does serve to emphasize the fact that we are not dealing with a new phenomenon. Evil has been with us for centuries. It is, nevertheless, interesting that contemporary reports from victims so closely correlate with the historical record.

ASSESSING DEGREE OF DAMAGE

Research has identified various factors that can increase the impact of abuse on a child. These factors, defined in Exhibit 5.3 include:

- The relationship of the molester to the victim
- The use of force and violence
- The degree of nonviolent coercion
- The severity of abuse
- The duration of abuse
- The frequency of abuse
- The age and developmental status of the victim
- The emotional climate of the child's family
- The reactions of significant adults to the report of abuse
- The guilt the child feels
- The meaning of the event to the child

Because there have been very few practical efforts to bring this information together for the clinician, I have prepared a form that allows the counselor to make an objective summary of the effects of abuse on a particular child. With each of these factors the counselor uses a rating scale to assign values ranging from one to five. A rating of "one" indicates an extremely minimal presence of that factor, a rating of "three" reflects a moderate degree of influence or impact, and a "five" suggests an extreme degree of the negative factor being present. The counselor's rating of the severity of the factors is certainly a subjective decision, but the table can be a useful clinical tool in formulating an initial impression about the total traumatic impact of the abuse.

Another major ingredient in determining the impact of child sexual abuse is an understanding of the adaptive or coping abilities of the child. Instruments such as the Vineland Adaptive Behavior Scales, which is based on an a structured interview with the parent(s), can provide an objective measure of the child's performance of the daily activities required for personal and social sufficiency.[20]

The Vineland Adaptive Behavior Composite Score, with a mean of 100 and a standard deviation of 15, can be converted to one of five adaptive levels ranging from Low to Adequate to High. This data gives an estimate of the coping skills of the child. It might even be useful to obtain before and after descriptions of the child from the parents to see if the adaptive skills have deteriorated since the abuse began or was disclosed.

Other measures of developmental abilities may be necessary in some cases. For children under two and a half, the Bayley Scales of Infant Development is useful. For children over two and a half, either the McCarthy Scales of Children's Abilities or the Kaufman Assessment Battery for Children are appropriate. The Wechsler Preschool and Primary Scale of Intelligence for preschool children, and the newly revised Wechsler Intelligence Scale for Children-III for elementary through high school students are both excellent measures of intelligence. These IQ tests are necessary to assess the learning potential of a child. Being aware of that potential, the counselor can compare measures of adaptation, much as academic achievement scores are measured to determine discrepancies.

Exhibit 5.3

Damage Factor and Adaptive Level Chart for Child Sexual Abuse

A. Degree of Damaging Factors   (circle one)

	Low Moderate High
1. *The relationship of the molester to the victim:* The more closely related or highly trusted the molester, the more damage to the child.	1 2 3 4 5
2. *The amount of force or violence:* The more force or violence, the greater the damage, especially if serious physical injuries result.	1 2 3 4 5
3. *The degree of nonviolent coercion:* The greater the amount of fear and guilt used in controlling the victim, the more serious the damage.	1 2 3 4 5
4. *The severity of abuse:* Intercourse is more emotionally harmful than genital exposure or other noncontact forms of abuse. However, extensive and long-term fondling has been found in some instances to rival the damage caused by intercourse.	1 2 3 4 5
5. *The duration of abuse:* Sexual abuse which takes place over a long period of time more harmful because the child has greater opportunity to utilize and refine defense mechanisms, such as dissociation, which can become more problematic as the child gets older.	1 2 3 4 5
6. *The frequency of incidents:* The more chronic and frequent the incident, the greater the emotional damage as the child experiences a greater sense of helplessness and vulnerability.	1 2 3 4 5
7. *The age and developmental status of the victim:* Some discrepancy exists in the research here. There is some trend to viewing the younger child as more vulnerable to damage.	1 2 3 4 5
8. *The emotional climate of the child's family:* Dysfunctional families with characteristics such as family discord, mental health problems, divorce, drug and alcohol dependence, spouse abuse, social isolation and insufficient income, can add to the emotional damage an abused child experiences, as well as be harmful, separate and distinct from the abuse.	1 2 3 4 5
9. *The reactions of significant adults to the report of abuse:* The less emotional support the victim receives from the family members and the community, the greater the degree of damage.	1 2 3 4 5
10. *The guilt the child feels:* The greater the amount of guilt a child feels for having felt pleasure, for causing the abuse, or for the disruption following disclosure, the greater the impact.	1 2 3 4 5
11. *The meaning of the event to the child:* The greater the traumatic impact in the eyes of the child, the greater the impact.	1 2 3 4 5
Total of Damage Factors (Range will be 11-55)	

B. Level of Adaptive Behavior of Child   Adaptive Level

	L	ML	A	MH	H
1. Level of Adaptive Behavior Composite Score from Vineland Adaptive Behavior Scales	1	2	3	4	5
(Based on Standard Score from administration of Expanded Form, Interview Edition)					

When there is a significant difference between potential and current functioning, environmental factors such as abuse may explain part of the differences.

Completing the Damage Factor and Adaptive Level Chart in exhibit 5.3 will give the counselor a fairly accurate idea of the severity of the child's experience. One implication is the more severe the abusive experience, and the lower the adaptive functioning, the more support the child is going to need, immediately and over the long term.

For example, a child might appear to be dealing fairly well with things a month or so after the disclosure, and the family may report very few symptoms. But the impact factors show that the child was raped by her father over a period of four years, she received numerous violent threats, and her mother is minimizing the importance of the whole ordeal. (On the Damage Factor Chart the toal of part A is 43, an average rating of almost 4 for each item, and the rating on part B, the Adaptive Functioning on the Vineland, is Low.) From these indices, the counselor concludes that it is vital that the child have maximum emotional, physical, and educational support. A recommendation to the court or social service organizations would be that the child probably needs long-term care. Also, the mother needs support for her own issues and will need to be encouraged to make sure the daughter is kept safe.

A case study illustrating an example of suspected child ritual abuse is presented in Appendix II.

SUMMARY

The concept of traumagenic states allows the counselor to examine the specific dynamics of a child's situation, assess the degree of psychological impact, and look for the behavioral symptoms. The traumagenic categories described are: self-blame, powerlessness, loss and betrayal, stigmatization, eroticization, destructiveness, dissociative disorder, and attachment disorder.

Traumatizing events such as sexual abuse can be a predisposing factor in the formation of dissociative disorders in children. Dissociation is a complex psychophysiological process that produces a separation of the child's mental processes. This produces a disturbance in the child's sense of self-identity and a loss of memory for the events involved.

Multiple personality disorder (MPD) is at the extreme end of the dissociative continuum. It produces two or more distinct personalities. While not usually diagnosed until adulthood, these personalities begin forming in childhood. The sources of MPD are thought to be a result of the biological incapacity to dissociate, severe trauma, a high level of intrapsychic organization, and the continuing existence of abuse and lack of nurturing or emotional support.

Ritualistic child abuse is a brutal form of abuse that consists of physical, sexual, and psychological abuse and involves the use of rituals. It usually takes place in a context that is linked to symbols or group activities that have religious, magical, or supernatural connotations. There are certain signs and symptoms of ritual abuse in children. These, along with activities common in adolescent victims, are shown in exhibit 5.2.

The Damage Factor and Adaptive Level chart for child sexual and ritual abuse shown in exhibit 5.3 can be used by the counselor to estimate the level of severity or impact of a abusive experience.

Many of the symptoms of a severely abused, and possibly ritualistically abused, young child are described in the case study included in Appendix II.

NOTES

1. Beverly James, *Treating Traumatized Children* (Lexington, Mass.: Lexington Books, 1989) 21–38.

2. D. Finkelhor and A. Browne, "The Traumatic Impact of Child Sexual Abuse: A Conceptualization," *Annual Progress in Child Psychiatry & Child Development* (1986): 632–648.

3. James, *Treating Traumatized Children*, 21–38.

4. Ibid., 21–38.

5. James, *Treating Traumatized Children*, 50–52

6. C. A. Ross, et al., "Abuse Histories in 102 Cases of Multiple Personality Disorder," *Canadian Journal of Psychiatry*, 36.2 (1991): 97–101; B. G. Braun, "Multiple Personality Disorder: An Overview. Special Issue: Multiple Personality Disorder," *American Journal of Occupational Therapy*, 44.11 (1990): 971–976.

7. James G. Friesen, *Uncovering the Mystery of MPD*, (San Bernardino, Calif.: Here's Life, 1991); L. C. Baldwin, "Child Abuse as an Antecedent of Multiple Personality Disorder. Special Issue: Multiple Personality Disorder," *American Journal of Occupational Therapy*, 44.11 (1990): 978–983; Richard P. Kluft, ed., *Childhood Antecedents of Multiple Personality*, (Washington, D. C.: American Psychiatric Press, 1985).

8. Frank W. Putnam, "Dissociation as a Response to Extreme Trauma," *Childhood Antecedents of Multiple Personality*, R. P. Kluft, ed. (Washington, D.C.: American Psychiatric Press, 1985) 66–97.

9. Ibid. 67–68.

10. A valuable addition to our understanding of MPD from the Christian perspective is provided by Dr. James Friesen in *Uncovering the Mystery of MPD*. A close reading of the book will give you insight on diagnosis and treatment strategies appropriate for both the psychological and spiritual forms of intervention. See also the American Psychiatric Association's *Diagnostic and Statistical Manual of Mental Disorders*, Third Edition, Revised (Washington, D.C.: American Psychiatric Press, 1986).

11. Finkelhor and Browne, "The Traumatic Impact of Child Sexual Abuse,". 632–48.

12. J. T. Richardson, J. Best, and D. G. Bromley, *The Satanism Scare* (Hawthorne, N.Y.: Aldine de Gruyter, 1991); Robert D. Hicks, *In Pursuit of Satan: The Police and the Occult* (Buffalo, N.Y.: Prometheus Books, 1991).

13. S. C. Van Benschoten, "Multiple Personality Disorder and Satanic Ritual Abuse: The Issue of Credibility," *Dissociation: Progress in the Dissociative Disorders*, 3.1 (1990): 22–30; G. K. Ganaway, "Historical Truth Versus Narrative Truth: Clarifying the Role of Exogenous Trauma in the Etiolgy of Multiple Personality Disorder and its Variants," *Dissociation*, 2 (1989): 205–220; P. S. Hudson, "Ritual Child Abuse: A Survey of Symptoms and Allegations," *Journal of Child and Youth Care: Special Issue: In the Shadow of Satan: The Ritual Abuse of Children* (1990): 27–53; J. Crewdson, *By Silence Betrayed: Sexual Abuse of Children in America* (Boston: Little, Brown and Company, 1988); K. Marron, *Ritual Abuse: Canada's Most Infamous Trial on Child Abuse* (Toronto: McClelland-Bantam, Inc., 1988); J. Hollingworth, *Unspeakable Acts* (New York: Cogdon & Weed, 1986).

14. W. C. Young, et al., "Patients Reporting Ritual Abuse in Childhood: A Clinical Syndrome: Report of 37 Cases.," *Child Abuse & Neglect*, 15.3 (1991): 181–189; V. Graham-Costain and C. Gould, "Play Therapy with Ritually Abused Children," Presented at The Seventh International Conference on Multiple Personality/Disociative States (November 10, 1990); *Ritual Abuse*, Report of the Ritual Abuse Task Force, (Los Angeles: Los Angeles County Commission for

Women, 1989); D. Finklehor, L. M. Williams, and N. Burns, *Nursery Crimes: Sexual Abuse in Day Care* (Newbury Park, Calif.: Sage Press, 1988).

15. L. J. Cozolino, "The Ritual Abuse of Children: Implications for Clinical Practice and Research," *Journal of Sex Research*, 26.1 (1989): 131–138; and "Religious Expression and Ritual Child Abuse," *Psychologists Interested in Religious Issues Newsletter (APA Division 36)*, 14.1 (1989): 3–6.

16. Finkelhor, Williams and Burns, *Nursery Crimes*, 155.

17. Exhibit 5.2 was prepared by Louis Cozolino and represents an abridged version of an extensive document prepared by Dr. Catherine Gould. See C. Gould, "Signs and Symptoms of Ritualistic Child Abuse," Unpublished document (Catherine Gould, Ph.D., 12011 San Vicente Blvd., Suite 402, Brentwood, CA 90049, 1988) and "Satanic Ritual Abuse: Child Victims, Adult Survivors, System Presponse," *California Psychologist*, 22.3 (1987): 9–15. Hudson describes a similar list of symptoms, allegations, and reported forms of abuses. See P. S. Hudson, "Ritual Child Abuse: A Survey of Symptoms and Allegations," *Journal of Child and Youth Care*, 27–52.

18. Lyle J. Rapacki, *Satanism—The Not So New Problem*, 3rd. ed. (Flagstaff, Ariz.: Crossroad Ministries, Inc./INTEL, 1988).

19. S. Hill and L. Goodwin, "Satanism: Similarities Between Patient Accounts and Pre-Inquisition Historical Sources," *Dissociation* 2.1 (1989): 39–44.

20. S. S. Sparrow, D. A. Balla, amd D. V. Cicchetti eds., *Expanded Form Manual, Vineland Adaptive Behavior Scales*, interview edition (Circle Pines, Minn.: American Guidance Service, 1984).

Chapter Six

Custody Evaluations: Initial Considerations

Most counselors who work with children and youth do not set out to practice forensic psychology. The image of being cross-examined by Perry Mason and trying to respond to a complicated question about human behavior with a simple yes or no answer does not appeal to most counselors. But if you work with children, the chances are good that you will have some type of contact with the court system. The most probable court-related process that counselors will face is a custody determination. Even counselors who do not conduct independent custody evaluations need to know how to handle the inevitable requests for declarations or opinions about clients. Also likely is the surprise visit by a courier who delivers a subpoena and then vanishes, leaving the counselor to wade through the legal language mandating that everything known about a particular client be revealed.

This chapter introduces the process of custody evaluations, and the next chapter provides specific tools and procedures for conducting the evaluations.

BACKGROUND AND HISTORY OF CHILD CUSTODY DETERMINATIONS

Divorce is an obvious sign of a collapsing family system. One out of two to three marriages now ends in divorce. The most frequent and major issues in these dissolutions are property rights and child custody. The process of divorce is now simpler than ever—nearly all fifty states have "no-fault" laws.[1] This makes it easier for couples to end their relationships, but it also means increasing numbers of children are becoming embroiled in a legal tug-of-war.

Disputes concerning the custody of children are among the most difficult and troubling decisions to adjudicate. Often the court is asked to choose between custody alternatives that are either equally good or equally not in the best interests of the child. Such is the case if two parents who claim to love their child appear to be equally flawed and equally capable.

It really is not much different from the dilemma Solomon faced some three thousand years ago. According to the description in 1 Kings (3:16–27), both women who came before Solomon were prostitutes. Each had given birth to a baby just three days apart while living together, probably in a brothel. One child had died, perhaps after the mother rolled on top of it in her sleep. (Another hypothesis is that this was an early instance of sudden infant death syndrome or SIDS). Whatever the reason, Solomon was asked to render a decision regarding the "best interests" of the surviving child. God's wisdom was obviously needed, because neither of these ladies brought glowing endorsements and neither led an exemplary life.

Like Solomon, judges in custody disputes today are faced with the task of making decisions that will determine the future of entirely innocent children. To help with this process, the courts frequently request the assistance of "expert" witnesses. And it is in these highly charged emotional settings that the mental health professional contributes his or her opinion. The goal is to perform a comprehensive job of evaluating and reporting that will serve the needs of the children who are already experiencing high levels of stress.

Historically, courts have followed traditional social role definitions of parents when determining which parent should be granted custody following a divorce. Unless that parent was deemed unfit as a caretaker, the parent whose social role was believed to be most important for the care of the child was given custody. Prior to the eighteenth century, the social role definitions of parental responsibilities gave the father complete legal control over the family. Going back to Roman legal precedent, the Law of the Twelve Tables granted the father the absolute right to sell his children, as well as the power of life and death over them. That authority, known in Roman jurisprudence as *patria potestas*, is one of the most far-reaching legacies of the private law of Rome. Children were considered to be the father's property, much the same way as material goods. Women held no rights over their husbands. They could neither question the father's ability as a parent nor exert any legal influence over him.

One of the earliest instances of courts showing some concern for the welfare of the child occurred in Britain in 1817, when Shelley, the poet, lost custody of his children after his wife Harriet's suicide. The judgment was made because he was an atheist and had engaged in immoral conduct.[2] For the first time in Western history, children were awarded rights as individuals. The English parliament established this change in the social status of children in 1817 by instituting the doctrine of *parens patriae*. This doctrine held that the Crown should defend the rights of those who had no other protection.[3] For the first time in history, although it did not happen very often, the father's rights over his children could be superseded by the rights of the child.

The presumption that fathers had priority over mothers, unless the father could be shown to be unfit, continued until the early 1900s. By the 1920s, however, the courts had shifted to favor maternal custody based on the "tender years" doctrine. At that time, the mother's care was seen as necessary and more important than paternal care for development through the early years of life. The courts began to refer to the assumption that young children needed a mother's care to facilitate their growth and development. Under this presumption, and through the 1920s, custody awards were often given to mothers. But fathers still won most of the custody determinations.[4]

Initially, the first four years of a child's life were thought to require maternal care. As the importance of a mother's care was expanded, the time was extended. The courts reflected this rise in the social status of the mother, so that by the mid-1900s about 90 percent of the cases were settled in favor of the mother.[5] This altered the burden of proof so that the father had to prove the mother unfit in order to gain custody.

The pendulum eventually became more centered by the 1970s as the courts began to recognize the "best interest of the child" standard. This presumption, suggesting a more sex-neutral stance, was codified in the Uniform Marriage and Divorce Act of 1970, and has since been adopted by all states. The Act states that "the court shall determine custody in accordance with the best interest of the child." All relevant factors are to be considered, including the wishes of the child's parent(s); the wishes of the child; the child's interaction and interrelationships with other family members; the child's adjustment to school, home, and community; the mental and physical health of all persons involved; and the presence of potential violence or abuse. The court is not to consider any conduct of the present or proposed custodian that does not affect the relationship to the child.[6]

The 1980s marked a growing trend to recognize, and even encourage, joint custody. It is now permitted in every state, and the majority of states have statutes that specifically recognize it.[7] The premise for joint custody is to keep both parents actively involved in the life of the child. While it appears to be a sensible idea, the conflicts that bring a couple to divorce also make it difficult for most divorcing parents to cooperate and communicate objectively about the logistics of joint custody. Research to date has not supported the assumption that joint custody will promote cooperation between previously conflicting parents.[8]

CAUTIONS REGARDING THE CUSTODY DETERMINATION PROCESS

The state of the law relating to the custody of the persons of infants is not very satisfactory. Not only are

there defects which can, perhaps, be remedied only
by the authority of the legislature, but there prevails
an uncertainty in the application of the law as it exists to the difficult cases which frequently arise in
connection with the disposition of minor children.[9]

This statement, written in 1850, is as accurate today as it was
over 140 years ago. Our legal system is still struggling to determine how best to deal with the breakup of family units. We
are looking for a way that is just, fair, and equitable, and which
minimizes the emotional trauma of the participants. Unfortunately, the U. S. court system, in both criminal and civil action,
is based on the adversarial form of presenting a case.

ADVERSARIAL SYSTEM

Some would argue that the adversary system used in the
United States is the worst conceivable method for resolving
child custody disputes.[10] The system is based on the theory that
the best way to resolve a dispute is for both parties to present
their arguments before a presumably impartial third party.
Each side is represented by an advocate who does everything
possible to support the contentions of his or her client. Information that might weaken the position of the litigant is
withheld or minimized whenever possible. Information that
strengthens their position is emphasized. Out of this conflict
of presentations, the impartial party (judge or jury) is presumably in the best position to determine who is telling the truth.
The impartial party then makes a decision regarding the resolution of the dispute.[11]

The system was designed to determine whether an accused
party did, in fact, commit a crime. This same system is now
being utilized to decide which of two parents, who are often
quite equal, albeit different, in their parenting capacities, would
better serve as the primary custodial parent for their children.
The adversarial system can intensify the stress of a marital
breakup. Children feel pressured to verbalize a parental
preference. The stress of the legal conflict can exacerbate pre-
existent psychopathology and can even cause problems such
as parental alienation syndrome. I have worked with clients

who, at the time I saw them, were, indeed, abnormally suspicious or fearful to the degree that they were not able to function as a safe parent. But I was convinced their condition had arisen as a result of a protracted divorce dispute along with all the threats and power plays that typically accompany the process. This is not to lay all the blame on the legal process. An abusive and manipulative power addict can find ways to harass a spouse even outside the court system. The point is that the use of adversarial litigation as the primary way to settle domestic disputes is as much a cause of many problems as it is a solution.

You may not agree with the adversary system, but if you expect to serve as an expert witness, you must understand the mechanics and logic of the process. By reading literature on the counselor and the court system, talking to colleagues familiar with forensic work, attending a few civil trials, and discussing the issues with an attorney or two who will give some pointers, the counselor can derive a basic understanding of the process and its influence on counseling. The concepts and terms used in the court system influence the way the counselor gathers data, examines the results, and prepares the report. A counselor who doesn't understand the system is very likely to make a technical error or omission that will render the work uncredible.

TRAITS OF THE MENTAL HEALTH PROFESSIONAL

The typical mental health professional is not trained for, and usually does not have the temperament to function at maximum effectiveness in the legal process. Counselors tend to want to facilitate communication, work toward compromises, and bring peace to a conflictual setting. With that orientation, and without a proper understanding of the rules of court conduct, counselors can add to the problem rather than help.

To work successfully within the court system, a counselor must have clear thinking skills, must not be easily rattled, and must have a constitution strong enough to withstand the cross-examination procedures and the inevitable criticism and complaints from unsuccessful clients. It also helps to have some obsessive-compulsive qualities and good attention to detail. Unfortunately, none of this information is covered sufficiently in graduate school. More often it is learned in a trial by fire. Be forewarned. It is frustrating work.

REASONS FOR CUSTODY DISPUTES

Some custody battles occur for reasons other than a desire to have residential and decision-making control of the children. Requests for custody can stem simply from anger, manipulation, and power issues. I remember one situation where the father didn't want the hassle of taking care of the children on a daily basis, he just didn't want the mother to "win." The parent may request custody as a continuation of power or control battles within the dissolving marriage. At other times the motive may be to get revenge or to hurt the other parent. It is also possible that one of the parents has become dependent on the child, and the request is primarily an effort to continue an addictive and reversed relationship. At times, custody battles are used as bargaining tools in the divorce. For example, the father may say, "I will drop my request for custody if you will accept a lower child support payment." Another situation arises when a parent finds himself or herself dealing with unresolved issues from childhood. "I had to live with my critical mother and abusive stepfather, so I won't ever let that happen to my children." The custody battle then becomes an attempt to work out unresolved inner conflicts.

These are not reasons for avoiding an independent evaluator role. These are just examples of the complex dynamics that are involved. The feelings will be as intense as anything you have ever seen in therapy or counseling.

PROFESSIONAL BIASES

Another issue that has impact in these situations is professional and personal bias. I have been asked to issue opinions in cases where one parent has left the home and is living with another person. The remaining parent wanted me to be an advocate for her side, documenting that her husband's infidelity and lifestyle was harmful to the child. In today's society that is a very tough thing to prove. In fact, the court often excludes the offending parent's lifestyle as not having any bearing on the ability to parent. While we may agree with the offended spouse about the definitions of sin and wrongdoing, as professionals we must support any contentions we make in court with precise data that shows a solid connection to child development.

We need to be aware of our biases and values and how they might affect our interpretation of the data we collect. We need to be particularly sensitive to attitudes about sex roles and psychological health. For example, some studies have suggested that mental health professionals place more emphasis on exhaustively evaluating the degree to which the mother meets traditional sexual role stereotypes than in evaluating the father.[12] The implication is that if the evaluator believes the mother does not live up to the sex role stereotypes, the recommendation for custody should be in favor of the father, yet the father would not have to measure up to comparable standards.

The key to serving the best interests of the child is to do all we can to remain objective and know the presence of and effects of our values. We cannot be without values; we just need to know how and where they operate.

RISK OF PERSONAL HARM

Another consideration in taking on custody evaluations is the risk of personal harm. Any work with angry clients involves the possibility that they may choose to respond in a form that could be dangerous to the therapist. The nature of custody conflicts makes this likelihood even more probable.

I recall a time several years ago when I called the attorney representing the mother of two boys I was counseling. The boys had come to me with a background of physical and sexual abuse. Initially, I was asked simply to validate the existence of abuse. But before I was very far into the case, the issues included visitation rights for the father. When I talked to the attorney, the first thing he asked me was what kind of security force existed at my office complex. He added that since taking this particular case he had started carrying a gun. The father of these boys had a violent history, had made numerous threats, and demonstrated a preoccupation with guns, knives, and war games. He had also verbalized a strong hatred for anyone who supported or assisted his wife, and for counselors who might interfere with his parental rights. I did eventually recommend against any contact with the father, and when I went to court to testify, I was greeted by two police officers who were sent to frisk the father for weapons before entering the courtroom. The attorney, I believe, intentionally arrived late to the proceedings as a personal safety precaution.

I have been told by clients that I was on the hit list of disgruntled spouses who were quoted as saying, "If I can't have my kids, nobody else will have them either." And, "If I go down I'm going to take a bunch of people with me." Other types of clinical work can have risks, but custody conflicts certainly involve a degree of peril not found in giving an IQ test to a ten-year-old.

NONPAYMENT FOR SERVICES

Nonpayment for services rendered is another problem that arises in custody evaluations. I expect every counselor has had at least one client who refused to pay for services because they did not like the recommendations made or the outcome of the court's decisions. Angry parents who do not like the counselor's opinion are often reluctant to pay. One such father told me I was a Judas and I could very well get my "thirty pieces of silver" from his ex-wife if I expected to receive anything else for the work I had done. He took this stand, flaunting the authority of a signed document spelling out the mutual responsibilities to pay.

PERSONAL AGONY

Perhaps the most distressful aspect of custody evaluations is the agony and stress of making Solomon-type decisions. Most often counselors are required to evaluate the strengths and weaknesses of two parents who are more alike than different. Sometimes there are clear indicators of preference or unfit characteristics, but usually the decision is an agonizing choice made by sifting through differing types of data, much of it subjective. Thankfully, more objective measures of parent effectiveness and child bonding are becoming available to the evaluator. It will never be easy, however. Counselors will never be able to add up the pluses and minuses for each parent and give the child to the one with the highest score.

I recently wrote a letter to a father telling him I had finally decided to terminate all visits between him and his children. This case had gone on for two and a half years. He had abused one of the children, and I became involved in treating the boys for the trauma of the abuse, parental separation, and behavior problems. In the process, my observations were used by the court to award sole custody to the mother. However, I was designated as the one to decide if visitations were to be allowed. We tried numerous cycles of visitation, observation, and treatment to see if visits could occur without causing major disruptions for the children. It just did not work. This was a classic example of the parent alienation syndrome (discussed in chapter seven). I agonized for months over how to resolve this situation, eventually collecting enough observations from numerous sources to feel confident about my final recommendation. The father had made all kinds of threats, but given all the information available to me, terminating visitation was the best decision even though the emotional cost was high.

A counselor taking on custody cases must have a reasonable tolerance for this type of stress and a good system for managing personal stressors. I guarantee your blood pressure and stomach acid will rise to harmful levels at various times. So why do it? We need also to ask ourselves, if Christians don't become involved in these hard decisions with the promise of God's direction and strength, who will?

DISCERNMENT

Discernment is a key ingredient in the custody process. Solomon gives us some background on the definition of this form of wisdom. Motive is crucial to the employment of discernment. In 1 Kings 3, Solomon's motivation is apparent. God appears to Solomon in a dream and informs Solomon he can "Ask for whatever you want me to give you." (1 Kings 3:5). Solomon, who was only about twenty years old, lacked experience in assuming the responsibilities of his office. He responds by asking God to ". . . give your servant a discerning heart to govern your people and to distinguish between right and wrong . . ." (1 Kings 3:9). Right and wrong are used here in a judicial sense. The basis of Solomon's request was that he might judge the people in equity and truth.

God was pleased, and answered Solomon's request by saying, "Since you have asked for this and not for long life or wealth for yourself, nor have asked for the death of your enemies but for discernment in administering justice, I will do what you have asked. I will give you a wise and discerning heart, . . ." (1 Kings 3:11,12).

Discernment means to make a judgment or a distinction. It has one function—to distinguish right from wrong so the right can be promoted and the wrong can be eliminated. Discernment is not so much a function of the mind as it is a function of the Holy Spirit in concert with our thoughts and experiences.[13] The motive for discernment is not to promote ourselves or secure an advantage over another person.

We are instructed, "If any of you lacks wisdom, he should ask God, who gives generously to all without finding fault, and it will be given to him" (James 1:5). It is instructive to note there are conditions attached to God's promise. Obviously, we must ask. But the request must also be made in faith, nothing wavering. We must believe and not doubt. When we come to God, we must be sure we want what we are requesting. We are to avoid divided allegiance. A double-minded person has reservations about prayer and about the certainty of God granting the request.

God's promise comes after James has told us to count it "pure joy" when we face trials of many kinds. These difficult circumstances help us develop perseverance. The wisdom we request from God will allow us to face these inevitable difficulties with patience and practical insights into life.

Applied to the process of custody evaluations, I see no more difficult or trying situation facing the Christian counselor. Our advantage is that we have access to both God's revealed and inspired knowledge. Revealed, or natural truth, is found in the body of knowledge we call psychology. Of course, we need discernment to sort through the truth and fiction within our field of practice, but there is relevant information there. We should utilize our science just as an engineer uses the laws of physics in designing a car.

Yet we must be even more diligent about seeking God's inspired knowledge as found in Scripture. Without this foundation for comparison and examination, we will certainly become confused, misled, and double-minded. Revealed truth can be used in our evaluation process only if it is not contaminated by secular assumptions about morality and ultimate meanings.[14]

THE VALUE OF EXPERT OPINION

Custody cases are intellectually and emotionally difficult when a court is forced to choose between custody alternatives which are neither clearly best nor clearly harmful for the child. Regardless of the outcome, when such an adversarial process is used, some person(s) will suffer great heartbreak. Even the move to a presumption of joint custody or the use of parenting plans does not solve the problem. Couples who are at great odds over their relationship are seldom able to achieve agreement concerning the specifics of joint custody or parenting plan arrangements.

Because of the difficulty of the decisions, expert opinion has come to play an important part in the determination process. However, the use of experts from the field of psychology has been criticized. Some have argued that psychological and psychiatric professions have nothing meaningful to contribute.[15]

Properly circumscribed, there is a legitimate, useful, and important role for expert psychological testimony in custody cases. As long as the adversarial system is being used and custody disputes are going to be determined by fixed and unbending rules, somebody is going to have to make some predictions about what are the "best interests of the child." The question then becomes, Should the court try to make these difficult decisions with or without the input from mental health experts? Psychological testimony can provide the court with information not otherwise readily available. As long as psychological testimony is more likely to add than detract from the accuracy of the court's prediction, it has a useful and necessary function.[16]

WAYS THE EVALUATOR CAN HELP THE COURT

The mental health professional can be a valuable asset to the court. There are four categories of assistance identified by Litwack, et al., that seem to be relevant: discovering, articulating, highlighting, and analyzing.[17]

DISCOVERING

Through interviews and testing, the counselor can identify and then bring to the attention of the court the feelings, attitudes, and personality traits of the children in the custody dispute. Patterns of interaction among all family members, patterns not otherwise evident to the court, can be discovered.

For example, out of fear of incurring parental displeasure, a child may profess to love and feel bonded to both parents equally, but interviews and testing reveal the child actually has a stronger relationship with one of the parents. Similarly, an in-depth investigation may reveal the adult's feelings toward a child are more complex than professed. A mother may say she loves her oldest daughter and wants to have her and the rest of the children live with her, while interviews reveal the mother has always treated the daughter harshly. Detailed questioning about parenting suggests the mother believes this daughter has always been defiant, resistant, and angry. Observation of the interaction reveals the mother is indifferent to the daughter but attentive and supportive toward the other children.

Based on this information, the mother is not an unfit parent, but the observations certainly do differ from her alleged feelings and need to be presented in the process of determining the best interests of that daughter. This type of data would not have been readily available to the court without the aid of an expert interviewer-witness. But it may not be the expert's conclusions or opinions that influence the court to the most significant degree—it may be the concrete and relevant observations that the professional has been able to discover and describe. "The best indication of an individual's true feelings and intentions is not what he or she claims those feelings and intentions to be, but how he or she acts and responds to situations, including the situations presented by psychological tests."[18] The trained eye or methodology of the mental health professional can help unearth these contradictions.

ARTICULATING

Another function of the mental health professional can be to articulate to the court the emotions and beliefs the family members may find difficult to express. In personal injury cases a physician may articulate or describe the nature of the damage suffered in a way unavailable to the injured layperson. Similarly, a psychologist or psychiatrist will often testify as to the emotional damage suffered by a victim. This is done not because the person is unaware of the damage or is seeking to hide it but because the victim finds it difficult to articulate the exact nature of the emotional injury.

The same is true for a child in custody disputes. Most children have trouble expressing their true feelings and experiences. A trained professional, after interviewing the child, may be able to articulate those thoughts and feelings more precisely for the court. The psychological witness can also communicate the nature and strength of the child's emotional attachment to each of the parents and can describe for the court the expectations and anxieties the child is experiencing as a result of the proposed changes.

An example might be a child who refers to his biological father as "Daddy," has an enthusiastic expression while talking about his daddy, and describes many positive experiences with him. Testing shows a clear preference of the child toward the father's characteristics. On the other hand, the boy refers to his mother by her first name only and seems tense and withdrawn while interacting with her; testing shows the child views the mother in a very distant manner. These observations need to be articulated and brought to the attention of the court in clear terms, unencumbered by too many theoretical assumptions or explanations.

HIGHLIGHTING

The expert witness can also serve the function of bringing to the courts's attention factors and observations that are relevant but that otherwise might have been neglected and given too little weight.

An example would be a custody dispute in which a biological parent is seeking to regain custody from a foster parent who has become the child's "psychological parent." The mental health professional can explain the concept of the psychological parent and discuss why maintaining the continuity of a stable, loving parent-child bond is important to the healthy development of children. Conversely, an explanation for why disrupting such bonds could be potentially harmful, would also be highlighted for the court. While this is certainly not the extent of all the court must examine in its attempt to do what is best for the child, it is one example of the need to bring all relevant data and considerations to the attention of the court.

ANALYZING

A psychological witness can also apply psychological logic to aspects of the evidence before the court to help it discern the implications of that evidence. An expert witness can articulate reasons the various custody alternatives are likely to affect the specific circumstances of the case at hand. An example might be pointing out the significant pattern of inconsistent behavior of one parent in the context of discipline. The testimony would then describe the negative and harmful effects on the child. The logic is accepted not strictly because of the expert's credentials, but because it makes rational sense. Another example of the analytical contribution relates to making predictions about behavior. Such predictions need not be based on any theory of personality or concepts of psychopathology, they can be based on the common sense assumption that people will continue to act in the future as they tend to act now and have acted in the past. The expert's training and experience allow him or her to observe and report such logic as it applies to a specific custody determination. Again, the expert's testimony enables the court to more equitably weigh all the factors relevant to the court's ultimate decision.

THE EVALUATOR AS ADVOCATE OR IMPARTIAL EXAMINER

Usually, mental health professionals enter the litigation process as a child custody evaluator in one of two ways. They may be hired by a parent for a specific purpose, perhaps to validate allegations of sexual abuse or to prove that he or she is fit to have custody. Or they may be appointed by the court to prepare a comprehensive evaluation of the family with recommendation for custody arrangements.

Several types of problems occur when the evaluator is hired by one parent. The opposing parent, who has hired his or her own expert, will likely refuse to be interviewed. Or the recommendation in your report may not be used by the attorneys if the advice is not beneficial to their client. It is also possible for the clinician to lose objectivity. This can happen when the counselor becomes emotionally invested in the hiring parent and then becomes influenced by hearsay statements made about the other parent. Seeing only one parent limits data and keeps the counselor from making any comparative statements. Statements about the parenting skills of the hiring parent can be made, but without access to the other parent, there is no opportunity to hear concerns the other parent might be able to describe that your client has kept secret.

Another consequence of taking on the role of advocate is the net effect of experts cancelling each other out. If the judge hears two contrasting professionals, with equivalent qualifications, each describe his or her client as an imperfect but satisfactory parent, little information has been gained.[19]

I prefer to serve as an impartial examiner and avoid the possibility of being used as a "hired gun." Counselors are on safer ground when they represent the best interests of the child or both parents, rather than the interests of one parent. Richard A. Gardner prefers to use the best interests of the family presumption and to make recommendations that take into consideration the best interests of all concerned.[20]

Impartial examiners are in the best position to make custody recommendations to the court. They have the flexibility to gather the most extensive and accurate information from both sides, and they are not constrained by courtroom procedure. Court-appointed evaluators come to the process without the burden of a particular point of view or preset conclusions. Under these conditions the counselor has the greatest degree of professional freedom to prepare a set of recommendations.

EVALUATOR'S ROLE AS COURT-APPOINTED EXAMINER

The nature and scope of the evaluator's role, along with terms of payment, should be clearly defined by court order. This order can be submitted by one or both of the attorneys. It should name the evaluator as the agent of the court for the purpose of making the evaluation. The order must confer on the evaluator the power of the court to compel the disclosure of information and the appearance of the parties and their children for evaluations as often as is necessary to complete a competent evaluation. The order should set forth the purpose of the evaluator's involvement and should make clear the responsibilities of each party for payment. A sample order can be found in Appendix III. The sample order does nothing more than appoint the evaluator and grant him or her the authority to investigate the situation. (Special circumstances require more complex documents.)

Once appointed, the evaluator takes on a quasi-judicial role and must avoid all appearance of impropriety with clients or their attorneys. Contact must be carefully controlled and documented, and expressions of sympathy or agreement to either of the clients or their counsel avoided. All information received will be shared with the other side. Clarifying this fact can prevent a lot of hassling or posturing by the various parties. If the counselor maintains an objective and professional relationship with the parents, children, and attorneys, the custody process is strengthened and the weight of the counselor's expert opinion is enhanced in the eyes of the court.[21]

WHEN THE EVALUATOR IS TREATING ONE OF THE CHILDREN

I have learned several difficult lessons. On numerous occasions while a child has been under my care, one or both parents have asked me to provide a recommendation to the court regarding custody issues. Often this has been in the context of validating allegations of physical or sexual abuse. Usually the mother has brought the child to me offering symptoms of abuse, along with suspicions that the father is the perpetrator. Regardless of whether the existence of abuse is validated, the mother may proceed to file for divorce. In such a situation the custody and visitation conflicts emerge.

In these cases another professional needs to provide the total evaluation. If I prepare a declaration or report for the court regarding the preference of one parent over the other, the therapy relationship will be severely jeopardized. The non-supported parent will become angry toward the therapist and this will undoubtedly be communicated to the child. Most often this will compromise the child's feelings toward the therapist. An exception to this might be the situation of abuse by the parent, in which circumstances the child sees the therapist as an ally who is helping to keep the child safe from further abuse. Even here, when a full custody evaluation is needed, I can offer only my observations about treatment issues.

Suppose a parent contacts you and is unclear about whether he or she wants a therapist, an advocate for the parent, or an impartial examiner. You should make clear that these are separate roles and cannot be combined. You should not even schedule a session until this is clarified because, if you later agree to serve as an impartial evaluator, you have already compromised your position by meeting with the one parent. This can be avoided by meeting only with both parents to discuss the options and subsequent procedures. Gardner offers some suggestions on this point and even has the parents sign a statement precluding his involvement in any custody/evaluation if the parents decide that only therapy is desired.[22]

I tell ongoing clients that, while I cannot prevent them from requesting my declaration or report to the court, such involvement would likely have an adverse effect on treatment. They alone must be held accountable. In Washington state, the best interests of the child presumption denies the parents' rights of confidentiality in custody determinations. If requested by the court, the counselor must divulge all pertinent data. State laws vary. In some states, both parents must give consent before an expert can testify.

DECISION VS. RECOMMENDATION

Attorneys and parents will often refer to the information and recommendations the mental health professional makes to the court as "decisions." In the context of a court-appointed evaluator, this in an incorrect use of the term. Its use is an abdication of the parents' responsibility for their children's future. The parents are accountable for the future of their children. Struggling with problems in the marriage does not relieve them of that commitment. Yet, the case comes to litigation because the parents have been unable or unwilling to make the decisions about child custody matters. If the parents can't make these decisions, the responsiblity becomes the province of the judge. The judge makes the decision, not the evaluator. During the evaluation process the counselor must remain vigilant against being cast in the role of the decision-maker.[23]

The counselor should encourage the parents to make decisions based on the recommendations given. Because people support best what they help create, custody arrangements that both parents help prepare are always going to be superior. And future problems are more likely to be handled better through compromise and resolution if the parents are able to maintain a sense of participation and agreement with the initial parenting plan. The evaluator should do everything possible to make sure each parent feels thoroughly understood in his or her positions. The more the counselor conveys unbiased acceptance and understanding, the more likely both parties will accept his or her input into the decisions about their child.

THE PROCESS OF CONDUCTING A CUSTODY EVALUATION

Robert Halon proposes a three-phase child custody evaluation process that attempts to structure a setting where a neutral, scientific evaluation can be conducted. It also attempts to address and control the damage that can occur when parents fight over the children. Parents are encouraged to agree and to decide themselves on the custody of their children. The clear distinction between making decisions and providing recommendations is explained, and a context for possible agreements is provided. The evaluator clarifies that his or her role is to be impartial to the parents and to the data; the evaluator is an advocate for the child, and as such, is an advocate for the family.[24]

Phase one of the process is discussed in this chapter. Phases two and three are discussed in chapter 7.

PHASE ONE: INITIAL MEETING

A major goal of the initial meeting is to establish the evaluator's neutrality and role as advocate for the child. Gardner and Halon advocate having both parents and attorneys present at the initial contacting interview. Others recommend at least both parents be present.[25] To see a parent individually always means somebody was seen first; this can erode the impartial nature of the counselor's role. However, where there has been a history of violence or extreme fear expressed by a parent, the mother and father can be scheduled separately.

The first interview can be primarily a business interview. The evaluator has several tasks and points to cover. Shutz, et al., recommend the following agenda for the first meeting.

1. *The evaluator describes his or her role and explains the model used for the evaluation.* The goal is to conduct an impartial, objective evaluation in the best interests of the child. The evaluator might stress that every parent has strengths and weaknesses, and that the purpose of the evaluation is to assess these unique abilities and relate them to the child's specific needs. This is an evaluation about current functioning and the best match; it is not a predictive evaluation determining the current and future status of the child.

2. *Next, the evaluator explains the entire evaluation sequence.* Details of the procedure—questionnaires, tests, interviews, observations, home visits, collaborative sources—are explained. The details and logistics of each phase are carefully explained with instructions that these guidelines must be followed for the procedure to be valid.

3. *The limits of confidentiality need to be carefully explained.* Since the purpose of the evaluation is to provide information to the court, any and all information gathered may be included in the final report or produced in court. Also, the parents must be informed of the duty of the evaluator to inform the proper authorities if there is any suspicion of unreported child abuse or if any party is in eminent danger to his or herself or someone else. Also, state licensing regulations for mental health professionals may mandate initial disclosure procedures.

PROVISIONS DOCUMENT

The items described thus far should be available in written form in a provisions document. The provisions document should state clearly the terms, conditions, and agreements for the custody evaluation.[26] This document can also be sent to potential clients to inform them of the evaluation procedures and to let them know what will be expected from each party.

The first section of a provisions document is a statement about general considerations and agreements. This can include a statement about the parents' responsibility to reach a decision and the desire to work toward a harmonious resolution. Statements about mandated reporting, written reports, and the distinction between psychological evaluations and child custody evaluations can also be made. Halon also includes a specific section on the selection of the pertinent custody factors, including the specific focal issues that have been defined by the parents and their attorneys.

The second major section of the provisions document is a description of the conduct and process of the evaluation. This section describes the interviews, testing, and other activities the evaluator will use. An agreement to release all necessary information is provided, along with a statement of the right of either party to refuse the release of certain information and the resulting consequences to the evaluation process.

Specifications of the evaluating and reporting process are described next. These include a statement about the voluntary participation of each client, the right to terminate the evaluation, the limits of confidentiality, and the evaluator's procedure for presenting conclusions and recommendations. An example would be a joint summary conference where all parties, with legal counsel, are invited to hear the recommendations prior to a final written report.

The next section of the provisions document describes basic fees and retainers along with the financial responsibility of each individual. This can be quite detailed and is a crucial part of the agreement. The final section delineates the limits of communication and contacts with other than family members. For example, a statement is included that the evaluator will not speak to either attorney separately concerning the findings or recommendations.

FOCUS OF EVALUATION

The evaluator makes the final judgment about the ultimate focus of the evaluation process. But it is beneficial to have all parties identify what they consider to be the central focus of the evaluation. The evaluator is essentially asking what the parents want to know. They are asked to outline their views about what the focus of the evaluation should include. This is recorded and later can be summarized in the provisions document. It is crucial to have the focus of the evaluation agreed upon before attempting to answer specific questions.

An example of a general area of focus for the custody evaluation is shown below. These categories, from Washington law, provide that the court shall consider them in trying to assess the conditions that are in the child's best interests.

1. The relative strength, nature, and stability of the child's relationship with each parent, including whether a parent has taken greater responsibility for performing parenting functions relating to the daily needs of the child
2. The agreements of the parties, provided they were entered into knowingly and voluntarily
3. Each parent's past and potential for future performance of parenting functions
4. The emotional needs and developmental level of the child
5. The child's relationship with siblings and with other significant adults, as well as the child's involvement with his or her physical surroundings
6. The wishes of the parents and the wishes of a child who is sufficiently mature to express reasoned and independent preferences as to his or her residential schedule.[27]

While establishing the areas of focus, the evaluator should take care to identify the expectations of the court. This information may come from the body of the court order appointing the independent evaluator, from previous depositions or declarations of the parents, and from state guidelines. The specifics of the family should be incorporated into the process, but the general categories (such as those described above) should be addressed. It is also helpful to provide the respective parties a copy of such a list and use it to elicit specific areas of evaluation.

RECORD KEEPING

As with any forensic work, keeping careful records is crucial. The evaluator should keep careful notes of all contacts, whether in person or by phone, logging the date, time and name of each contact. He or she should also note when written records were requested so their arrival can be documented, as can the procedure to obtain the information. A comprehensive, organized file is necessary since the entire file is likely to be subpoenaed.

SCHEDULING

The initial meeting ends with scheduling future contacts with the participants. It is a good idea to counterbalance the appointments. Alternate from one parent to the other to prevent one parent's need to rebut a fully presented case. This also allows for a cross-currrent of information, which facilitates the process of validating data.

FORMS

The evaluator should distribute and explain all forms and questionnaires the parents need to complete. Some evaluators prefer to have background questionnaires completed in the office under supervision to ensure they are completed independently. This way, a parent who is uninformed about the needs of the child will not be able to research the answers while completing the form. Nor will a parent be able to consult their attorney about altering answers to present the most favorable impression. Some mental health professionals argue that the clinical interviews allow the determining of a person's actual knowledge and background. If forms are handed out at at this time, they should be returned prior to the first interview so the evaluator has access to the data before seeing each person in the clinical setting.

OUTSIDE INFORMATION

By now, the evaluator should have a good idea of the nature and extent of outside information needed in the case.

Written information should be requested from the child's teacher(s), the current day-care provider(s), physician(s), and any other significant professional source. Any mental health records for the parents and child also should be requested. If any type of educational evaluation has been done on the child, this should be obtained in addition to the teacher's report.

Other information that might be needed includes records from the police, probation, official court, military, or state or federal social service offices. Due to the complex laws and procedures governing some of the records, it is best to have the parent's attorney procure and forward these records. The attorney has the power and expertise to do this. Consent for release of information is a part of the provisions document, but at times a separate consent for exchange of information form will be needed for each agency and for each person.

When sending your requests along with the consent forms, state that only written replies are accepted. Also convey that this information is for use in a legal proceeding and ask for a prompt reply.

MEDIATION

Prior to 1981, none of the books on divorce, children of divorce, or child custody included mediation as a topic. In fact, mediation as an alternative to custody disputes is a recent phenomenon, although the early Quakers did practice mediation and arbitration, which sometimes included marital disruption.[28]

Much of the reason for the rise of mediation services is the recognition that the adversarial court system is not well suited to helping families dissolve a marriage while protecting the bonds between parents and children. A number of mediation services have been founded to help meet this need, including the Christian Conciliation Service, which is sponsored in many areas by the Christian Legal Society.[29] Based on the principles of injunction against litigation between Christians (1 Cor. 6:1) a mandate to promote justice (Amos 5:24) and exhortation to love and forgiveness (Eph. 4:32), Christian Conciliation Services emphasizes mutual consideration rather than individual rights. Another organization is the Academy of Family Mediators, which has established training and ethical standards for professional mediation practice.[30]

Divorce mediation in which parents work together with one or more mediators in as nonadversarial a climate as possible can reduce the conflict and the resulting trauma on both the parents and children. In this model, the needs of the parents and children take precedence over blame.[31] Restoring harmony rather than winning the dispute may sound idealistic, but it certainly seems more consistent with the principles of Christian living.

ASSUMPTIONS OF MEDIATION

Mediation attempts to provide a setting where the participants can feel that the divorce does not have to be a win-lose battle. Each parent should feel that his or her needs can be addressed in some reasonable way, that the other person has needs also, and that the welfare of the children will take precedence over anger or retaliation. The process is based on the assumption that both parents have equal power or opportunity to have their needs or expectations met. The role of the mediator is to empower each participant and to facilitate the process so that a fair and equitable settlement can be made.

Brown identified five basic beliefs inherent in mediation: (1) the availability of mutually acceptable solutions, (2) the desirability of mutually acceptable solutions, (3) the right of the other party to be valued and respected and to be heard and understood, (4) the existence of superordinate goals that transcend special interests and are in the common good of the children and family, and (5) the fairness and integrity of the mediator.[32]

Family court mediation is required in many states when custody issues arise, unless abuse has been validated. The problem is that it is often attempted by overworked caseworkers who must try to get closure in one or two sessions. Mediation takes time and skill, but is still cost effective and less traumatic than a court battle.

Even though some states such as California attempt to mediate all custody disputes at the outset, many custody disputes are not settled in a mediation format.[33] This is unfortunate because the majority of custody disputes are eventually settled outside the courtroom, after all of the expense of dual attorney fees and evaluation costs, not to mention extensive emotional wear and tear.

The mental health professional can help by being alert to any facilitating resolution and mediation opportunity during the initial phases of the evaluation process. He or she can suggest this solution when the evaluation data shows the parents might be amenable to it. Even if an earlier attempt was made, with the intervening experiences the couple may now be more open to a mediated resolution. An evaluation may still be needed to help the family identify their strengths and weaknesses, but the process would be removed from the adversarial proceedings and the focus placed on points of agreement rather than difference.

The Christian Legal Society publishes a number of helpful materials regarding Christian conciliation, including the workbook *Readiness for Reconciliation*. This is a seven-part Bible study designed to assist persons in assessing their readiness for reconciliation in the midst of conflicts and disputes. It is not limited to custody disputes, and is not intended to provide answers for the dispute itself, but it can help the participants become open to God's direction.[34]

SUMMARY

This chapter began with a background and history of child custody determinations. The early presumption in domestic disputes was that fathers had priority over mothers. By the 1920s the courts had shifted to a "tender years" doctrine that favored maternal custody. By the mid-1970s the courts had begun to recognize the "best interest of the child" standard. More recently, joint custody has enjoyed an emphasis in many states, but there are factors that mitigate against its blind application.

The adversarial nature of the court system works against an unbiased assessment of the needs of the child. The counselor needs to recognize the qualities necessary to be successful in this type of work. Issues include professional bias, risk of personal harm, nonpayment for services, personal agony, and the need for discernment.

The evaluator can help the court through four categories of assistance: discovering, articulating, highlighting, and analyzing. For many reasons, the court-appointed role of impartial examiner is far superior to that of an advocate. There are many guidelines for responding to requests from a parent for declarations when serving as an existing therapist for the child. It is important to maintain the distinction that the evaluator provides information for the court to make the final decision. The ultimate decisions regarding custody issues are not made by the evaluator. Further, this state of affairs is reached only because the parents have been unable to decide responsibility for their child's future.

The first phase of the custody evaluation is the initial meeting where structure, focus, and agreement between parties is established. The focus of the evaluation is on identifying the needs of the child and how best to match the strengths of each parent to meet those needs. A provisions document clearly states the terms, conditions, and agreements for the custody evaluation.

Mediation as an alternative to the adversarial approach can be used to reduce the conflict and the resulting trauma to both the parents and children. The process is based on the assumption that both parents have equal power or opportunity to have their needs or expectations met. The role of the mediator is to empower each participant and facilitate a fair and equitable settlement.

NOTES

1. Theodore H. Blau, *The Psychologist as Expert Witness* (New York: John Wiley & Sons, 1984).

2. H. H. Foster, and D. J. Freed, "Life with Father," *Family Law Quarterly* 11.4 (1978): 321–42.

3. Andre Derdeyn, "Child Custody Contests in Historical Perspective," *The American Journal of Psychiatry* 133 (1976): 1369–1376.

4. Erik D. Sorensen and Jacquelin Goldman, "Custody Determinations and Child Development," *Journal of Divorce* 13.4 (1990): 53–67.

5. Derdeyn, "Child Custody Contests" 1371.

6. Uniform Marriage and Divorce Act 402 9A UCA, 197–198, 1979).

7. V. Simmons and K. G. Meyer, "The Child Custody Evaluation: Issues and Trends," *Behavioral Sciences & the Law* 4.2 (1986): 137–156.

8. Ibid. 140.

9. W. Forsyth, *Cases of Difference Between Parents or Guardians* (Philadelphia: T. & J. W. Johnson, 1850).

10. Richard A. Gardner, *Family Evaluation in Child Custody Mediation, Arbitration, and Litigation* (Cresskil, N.J.: Creative Therapeutics, 1989).

11. Ibid. 7.

12. R. T. Hare-Mustin, "The Biased Professional in Divorce Litigation," *Psychology of Women Quarterly* 1.2 (1976): 216–222.

13. N. T. Anderson, *The Bondage Breaker* (Eugene, Ore.: Harvest House, 1990).

14. See D. S. Browning, *Religious Thought and the Modern Psychologies: A Critical Conversation in the Theology of Culture* (Philadelphia: Fortress, 1987); Kirk E. Farnsworth, *Servanthood Now* (CRISTA Counseling Service, 1991); Kirk E. Farnsworth, *Whole-Hearted Integration. Harmonizing Psychology and Christianity Through Word and Deed* (Grand Rapids: Baker Book House, 1985); and Gary R. Collins, *The Rebuilding of Psychology. An Integration of Psychology and Christianity* (Wheaton, Ill.: Tyndale House, 1977).

15. See Jay Ziskin, *Coping with Psychiatric and Psychological Testimony*, 3rd. ed. (Marina del Ray: Law and Psychology Press, 1981); J. Ziskin and D. Faust, "Psychiatric and Psychological Evidence in Child Custody Cases," *Trial*, (August 1989): 45–49; and S. R. Okpaku, "Psychology: Impediment or Aid in Child Custody Cases?" *Rutgers Law Review* 29 (1987): 1117–1145.

16. T. R. Litwack, G. L. Gerber, and C. A. Fenster, "The Proper Role of Psychology in Child Custody Disputes," *Journal of Family Law* 18.2 (1980): 269–300.

17. Ibid. 283–94.

18. Ibid. 288.

19. Andre P. Derdeyn, "Child Custody Consultation," *American Journal of Orthopsychiatry* 45.5 (1975): 791–801.

20. Gardner, *Family Evaluation*, 340.

21. B. M. Schutz, et al., *Solomon's Sword: A Practical Guide to Conducting Child Custody Evaluations* (San Francisco: Jossey-Bass Inc., 1989) 52.

22. Gardner, *Family Evaluation*, 100–122.

23. Robert L. Halon, "The Comprehensive Child Custody Evaluation," *American Journal of Forensic Psychology* 8.3 (1990): 19–46.

24. Halon, Ibid. 35–43.

25. Schutz, *Solomon's Sword*, 53.

26. Both Gardner and Halon provide illustrations of such provisions documents. Also, a fourteen-page sample provisions document is available (for a small fee) from Dr. Grant L. Martin CRISTA Counseling Service, 19303 Fremont Avenue N., Seattle, WA 98133.

27. Uniform Marriage and Divorce Act, "Chapter 26.09—Dissolution of Marriage," RCWA 26.09.010 to 26.09.902 (1987).

28. D. G. Brown, "Divorce and Family Mediation: History, Review Future Directions," *Conciliation Courts Review* 20.2 (1982): 1–44.

29. Christian Legal Society, P. O Box 1492, Merrifield, VA 229–96, (703) 560–7314.

30. For more information, contact the Academy of Family Mediators, P.O. Box 10501, Euguene, OR 97440, (503) 345–1205.

31. William F. Hodges, *Interventions for Children of Divorce: Custody, Access, and Psychotherapy* (New York: John Wiley & Sons, 1986).

32. Brown, "Divorce and Family Mediation," 1–44.

33. H. McIsaac, *Family Mediation and Conciliation Service: Standards and Procedures* (Los Angeles, Calif: The Conciliation Court of the Los Angeles Superior Court, 1984).

34. L. Buzzard, J. Buzzard, and E. Eck, *Readiness for Reconciliation* (Marrifield, Va.: Christian Legal Society. Their address is P.O. Box 1492, Marrifield, VA 22116–1492, (703) 560–7314, 1987).

Chapter Seven

Custody Evaluations: The Assessment Process

PHASE TWO OF THE CUSTODY OR PARENTING PLAN EVALUATION is the data-gathering process. Based on the information gleaned from the initial contacts, the evaluator will have areas of focus and hypotheses in place. At this point the task is to gather data that will answer the focal questions. The child's developmental needs must be assessed and defined, and the parents' strengths and weaknesses must be assessed in terms of how their past behavior aligns with stated intentions as parents. These descriptions of strengths and weaknesses are then compared to their respective complaints, values, and expectations.

PHASE TWO: DATA GATHERING

The second phase in the custody evaluation process is the data gathering phase.

PARENT BACKGROUND INFORMATION

Prior to the first clinical interview, the evaluator should review all the completed forms given to the parents during the joint "business" session or completed by the parents under supervision. Whenever possible, reports from outside sources should be reviewed before the clinical interviews, but this information can be slow arriving, and you may decide to go ahead with the interviews and observations. Any questions arising from the outside reports can be covered at a later time.

Most clinicians have personal data, social history, or background information forms to use when taking on new clients. These forms can be used here, as well. Schutz, et al., and Gardner include examples of parent background and child questionnaires in their books.[1]

Questionnaires are intended to elicit primarily factual information and to identify areas to be investigated further in the interviews. Standard information is sought about the parent's family, education, work, religious affiliation, marriage, physical and mental health, military service, arrest and legal involvement, alcohol and drug use, as well as areas of concerns regarding the other parent. Upon reviewing the completed forms, areas of concern such as suicidal potential or drug and alcohol use need to be explored more deeply with detailed questioning.

Each parent should also be given a questionnaire to complete for each child involved in the litigation. This form should provide basic facts about the child and his or her current functioning. It can include information about day-care, school, special needs or difficulties, medical history, developmental descriptions, methods of discipline, and the current custody or visitation arrangement.

Clinical interview. The clinical interview will amplify areas of inquiry from the questionnaires, perhaps adding others. The areas of content should include personal and marital history, parenting, and custody and visitation rights. The interview is intended to provide information about the accuracy of the parents' perceptions and the appropriateness of their expectations relative to the needs of the child. The counselor will want to evaluate their attitudes and behavior toward the child, as well as their feelings and beliefs about each other and their thoughts about the other parent's relationship with the child.

While these interviews provide a self-report of parenting behaviors, such data will need to be corroborated by direct observation and reports from others. The historical information is not weighted as heavily, but can provide contextual and explanatory information for some of your conclusions. Any discrepancies that appear between individual parental reports should be clarified by further questioning, and areas of alert will need to be highlighted. For example, if drug and alcohol use or abuse is mentioned, these topics should be thoroughly investigated. If one parent makes allegations about the conduct of the other, the issue must be explored.

Throughout the interview, the evaluator must be alert to fabrications, lies, and exaggerations. Standardized procedures, careful record keeping, detailed questioning, corroborative data, thorough preparation, an objective and cautious attitude, continued prayer for discernment, and sensitivity to God's leading will all contribute to your ability to know the truth. But it is not easy.

Richard Gardner uses the joint interview to help "smoke out" the fabrication and lying that are often present in custody litigation. Both couple and family sessions can be used to bring about confrontation on crucial issues. By carefully observing and recording the interview process, the sensitive therapist will be able to clarify truth about the family needs and relationships[2]

Custody Quotient evaluation. Once the background information is obtained and reviewed, it is useful to employ an instrument designed specifically to measure parental skills objectively. For example, the Custody Quotient (CQ), authored by Gordon and Peek and published by the Wilmington Institute, is a system of mapping examiner judgment of a person's capacity to be an effective parent.[3] Its purpose is to assist the mental health professional in providing objective information about the knowledge, attributes, and skills of the adults seeking parental rights and duties. It is useful in providing information relevant to the child's best interests.

The Custody Quotient helps identify parents' strengths and deficits so they can be related to specified parenting duties. The CQ reflects current empirical research in child psychology, psychiatry, and child development. It is anchored in case law and statute, and there is direct or reasonably inferred multi-state legal authority for each test item.

The authors define good parenting as "those collections of attributes, skills and behaviors which adults rely on and use in raising the next generation. Good parenting occurs when adult practices lead the child to live independently and fulfill his or her biological, psychological and social potential. Good parenting specifically includes those attributes, skills and behaviors which the CQ scales comprise."[4]

The test is organized into nine categories, including assessment of (1) the ability of the parents to meet the emotional needs of the child, now and in the future, (2) the ability to meet the physical needs of the child, (3)the presence of dangers to the child emotionally or physically, (4) good parenting based on knowledge, attributes, skills, abilities, and participation with the child, (5) the degree of parental assistance or support, (6) the ability of the parent to plan ahead for the child, (7) home stability, (8) acts or omissions, including misconduct by a parent, that would affect the safety of the child, (9) values, including parental beliefs, ethics, and religious-educational considerations.

The final score on the CQ is based on numerous structured questions given through the CQ interviews. Information for scoring is also drawn from the home study, psychological testing, collateral contacts with other professionals, and review of documents submitted to the evaluator. Items built into the Custody Quotient scale assess frankness or honesty. The CQ instrument also computes a joint custody quotient score for the parent being evaluated. This score reflects a parent's capacity to participate effectively in a joint custody arrangement.

Parent Awareness Skills Survey. Another instrument developed for use in custody evaluations is the Parent Awareness Skills Survey (PASS).[5] This survey is a clinical tool designed to illuminate the strengths and weaknesses in awareness skills the parent accesses in reaction to typical childcare situations. It presents a parent with eighteen childcare problems and asks how he or she would respond to each.

The PASS yields scores that reflect a parent's awareness of:

1. The elements that should be addressed or ignored in various situations to bring about positive solutions; a recognition of the critical issues involved
2. The necessity of selecting strategies adequate to bring about positive solutions
3. The need to respond in words and actions understandable to the child
4. The desirability of acknowledging the feelings aroused in the child by various situations
5. The desirability of taking a child's unique past history into account in deciding how to respond
6. So-called feedback data; a recognition that an effective communicator pays attention to whether and how an offered response is coming across to the child.[6]

Responses from the parent are obtained and scored at a spontaneous level, as well as at two levels of probing. Data generated by the PASS can be used by the clinician to pinpoint areas of strength and weakness. A conclusion can be formed as to whether the responses meet minimal standards of adequacy. Responses from each parent can be compared.

This instrument helps the evaluator understand the adequacy with which a parent becomes aware of the critical aspects of childcare issues, regardless of the age of the child. It also summarizes the effectiveness with which the parent is able to communicate with the child about these issues. There is a scoring system for the PASS, but no normative data. The evaluator must relate the results to the specific needs of the family being evaluated.

Other formal testing. Many evaluators use standardized psychological tests such as the Minnesota Multiphasic Personality Inventory (MMPI), Sixteen Personality Factor, California Psychological Inventory, and the Millon Clinical Multiaxial Inventory. While these tests do have a strong research base, they tend to measure attitudes and beliefs rather than parenting skills. Grisso and Schutz, et al., have proposed that a psychological test can contribute to a child custody evaluation if it directly measures or quantifies (1) the degree of congruence between the functional abilities of a parent and the specific needs of a child, (2) those mental health dimensions that might explain the presence of observed deficits and their remediability, or (3) a "special need" in the child. In addition, an adequate instrument has norms on the parents and children, good reliability, and measures of response distortion.[7] At the time, these writers did not find a single test that met a sufficient number of these criteria. Their conclusion was that tests such as the MMPI should be used only to provide causal explanations for observed deficits and to screen for high-risk characteristics such as acute depression, addictive personality, and schizophrenic or sociopathic individuals.

Projective tests such as the Thematic Apperception Test and Rorschach, in the hands of a skilled clinician, can provide descriptions of personality dynamics and hypotheses about behavior. Conclusions about parental capacity derived from projective tests, however, are highly speculative and are not likely to hold up well in court.

The challenge facing the evaluator is to relate personality test results to parental functioning. A psychological test contributes to the custody evaluation if it measures the ability of the parent to meet the needs of his or her particular child. Testing, without the direct implication for matching the needs of the child with the abilities of the parents, can lead to serious problems in cross-examination.

Sometimes other testing is needed for special concerns. For example, in one case I handled, the question was raised about the mother's ability to manage her two children because she was learning disabled. I gave the Wechsler Adult Intelligence Scale, along with subtests from the Woodcock-Johnson Psychoeducational Battery to define the nature and extent of her learning problems. The mother was taking some courses to prepare to enter the work force, but had to spend a large amount of time in study and course preparation. This requirement of time and energy affected how she related to her children. The test information was considered along with all the other variables in making the final recommendations.

Psychological testing in custody evaluations is a controversial subject. If you plan to use psychological tests, make sure you are skilled in their usage and circumspect in your interpretation.

Observation of parent with children. It is crucial to observe the parents' interactions with their children. This can be some of the most important data you obtain. Parents should be scheduled for direct observation with their children in a counterbalanced format. This reduces the appearance of evaluator bias, enables cross-checking of information, and gives the counselor a chance to see each parent at various stages in the process.[8]

The observation sequence should include the biological parents, stepparents, and significant caretakers. Each child will be seen twice under the same conditions. For example, a child will be observed twice in the office with the father, and likewise with the mother. Usually there will be one home visit with each parent. All children would be present at the single home observation. If there are stepparents or stepsiblings, observations must be scheduled to incorporate all of the combinations, both for office and home sessions.

The purpose of the observations is twofold: to obtain accurate data about the ability of the parent to meet the needs of the child, and to gather a clear picture of the child's needs. To this end, sessions should be equivalent and objective. A structured task format should be used during the observations, and specific observational targets should be identified and recorded for the sessions.

Several structured tasks can be used to provide an equivalent and objective context for observations. For example, each office observation can include a time of free play, followed by teaching and then cooperative and problem-solving tasks. The session might end with clean-up.

An example of a teaching task for a child six to eleven years old would be for the parent to teach the child how to sew on a button or how to play a new game, such as checkers. A cooperative task would be to give the parent and child an elaborate set of building blocks and ask them to construct something. The problem-solving task is a verbal discussion of some problem relating to the child. For example, if previous interviews have identified that homework is an ongoing issue for a student, the evaluator would ask the parent and child to discuss how they might improve the situation.[9]

The characteristics of good parenting can establish benchmarks for behaviors to look for. If the evaluator has used the Custody Quotient and Parent Awareness Skills Survey, the observation setting can be used to corroborate and verify the parents' reports.

Careful notetaking is essential. If possible making a video or at least an audio tape of the sessions is desirable. This allows the evaluator to review the session later, as well as to cross-check data that might come up in later sessions. Schutz has described clusters of behaviors that can be observed and recorded that seem to fit the "good enough" parent. The categories are positive emotional attachment, differentiated self, accurate perceptions of the child, reasonable expectations, and communication skills. Research is still needed to validate and extend these preliminary procedures, but this approach to observations does have much to offer.[10]

Interviews of collaterals.   Testimony may be sought from friends, neighbors, and relatives in reference to the parenting abilities of the parents. This material can be compared and contrasted with the parenting profiles that emerge from interviews, testing, and observations. Often, however, comments from the friends and family of each parent tend to cancel each other out. Also, some people, such as day-care providers, may be reluctant to tell the whole story for fear of losing the parent as a customer.

Usually some collateral sources are necessary. Have each parent submit a list, complete with addresses and phone numbers, of people who know them and their children and have observed the family interactions. Instruct each parent to inform these persons of the possibility of being contacted. Also, be sure a signed release is obtained. It is preferable to have the collateral witness's comments in writing. Since this may not always be possible, some information may be gained by phone.

The evaluator asks standardized questions that focus on current parental functioning and avoid value judgments or opinions of past failures.

EVALUATION OF CHILD

Clinical interview.   The evaluator attempts to understand the needs of the child and, from the child's perspective, determine how well each parent is able to respond to those needs. The evaluator also evaluates the child's perspective of each parent and the child's preferences regarding custody and visitation issues.

With young children, it is best to have both parents accompany the child to interview sessions. It is also preferable not to schedule a session with the child immediately after having spent a significant amount of time exclusively with one parent. Younger children may be especially vulnerable to coaching, bribery, and parental manipulation.

The initial goal of the interview is to build rapport between the child and the evaluator. The techniques described in earlier chapters will be of value here. Start with easy-to-answer, concrete questions about school, hobbies, friends, pets, or toys. From this point the session moves from rapport-building activities and questions to a statement about the purpose of the interview and the process to be used. Children's anxieties can be reduced if they know what is going to happen. Be truthful and direct, but use discretion about how much to tell each child. Make sure similar-aged children within the family receive the some orientation. This way, if they later compare notes, there is no significant discrepancy.

It is important to point out that your job as evaluator is to help the judge understand the situation. The child needs to know that you will not make the decisions, you will simply take the information about the family and summarize it for the court; the judge makes the final decision about custody and visitation issues.

The following areas can be explored, either through a structured or informal interview.

- Family
- Extended family
- Celebrations
- Pets
- Social and play activities

- School
- Day care and baby-sitting arrangements
- Medical problems and care
- Religion
- Daily routine and parental involvement
- Description of parent, positive and negative
- Sex education—who and what
- Parental social activities and alcohol or drug use
- Discipline and rules
- Separation/custody/visitation—current arrangements and preferences.[11]

Bricklin Perceptual Scales. The Bricklin Perceptual Scales (BPS) is a test developed specifically for child custody evaluations. The test elicits information about the child's perception of each parent's functioning in four areas: competence, supportiveness, follow-up consistency, and possession of admirable character traits—traits that match the positive parenting characteristics described earlier. Remember, the purpose of the evaluation is to determine the best fit between the needs of the child and the abilities of the parent. The Bricklin Perceptual Scales can illuminate a child's view of how well the parent meets his or her particular needs. A child's perception may or may not match the parent's actual abilities, but it does give an indication of the child's view.

The Bricklin Perceptual Scales test can be given to children age six or older. It consists of sixty-four items, thirty-two for each parent. Each item asks for a verbal and nonverbal response from the child. Only nonverbal responses are scored. The scale yields point scores for each parent in each of the four areas and a total point score for each parent.

The test assumes that nonverbal responses yield information about the child's unconscious or private preferences and evaluations. Bricklin also believes that the nonverbal responses are less vulnerable to contamination from parental coaching, bribing, and intimidation.[12] Validity studies have shown a high relationship between the test's results and judges' decisions, results from psychologists using other instruments, and clinical and life history data.

Perception of Relationships Test. The Perception of Relationships Test (PORT), also developed by Barry Bricklin, is designed for use with children age three years, two months and older. The test is designed to measure the degree to which the child seeks psychological "closeness" (positive interactions) with each parent, as well as the degree to which the child has been able to work out a comfortable, conflict-free style of relating to each parent.[13]

The instrument consists of seven tasks which are included in a single standardized protocol booklet. The child is asked to:

1. Draw each parent
2. Draw a self-representation on the same page as mother and as father
3. Draw a self-representation on the same page as both mother and father
4. Draw his or her family
5. Draw his or her family "doing something"
6. While viewing a picture of two stables and a horse, draw where the horse will go
7. Tell stories about a doggie's dreams and tell which dream is more pleasant

Criteria and examples to aid in scoring are provided. The better primary caretaking parent is suggested by the one who garners the greatest number of PORT choices. Test assumptions are the same as for the BPS. Validity studies since 1981 show high agreement between PORT results and external criteria, such as judges' decisions. They range between 90 and 95 percent.

Bricklin calls his approach to custody decision-making "access to parental strength." The aim is to make sure each child has access to what each parent can best offer to each child in the family. The child's view of a parent's behavior may not be the same as a decision-maker's. But we are trying to understand the child's ability to profit from a particular parent's style of doing things. An optimal custody plan should honor these complex considerations. Both the PORT and BPS provide data which allow the evaluator to note the unique strengths each parent can offer.[14]

Other tests.   The evaluator may also administer other tests such as the Thematic or Children's Apperception Test, Education Apperception Test, Projective Story Telling Cards, Draw-A-Person, House-Tree-Person, Kinetic Family Drawings, and Bender Gestalt.

Selective tests may be used to assess specialized needs. After looking at school or teacher reports, the evaluator may decide to administer intelligence and achievement tests. Tests to assess the child's preferred modality for learning or the existence and nature of learning disabilities or attention deficit disorder may be needed. It may be important to compare the learning style of the child with that of his or her parents. If so, the evaluator will need data from the parents as well as the child.

PARENT ALIENATION SYNDROME

Richard Gardner has identified the manifestations of a disorder he has called the *parental alienation syndrome*.[15] It is found particularly in children who have been involved in protracted custody litigation, but may be present, to some degree, in almost all conflictual custody determinations. The symptoms are outlined below.

A. *The child is obsessed with "hatred" of a parent*

1. Speaks in very negative terms without embarrassment or guilt
2. Denigration has quality of litany
3. Justifies alienation with memories of minor altercations
4. Most intense when both loved and hated parent are present
   a. When alone with hated parent, behavior may range from hatred to affection
   b. May realize he/she has done something "wrong" and suddenly resume expression of animosity
   c. Child may voice negative feelings about absent parent to "loved" parent, and ask loved parent for promise not to tell
   d. Hatred often spills over to parent's extended family. Child will accept all allegations of loved parent against hated parent

B. *Complete lack of ambivalence*
  1. Hated parent is all bad, loved parent is all good
  2. Memory of all positive experiences seems obliterated
C. *Guiltless disregard for feeling of hated parent*
  1. Lack of gratitude for gifts, financial support, and any other manifestations of involvement and affection
D. *Obsession with resentment above and beyond what might be expected in usual divorce*

It seems that in most of these cases the mother is favored and the father is denigrated. Gardner believes four factors contribute to parental alienation syndrome (PAS). These factors are outlined below.

A. *Brainwashing.* Brought about by one or more of the following:
  1. Denigration of one parent by the other
  2. Delusional thoughts
  3. Complaints about lack of financial support
  4. Exaggeration of parent's minor psychological problems
  5. Selected use of pictures
  6. Sarcasm
  7. Telling children to tell father they are not home when he calls
  8. Unwilling to forward information such as mail and school reports
  9. Labeling father's attempts to contact family as harassment
B. *Subtle and often unconscious programming.* Brought about by one or more of the following:
  1. "There are things I could say about your father that would make your hair stand up, but I'm not that kind of person."
  2. Expressing neutrality regarding visitation; insists the child must make the decision
  3. Guilt trips
  4. Moving to distant city
  5. Doing and undoing (i.e., "Your father is a jerk. Oh, I didn't mean it.")

C. *Factors arising within the child*
   1. The child has a stronger bond with loved parent than hated parent; the PAS campaign is attempt to maintain that tie, which is threatened by litigation; child fears loss of preferred parent's love
   2. Vehicle for expression of anger toward parent who has left
D. *Situational factors*
   1. Child has lived with custodial parent and is fearful of moving
   2. Child has observed sibling being treated harshly for expressing affection for hated parent
   3. Fear; identification with aggressor as result of seeing one parent mistreat the other (if you can't beat them join them)
   4. Instantaneous identification; for example, mother killed in auto wreck, child takes on beliefs of mother and blames father
   5. History of abuse

Gardner provides some guidelines for dealing with parent alienation children and their families depending on whether the case is severe, moderate, or mild. A counselor's recommendations to the court may need to include procedures for moderating the effects of parental alienation syndrome.

ALLEGATIONS OF SEXUAL ABUSE

Allegation of sexual abuse is one of the most difficult topics in custody evaluations. Only five to ten years ago the common professional opinion was that children seldom fabricated details of sexual abuse. This can no longer be assumed to be correct. The incidence of false allegations of sexual abuse in custody litigation is significant. One study found 77 percent of the custody cases where allegations of sexual abuse arose were adjudicated as having no abuse.[16] This figure doesn't tell us whether there was actually no abuse or whether there was just not enough evidence to prove it. Either way, custody battles are bound to produce such accusations. Therefore, professionals working in this area are going to be confronted with the task of discriminating between true and false allegations.

To assist in the investigation, the evaluator needs to be well versed in current methodology. The material described in chapter 4 on validating sexual abuse will be important in this context.[17]

If allegations of abuse arise prior to the start of the evaluation, it may be best to delay initiating the process until there is a validation report. Perhaps another professional can focus on this specific topic and leave you free to focus on the "best fit" strategy. If allegations arise during the evaluation process, there is no choice but to make the validation of abuse a part of the evaluation process.

Phase Three: Conclusions and Recommendations

The prime purpose of the evaluation is to recommend a custody plan providing the best possible match between the parent's strengths and the child's needs. The correct "fit" is established when the demands and expectations of the parents are compatible with the child's personality, abilities, and needs. When there is a good fit, healthy development can be assumed.

Goals

Several essential objectives or goals of a custody report are discussed by Bricklin. A summary of these goals follows. The goals are helpful when trying to understand how to interpret and organize the data and formulate recommendations. The goals of a custody report are:

Goal 1. To suggest a creative plan which maximizes the child's exposure to the strengths each parent has to offer and minimizes exposure to weaknesses

Goal 2. To increase the chances the parents will cooperate with the recommendations. The evaluator should use maximum communication skills to insure that the parents believe in the report

Goal 3. To provide motivation for each parent to improve himself or herself in any areas of weakness

Goal 4. To promote self-healing from each participant. This is done with the use of caring and value-free words, and by complementing all strengths identified

Goal 5. To gain the respect of the judge or decision maker who will be involved in the custody decision. This is done by writing a balanced report that is obviously objective and fair and that clearly shows the strengths and weaknesses of each parent

Goal 6. To provide recommendations for a method of monitoring the adequacy and effectiveness of the arrangements

Goal 7. To address the concerns of each parent carefully and clearly in at least one specific recommendation

Goal 8. To make available to the child the important strengths possessed by each parent. The report must emphasize there are no winners or losers

Goal 9. To be clear and direct and avoid terms that are offensive or clinical[18]

KEY PARENTAL FEATURES

Key parental features differentiate the good parents from deficient ones. While not all-inclusive, the list below is representative of the essential characteristics that can be used to evaluate the presence of an effective match between the parent's abilities and the child's needs.

1. Positive emotional attachment to the child on the part of the parent, which the parent is able to communicate

2. Ability to recognize the child as a totally separate entity, to appropriately foster the child's autonomy, and to place the child's needs before the parent's needs

3. Ability to perceive the child accurately without distortion or overinterpretation, and to recognize and validate the unique needs and characteristics of the individual child

4. Positive self-esteem and realistic self-confidence within the parent

5. Knowledge of the general developmental needs and characteristics of children at different stages, and the ability to respond appropriately
6. Willingness and ability to be adaptable and flexible in responding to the child's behavior
7. Two-way, open communication patterns characterized by clarity and respectfulness
8. Consistent enforcement of appropriate rules and standards[19]

ORGANIZATION OF REPORT

Preliminary information. The report should be clearly titled. An example is, "Psychological Custody Evaluation." The title page should include identifying information such as the date, the name and address of the judge, the names of the litigants, and the docket number.

The opening paragraph to the judge should indicate that the evaluation is submitted in compliance with a court order. This affirms the counselor's position as an impartial examiner who serves the court.

The next sections can include the qualifications of the evaluator, dates of the interviews, names of people interviewed, and the number of hours for each interview. Give a skeleton description of each of the persons interviewed, followed by a summary statement of the conclusions and recommendations. The balance of the report provides detailed background information and descriptions of the family members.

Body of report. Behavioral descriptions are often the key features for determining if there is a good fit between parent and child. A good way to begin the body of the report might be the following:

> The main objective of this evaluation is to devise a custody plan of maximum benefit to (name of child). This will be done by identifying the strengths of each important adult in his/her life, and then creating an arrangement that will offer (child) the widest possible exposure to these strengths. The best arrangement is

one that matches those things the child needs most
with those things each parent has to offer.[19]

Subsequent sections of the report cover the mother's assets
as a parent, the mother's liabilities as a parent, the father's assets as a parent, the father's liabilities as a parent, the child's
strengths, and any special needs of the child. The data will
come from questionnaires, collateral sources and records, interviews, test results, and observations collected over the
course of the evaluation. Here the evaluator's skill in synthe-
sizing and analyzing the results is important. Prayerful
discernment, as described earlier, is also important.

Clinical opinions or inferences should be supported by two
or more data sources. One of those sources should be either a
self-report or a direct observation.[20] The categories of good
parenting described earlier can be used as a guide for describing each parent. Clarify the relationship of the identified
characteristics to either the Uniform Marriage and Divorce Act
or your state divorce and parenting plan guidelines. The following characteristics of a good custody report are important
when analyzing the data and writing the report. A good report will include:

1. A full history. Have appropriate data been collected?
2. Credentials of the author, including appropriate area of
   expertise.
3. The possibility of replicating the findings. Are procedures and findings sufficiently detailed to permit
   replication of the process?
4. The amount of time involved in evaluation. Is it sufficient?
5. Provision of patterns or themes, not isolated facts. One
   fact does not make a case.
6. Consulting or supportive opinions. Was collaboration
   used? Team approach or experts drawn in as needed.
7. Relevant material. Were procedures and tests appropriate for the questions being asked? Relevant to the
   identified focus from Phase One?

8. Source of referral. Was the report potentially biased based on the source of the contact for hiring the professional?

9. Well-organized. Does the information flow logically from questions to data to conclusions and recommendations?

10. Understandable terms rather than technical terms or jargon. Is it neutral or adversarial?

11. Office behavior and testing reported in addition to behavioral observations outside of office. Were home visits made? In what context were observations made, and can conclusions be generalized?

12. Indications of the report's own limitations.

13. Conclusions. Were conclusions based on the material used for the evaluation? Do conclusions speak to the best interests of the child (family) and questions specified by the court?[21]

Report recommendations.   As the evaluator sorts through the data, the guiding theme is to make recommendations that maximize the child's exposure to the strengths of each parent. There is no perfect parent. The evaluator's job is to articulate to the court the best way to arrange the child's life in order to minimize the destructive aspects of the divorce. The counselor will highlight the needs of the child and how those needs will best be met by the child's imperfect parents.

There are five general types of custody arrangements. These options for residential and decision-making arrangements are:

1. *Sole (or primary) custody.* Child lives with one parent, with visitations by the other. Residential parent makes most minor decisions, usually both parents participate in major decisions such as education, religious training, medical care, and vacations.

2. *Split custody.* Children are divided between the two parents. One or more children live with the mother, and one or more children live with the father. It is usually best to keep children together, but not always.

3. *Divided (alternating or shared) custody.* Children spend approximately half the time with one parent and half the

time with the other. While living with one parent, there are reciprocal visitation privileges.

4. *Joint custody.* Both parents have equal rights and responsibilities for their child's upbringing, and neither party's rights are superior.

5. *Parenting plan.* Residential and decision-making arrangements provide for child's physical care, maintain child's emotional stability, and provide for child's changing needs. Plan sets forth authority and responsibilities for each parent. The intent is to minimize child's exposure to harmful parental conflict. It encourages parents to meet their responsibilities through agreement rather than judicial intervention and to protect the best interests of the child.

The parenting plan is an attempt to avoid designating either parent as the custodial parent. Arrangements for place of residence, decision-making, and visitation must still be identified and followed. In Washington state, the parenting plan must contain the following components: (1) a provision for resolution of future disputes between parents, (2) allocation of decision-making authority, (3) residential provisions for the child, and (4) financial support for the child.

Whatever the custody arrangement is called, the evaluation must make recommendations to the court about how best to meet the child's (and family's) needs.

CRITERIA FOR JOINT CUSTODY ARRANGEMENT

It has been proven time and again, litigating parents have trouble cooperating. If not, why would they spend thousands of dollars going to court to resolve their disputes? Like most conflicting behavior, their communication is probably distorted. To presume that joint custody is the best solution, unless proven otherwise, is not realistic. Joint custody is viable only when these provisions are met:

1. Both parents have a clear understanding of what joint custody involves and have the desire for such an arrangement.

2. The parents have the psychological flexibility and maturity to make the sacrifices and compromises necessary for the arrangement to work.

3. Both parents exhibit strong parental capacity.

4. The parents can cooperate significantly well with one another.

5. The parents live close enough to one another to ensure that travel arrangements will not become cumbersome or unrealistic.[22]

Criteria that contraindicate a joint custody recommendation include the following characteristics:

1. High level of current conflict between parents, especially if children are drawn into it

2. Lack of physical proximity

3. Markedly discrepant lifestyles in the two homes

4. Negative impact of frequent changes on very young children

5. Adolescent children who have a strong stated preference to stay with one parent

6. Implementation under duress (court order) and contrary to the wishes of one or both parents[23]

VISITATION GUIDELINES

Whether recommendations about visitations are included depends on the mandate from the court and the topics identified in the preliminary session. Often, the attorneys, judge, and parents work out such details, but sometimes recommendations are needed. The following visitation guidelines are based on the child's developmental age. Other factors related to the specific needs of each child and the abilities and availability of each parent will enter into the recommendation. These suggestions can serve as a point of departure for your report.[24]

Infant to age two. For children under two, the following guidelines for visitation are recommended.

1. One to two hours at least once a week, preferably in home of custodial parent

2. Visits away from the custodial home may be initiated after age of eight months, beginning with three hours and increasing gradually to a maximum of six hours. During this period, a brief (one-to two-hour) midweek visit in the custodial home may be considered.

3. Overnights considered only if the noncustodial parent has been an active participant in the ongoing care of the infant, including feeding, changing, bathing, and caring for illnesses.

4. The infant should always be returned at least two hours before bedtime.

Preschool age (two to five years).   Recommendations for visitations involving children aged two through five include:

1. One full day each weekend, or

2. If the child is accustomed to independent time with the noncustodial parent, alternate weekends consisting of two days and the night in-between. To provide consistency, these should be scheduled routinely for either the first and third, or second and fourth, weekends.

3. At least one midweek visit of two to three hours away from the custodial home

4. Child returned at least one hour before bedtime

5. One to two weeks during the noncustodial parent's available vacation period.

Grade school age (six to twelve years).   For children aged six through twelve, recommendations include:

1. Alternating weekends, Friday nights to Sunday nights, scheduled routinely for either the first and third or second and fourth weekends

2. At least one midweek visit from after school to one hour before bedtime

3. Child returned at least one hour before bedtime

4. Visits flexible enough not to deprive the child of participation in special events. When appropriate, the noncustodial parent may be responsible for taking the child to these activities during the visitation period

5. Summer vacation:

    a. Four weeks for children six to nine years old

    b. Four to six weeks for children ten to twelve years old.

    c. Weeks scheduled either consecutively or split into two- or three-week segments

    d. Child returned to the custodial home at least one week prior to the first day of school

Adolescent (thirteen to eighteen years). Visitation for children thirteen to eighteen should be flexible. Parents should be sensitive to the importance of the adolescent's peer and social activities. Also, frequent communication and flexible visitation should be encouraged.[25]

In addition to visitation, if it is important that the noncustodial (or nonresidential) parent have telephone contact with the child between visits. This should be specifically mentioned in the report. Include suggestions regarding the frequency and time duration of the telephone contact, as well as financial arrangements. If there is concern on the part of the evaluator that the custodial parent might not provide the noncustodial parent sufficient access to the children, this should be stated clearly, along with changes in custody arrangements, if necessary.

The children should have significant opportunity to be involved with the noncustodial or nonresidential parent. However, if the noncustodial parent is exposing the child to emotional or physical abuse, there should be restrictions placed on visitation. In cases where visitation proves to be emotionally and behaviorally disruptive to the child, the evaluator must consider why this is happening. If intervention cannot change the impact on the child, visits may have to be restricted.

The evaluator's descriptions of the strengths and weaknesses of the noncustodial parent can help structure the visits. For example, if the father is very good at helping with homework, a midweek visit during the school year may be helpful.

Research has suggested that the stability of the visitation is a more important positive factor for children than the frequency of the visits. In other words, the constructive development of the relationship between the parent and child is more important that how often they get together.[26]

Summary Conference

Gardner and others have recommended the evaluator present his or her recommendations to both parents and their attorneys in a conjoint conference prior to writing the final report. This gives the parents a chance to know the evaluator's recommendation at the earliest opportunity and saves them additional anxiety and apprehension associated with wondering what the evaluator has found. Also, any errors, omissions, or distortions can be identified and corrected before the report becomes public. This conference also gives the parents an opportunity to present any final data or arguments to the evaluator.

Although this conference will seldom bring about major changes in the recommendations, it contributes to the parents' assurance that they have been heard and understood and that they have been enlightened regarding the evaluator's comprehensive approach. This summary conference can sometimes lead to an outside-the-court settlement, saving the participants time and expense.

The findings, based on the evaluator's preliminary notes, are often put in the following order: (1) the father's assets as a parent, (2) the father's liabilities as a parent, (3) the mother's assets as a parent, (4) the mother's liabilities as a parent, (5) the important needs of the child(ren), and (6) the rationale, based on the previous data, for why the particular recommendations were made, as well as the recommendations.

Courtroom Testimony

Most custody cases are settled outside the courtroom. This often takes place just days or hours before the case is scheduled to go to court. But the evaluator must prepare as if every case will go to trial.

In summary, you are the one who offers information to the judge; it is the judge who makes the decision. You are not the ultimate decision-maker. This is still the responsibility of the parents until they give it to the court; then it becomes the responsibility of the court. The counselor is an important resource, but keep your perspective about who you are and what you can do. This attitude helps with the emotional drain of preparation, as well as the mental set you have when answering questions in court.

Be thorough and accurate in your evaluation. Offer your opinion based on the data obtained in a professional and acceptable manner. Don't be afraid to say, "I don't know." It is far better to do that than to go beyond your knowledge or to make unnecessary inferences.

SUMMARY

Custody evaluations are difficult for all involved. They are one of the most stressful events in a child's life. Conducting custody evaluations is not something every mental health professional will want to do. The procedures outlined in this chapter are designed to help mental health professionals work through the final two phases of the evaluative process, gathering data and preparing recommendations.

In addition to observations and interviews, the Custody Quotient Evaluation, Parent Awareness Skills Survey, and formal tests are often used to evaluate parents. Formal testing with children may include the Bricklin Perceptual Scales, Perception of Relationships Test, and others.

Goals and methods for presenting conclusions and recommendations are part of phase three of the process.

NOTES

1. See Benjamin M. Schutz, et al., *Solomon's Sword: A Practical Guide to Conducting Child Custody Evaluations* (San Francisco: Jossey-Bass Inc., 1989); and Richard A. Gardner, *Family Evaluation in Child Custody Mediation, Arbitration, and Litigation*, (Cresskill, N.J.: Creative Therapeutics, 1989).

2. Gardner, *Family Evaluation*,160.

3. The Custody Quotient currently has a minimal amount of normative research behind it and is considered to be in the research mode since the authors do not regard it as a fully developed psychological technique. Even in its present form, however, the CQ can be of great value, as long as the evaluator respects the limits of the data.

4. Robert Gordon and Leon A. Peek, *The Custody Quotient, Research Manual*, 1989 Revision (Dallas, Tex.: The Wilmington Institute, 1989).

5. Barry Bricklin, *Parent Awareness Skills Survey Manual* (Doylestown, Penn.: Village Publishing, Inc., 1991).

6. Bricklin, Ibid. 6.

7. T. Grisso, *Evaluating Competencies: Forensic Assessments and Instruments* (New York: Plenum Press, 1986).

8. Schutz, et al., *Solomon's Sword*, 75.

9. Schutz, et al., Ibid. 167–8.

10. Schutz, et al., Ibid. 78–81.

11. Schutz, et al., Ibid. 155–61.

12. Barry Bricklin, *Bricklin Perceptual Scales* (Doylestown, Penn.: Village Publishing, Inc., 1990).

13. Barry Bricklin, *PORT Handbook: Perception-of-Relationships Test* (Doylestown, Penn.: Village Publishing, Inc., 1990).

14. Ibid. 1–11.

15. Gardner, *Family Education*, 225.

16. H. Wakefield and R. C. Underwager, "Techniques for Interviewing Children in Sexual Abuse Cases," Paper presented at Fifth Annual Symposium of Forensic Psychology, San Diego, CA. April 8, 1989. (San Diego, Calif.: 1989); and *Accusations of Child Sexual Abuse* (Springfield, Ill.: C. C. Thomas, 1988).

17. See Richard A. Gardner, "Differentiating Between Bona Fide and Fabricated Allegations of Sexual Abuse of Children," *Journal of the American Academy of Matrimonial Lawyers*, 5 (1989): 1–25; "Differentiating Between Fabricated and Bona Bide Sex Abuse Allegations of Children," cassette recording (Cresskill, N.J.: Creative Therapeutics, 1987); M. de Young, "A Conceptual Model for Judging the Truthfulness of a Young Child's Allegation of Sexual Abuse," *American Journal of Orthopsychiatry* 56.4 (1986): 550–559; P. Bresee, et al., "Allegations of Child Sexual Abuse in Child Custody Disputes: A Therapeutic Assessment Model," *American Journal of Orthopsychiatry* 56.4 (1986): 560–569; A. H. Green, "True and False Allegations of Sexual Abuse in Child Custody Disputes," *Journal of the American Academy of Child Psychiatry* 25.4 (1986): 449–456; and C. M. Loveless, "Sexual Abuse Allegations in Child Custody Cases—Some Practical Considerations," *Journal of the American Academy of Matrimonial Lawyers* 5 (1989): 47–61.

18. Barry Bricklin, *The Bricklin Custody Evaluation Report* (Doylestown, Penn.: Village Publishing, Inc., 1990).

19. Ibid. 65.

20. L. A. Weithorn and T. Grisso, "Psychological Evaluation in Divorce Custody: Problems, Principles and Procedures," *Psychology and Child Custody Determinations: Knowledge, Roles and Expertise*, L. A. Weithorn ed. (Lincoln, Neb.: University of Nebraska Press, 1987).

21. S. S. Clawar, "How to Determine Whether a Family Report is Scientific," *Conciliation Courts Review* 22.2 (1984): 71–76.

22. See E. P. Benedek and R. S. Benedek, "Joint Custody: Solution or Illusion?" *American Journal of Psychiatry* 136.12 (1979): 1540–1544; E. D. Sorensen

and J. Goldman, "Custody Determinations and Child Development," *Journal of Divorce* 13.4 (1990): 53–67; D. R. Coller, "Joint Custody: Research, Theory, and Policy," *Family Process* 27.4 (1988): 459–469; A. P. Derdeyn and E. Scott, "Joint custody: A Critical Analysis and Appraisal," *American Journal of Orthopsychiatry* 54.2 (1984): 199–209; and S. S. Volgy and C. A. Everett, "Systemic Assessment Criteria for Joint Custody," *Journal of Psychotherapy and the Family* 1.3 (1985): 85–98.

23. R. D. Felner and L. Terre, "Child Custody Dispositions and Children's Adaptation Following Divorce," *Psychology and Child Custody Determinations: Knowledge, Roles and Expertise*, L. A. Weithorn ed. (Lincoln, Neb.: University of Nebraska Press, 1987) and J. Folberg, *Joint Custody and Shared Parenting*, (Washington, D.C.: Bureau of National Affairs, 1984).

24. William F. Hodges, *Interventions for Children of Divorce: Custody, Access, and Psychotherapy* (New York: John Wiley & Sons, 1986).

25. V. Simons and K. G. Meyer, "The Child Custody Evaluation: Issues and Trends," *Behavioral Sciences & the Law* 4.2 (1986): 137–156.

26. M. B. Isaacs, "The Visitation Schedule and Child Adjustment," *Family Process* 27 (1988): 251–256.

Appendix I

Resources for the Treatment of Attention-Deficit Hyperactivity Disorder

PARENT EDUCATION RESOURCES

There are many valuable resources available for parent education. Several are listed below.

- Goldstein and Goldstein provide details of their parent training program in their text. A list of practical ideas for home intervention also appears in their workshop manual, *Managing Attention Disorders in Children*.

- Russell Barkley provides some detail about his training program in his text, *Attention Deficit Hyperactivity Disorder, A Handbook for Diagnosis and Treatment*, and a complete description of Barkley's behaviorally based parent training program is found in *Defiant Children: A Clinician's Manual for Parent Training* (New York: The Guilford Press, 1978). *Defiant Children. Parent-Teacher Assignments*, is also available from the same publisher. It contains copies of handouts, rating scales, and worksheets.

- Harvey Parker has written *The ADD Hyperactivity Workbook* (Plantation, Fla.: Impact Publications, 1988). This text provides guidelines for home and classroom behavior management.

- An excellent book for parents is Michael Gordon's, *ADHD/ Hyperactivity: A Consumer's Guide* (Dewitt, N.Y.: GSI Publications, 1991). Gordon reviews the entire process, from identification to management ideas, and discusses thirty different principles that make life with an ADHD child more enjoyable.

- Another practical book is by Stephen McCarney, *The Parent's Guide to Attention Deficit Disorders* (Columbia, Mich.: Hawthorne, 1990). The text has a cookbook format and is organized into sections dealing with problems of inattention, impulsivity, and hyperactivity. Each section includes specific suggestions for dealing with problems such as "failure to complete chores," or "doesn't remember directions."

- My book *The Hyperactive Child* (Wheaton, Ill.: Victor, 1992), is written especially for Christian parents of ADHD children. It covers the basic concepts of definition, causes, and assessment, but most of the book deals with intervention suggestions for the home, school, and church, including the pros and cons of medication.

RESOURCES FOR SELF-CONTROL TRAINING

There are a number of resources that counselors, parents, and teachers can use to teach self-control and problem solving skills. A few of them are listed here.

- Mary Ann S. Bash and Bonnie Camp, *Think Aloud: Increasing Social and Cognitive Skills—A Problem-Solving Program for Children* (Champaign, Ill.: Research Press, 1985). Designed for elementary-school children, the book provides guides for different grades. The goal is to achieve verbal mediation training by teaching children to verbalize plans, solutions, and consequences in cognitive and social problem situations.

- Lauren Braswell and Michael L. Bloomquist, *Cognitive-Behavioral Therapy with ADHD Children* (New York: The Guilford Press, 1991). The authors discuss the application of cognitive-behavioral methods with elementary school-age children and adolescents presenting symptoms of ADHD and/or features of oppositional defiant and conduct disorder.

The detailed manual describes program for children eight to twelve.

- Philip C. Kendall, *Stop and Think Workbook* (238 Meeting House Lane, Merion Station, PA 19066, 1988). The sixteen-session program provides ideas and materials to teach cognitive strategies for psychoeducational tasks, games, social problems, and suggestions on how to deal effectively with emotions. Available from the author.

- Pat Huggins, *Helping Kids Handle Anger. Teaching Self-Control* (Longmont, Colo.: Sopris West, Inc., 1990). A very comprehensive set of lesson plans consisting of fifteen lessons for both primary and intermediate students. Teaches anger is normal and there are times when it is appropriate to be angry, but we must learn to express it so that it doesn't harm others. Also emphasizes the importance of changing our "inner speech" to dampen angry responses. Tested in the classroom, but can be adapted for the counseling setting.

- *Stop, Relax and Think Game* (The Fourth Street Company, P. O. Box 1721, Arlington, TX 76004–1721). An excellent game where each player learns to verbalize feelings, practice stopping motor activity, relax, problem solve and plan ahead. Good tool for supplementing other programs. Available from (Childswork/Childsplay) Center for Applied Psychology, Inc., 441 N. 5th St., Third Floor, Philadelphia, PA 19123, (800) 962-1141.

- Berthold Berg, *The Self Control Game* (Cognitive-Behavioral Resources, 265 Cantebury Dr., Dayton, OH 45429). One of several games by this author. Contains pretest questionnaire that can be used to tailor content of game cards to needs of player(s). A very helpful workbook is also available to reinforce cognitive skills. Other titles include *The Anger Control Game* and *The Conduct Management Game* available from Childswork/Childsplay.

- Patti Page, *Getting Along. A Set of Fun-filled Stories, Songs, and Activities to Help Children Work and Play Together* (San Francisco: Children's Television Resource & Education Center, 1989). An audio tape and read-along booklet with animated stories, songs and activities that help elementary-age children learn about issues like teasing, bullying, sharing, and respecting others.

Several children's books on the topic of ADHD are available. The following are written for primary and intermediate students.

- Michael Gordon, *Jumpin' Johnny, Get Back to Work: A Child's Guide to ADHD/Hyperactivity* (Dewitt, N.Y.: GSI Publications, 1991).
- Deborah M. Moss, *Shelley the Hyperactive Turtle* (Kesington, Md.: Woodbine House, 1989).
- Matthew Galvin, *Otto Learns about His Medicine: A Story About Medication for Hyperactive Children* (New York: Magination Press, 1988).
- Jeanne Gehret, *Eagle Eyes: A Child's Guide to Paying Attention* (Fairport, N.Y.: Verbal Images Press, 1991).
- Kathleen Nadeau & Ellen Dixon, *Learning to Slow Down and Pay Attention* (Annandale, VA: Chesapeake Psychological Services, 1991).
- Patricia Quinn and Judith Stern, *Putting on the Brakes: Young People's Guide to Understanding Attention Deficit Hyperactivity Disorder* (ADHD) (NY, NY: Magination Press, 1991).
- Roberta Parker, *Making the Grade: An Adoleslcent's Struggle with ADD* (Plantation, FL: Impact Publications, 1992).
- The Neurology, Learning & Behavior Center has produced several videos on attention disorder. "Why Won't my Child Pay Attention?" is directed to parents of ADHD children. "It's Just Attention Disorder: A Video Guide for Kids" can be extremely helpful in communicating to children the nature of ADHD. All these videos can be obtained from the Neurology, Learning & Behavior Center, 230 South 500 East, Suite 100, Salt Lake City, UT, 84102, (801) 532–1484.
- A list of books, tests, scales, and programs is available from A.D.D. WareHouse, 300 Northwest 70th Avenue, Suite 102, Plantation, FL, 33317, (800) 233–9273.

RESOURCES FOR TEACHING SOCIAL SKILLS

The materials listed below have been used successfully to

instruct children and adolescents in prosocial behavior. The list is not exhaustive, but provides a good starting point. Each program listed is complete and includes detailed instructions for use, often including handouts, lesson plans, and overhead transparency masters.

- Samual Goldstein and MichaelGoldstein, *Managing Attention Disorders in Children* (New York: John Wiley & Sons, 1990).
- Russell A. Barkley, *Attention Deficit Hyperactivity Disorders. A Handbook for Diagnosis and Treatment* (New York: The Guilford Press, 1990).
- H. M. Walker, et al., *The Walker Social Skills Curriculum: The ACCESS Program* (Austin, Tex.: Pro-Ed, 1988). Appropriate for children and adolescents. Consists of thirty-one sessions to be used in a small group setting. Each lesson includes a review of the previously taught skill, the introduction of the new skill, an opportunity to practice and develop an understanding of this skill through discussion and role play, and a contract in which the student makes a commitment regarding when and with whom the new skill will be practiced during the coming week.
- J. S. Hazel, et al., *Asset: A Social Skills Program for Adolescents* (Champaign, Ill.: Research Press, 1981). This is a video program for both normal adolescents and adolescents who are having significant interactional problems. There are eight videocassettes dealing with skills such as giving feedback, peer pressure, problem solving, negotiation, following instructions, and conversation. Student manuals and a leader's guide are included.
- Arnold P. Goldstein, *The Prepare Curriculum: Teaching Prosocial Competencies* (Champaign, Ill.: Research Press, 1988). Designed for both children and adolescents, especially those having aggressive or social withdrawal problems. The text provides detailed suggestions using games, role playing, and group discussions to facilitate group participation and motivation. The curriculum covers areas such as problem solving, interpersonal skills, controlling anger, managing stress, being cooperative, and

dealing effectively in groups.

- P. Elardo and M. Cooper, *AWARE: Activities for Social Development* (Menlo Park, Calif.: Addison-Wesley). To be used by both parents and professionals; this material is designed to help children understand the thoughts and feelings of others, to improve abilities to accept individual differences, to solve interpersonal problems, and to increase respect and concern for others. Can be used in small group or individual setting.

BACKGROUND RESOURCES FOR TEACHERS

Teachers can be educated about the definition, cause, and developmental nature of attention disorders through books, pamphlets, videos, workshops, and personal communication. While the schools often provide training resources for their teachers, it is also a good idea for the counselor to collect short texts, pamphlets, and handouts written especially for teachers. Several are listed below.

- The Neurology, Learning & Behavior Center booklet, *Teacher's Guide: Attention-Deficit Hyperactive Disorders in Children*, and their two-hour training video, "Educating Inattentive Children," are extremely useful.
- References that include intervention ideas include *The ADD Hyperactivity Workbook for Parents, Teachers and Kids*, by Parker (Impact, 1988); *Attention without Tension: A Teacher's Handbook on Attention Disorders (ADHD/ADD)*, by Copeland and Love (3 C's of Childhood, Inc., 1990); and the *Attention Deficit Disorders Intervention Manual: School Version*, by McCarney (Hawthorne, 1989).

Video resources include "Understanding Attention Deficit Disorders (ADD)," by Copeland (3 C's of Childhood, Inc., 1989), and "All about Attention Deficit Disorder," by Phelan (Child Management, 1989). All of these materials can be obtained by mail order through A.D.D. WareHouse.

RESOURCES FOR HELPING BUILD STUDY SKILLS

The following books represent the kinds of resources that the parent or teacher can use to assist the ADHD student.

- M. T. DeBrueys, *125 Ways to Be a Better Student: A Program for Study Skill Success*, (Moline, Ill.: LinguiSystems, 1986). A foundational text to facilitate basic study skills and problem solving as it relates to school survival and success in the classroom.

- D. B. Ellis, *Becoming a Master Student*, (Rapid City, S.D.: College Survival, Inc. 1985). Written for the freshman college student, this book can be adapted and translated for the junior high and high school student. It includes very good material on note taking, test anxiety, and increasing memory of subject matter.

Appendix II

Case Studies

Case Study of ADHD Assessment

The following report illustrates the assessment procedures I used on a seven-year-old boy. In this case, multiple coexisting conditions were present. This boy was found to have both ADHD and learning disabilities. The narrative will describe the instruments used, sample scores, and the interpretation of the data. (Some identifying features have been changed to protect the confidentiality of the client.)

Introductory Information

Mr. and Mrs. Carson have two children. Seven-year-old Robert is in the second grade at Heritage Elementary. Their six-year-old daughter, Rachael, is in kindergarten, also at Heritage. The parents' concern for Robert was to obtain a psychoeducational evaluation to determine whether learning disabilities or possibly an attention deficit disorder might explain some of his academic, social, and behavioral difficulties. Robert was described as not being careful with people. He constantly hurt others without showing remorse; he appeared not to comprehend consequences; he repeated himself when in front of a large group.

Robert's behavior at home included squirming in his seat or having difficulty remaining seated or waiting his turn. He had difficulty paying attention during tasks or playing games; he found it difficult to play quietly, and often did not listen to what was being said. He had boundless energy and poor judgment, accompanied with poor self-control. Robert displayed temper outbursts, sloppy table manners, and sudden outbursts of physical abuse or aggression toward other children.

The mother reported no complications in her pregnancy. Robert was born two weeks overdue, and labor was induced. Forceps and a vacuum were used in the delivery with no apparent complications. The balance of Robert's developmental history seemed rather normal other than the visual and medical difficulties described as follows.

An occupational therapist described Robert as having impaired motor skills due to Hypotonia Dyspraxia. These motor difficulties affected Robert's balance, equilibrium, motor spatial judgments, and visual motor skills. The evaluation also indicated that specific visual-motor control problems could be attributed to Robert's presenting problems. As a result, a referral was made to a pediatric optometrist.

A letter from the pediatric optometrist reported that Robert was not binocular and had decreased abilities in eye tracking saccades and pursuits. He had been receiving therapy for his perceptual skills. An ophthalmologist reported that Robert had 20/30 visual acuity in each eye as well as other visual impairments. He recommended that Robert continue with his vision therapy. If not successful, Robert might require additional strabismus surgery. Robert had already had two surgeries to correct such problems.

The classroom teacher believed Robert's difficulties were not academically related. He had problems organizing his material and himself to be able to work. His teacher, at that time, did not see his problem as being attention deficit. She did describe poor spatial and visual skills, which showed up in activities such as P.E. classes and observed difficulties in processing directions in a larger group setting. The teacher also said Robert had difficulty remaining seated in his chair and displayed an unusual need for touching things. She said, "One way or another, his body needs to be in movement."

Robert demonstrated strong intellectual skills. The Wechsler Primary and Preschool Intelligence Scale, given at age five, revealed a Full Scale IQ of 134, a Verbal IQ of 135 and a Performance IQ of 127. The profile on the WPSI was generally high, particularly in the Verbal Scale with no subtest scale being below 14. On the Performance Scale, Animal House was significantly lower than the balance of his performance subtests with a scale score of 9. This lower subtest score, being a measure of specific motor skills and coordination, was not surprising.

EVALUATION RESULTS

To begin collecting information, I asked Mrs. Carson to complete both the 48-item and 93-item versions of the Conners Rating Scale, as well as the Achenbach Child Behavior Checklist. The home version of the McCarney Attention Deficit Disorder Evaluation Scale was also completed by the mother. In addition, the classroom teacher completed the Conners Teacher Rating Scale and the school version of the McCarney Attention Deficit Disorder Evaluation Scale.

The Conners Parent Rating Scale showed generally high T scores on all of the categories of conduct problems, learning problems, impulsive-hyperactive, anxiety, and the general hyperactive index. On this rating scale a T score of 50 is the recognized cutoff score for significance. Most of the T scores for the categories just described were in the 70s and 80s. The hyperactivity index was a T score of 78.

On the other, longer version of the Conners, the hyperactivity index had a similar scale score of 87 where 50 is average and the standard deviation is 10. This would place Robert almost four standard deviations above normal on the hyperactive attention deficit types of behaviors.

The results on the McCarney Attention Deficit Disorder Evaluation Scale completed by the mother resulted in a less significant level. The results came out at the 36th percentile for the average of the inattentive, impulsive and hyperactive subscales. On this scale, the lower the percentile, the more likely the child has ADHD behaviors.

The scores on the Achenbach Child Behavioral Scale completed by the mother were at or above the 98th percentile on anxious,

uncommunicative, social withdrawal, aggressive, and delinquent categories. The hyperactive scale on the Achenbach
was at the 97th percentile, which is high but just one point below the T score cutoff of 70 and a 98th percentile ranking.

The classroom teacher's description on the Conners Teacher
Rating Scale was very high on asocial, anxious-passive, and
emotional-indulgence, and just a little above average on conduct problems. The Teacher's Scale Hyperactivity Index was
62 (50 is average).

On the other hand, the McCarney Attention Deficit Disorder Evaluation Scale was at a very significant level with an of
overall percentile of 11. Here again, the lower the percentile,
the more likely the child demonstrates significant problems in
the areas of inattention, impulsivity, and hyperactivity.

The teacher's written comments regarding Robert stated that
he continually had problems staying on task, being moody,
and fluctuating from week to week. He was able to complete
his work when he "understood" what he was to do. Generally, he was able to finish his work quickly and accurately;
however, if he did not understand how to do an assignment,
he became very fidgety.

The teacher also stated that Robert had difficulty during free
play activities and frequently ended up distracting others. He
could even be aggressive with other children during such unstructured class times. Finally, the teacher reported that Robert
seemed unable to learn from consequences. In spite of receiving discipline for an offense, he would repeat the same
behavior at the next recess.

TEST RESULTS

Testing began by administering the Beery Development Test
of Visual Motor Integration (VMI). We knew that Robert had
visual difficulties, and I wanted to get a current reading, since
these skills are often needed in school. His VMI age equivalent
was six years and ten months. This placed him at the 54th percentile for his age, which is average considering his
chronological age but is quite a bit below his mental age.

The Wechsler Intelligence Scale for Children, revised version, was then given. This resulted in a Full Scale IQ Score of

132, a Performance IQ Score of 132, and a Verbal Score of 124. The subtests follow:

Verbal Tests	Scale Scores	Performance Tests	Scale Scores
Information	11	Picture Completion	17
Similarities	13	Picture Arrangement	10
Arithmetic	14	Block Design	17
Vocabulary	17	Object Assembly	16
Comprehension	15	Coding	13
(Digit Span)	8	(Mazes)	16

While his general intellectual ability was in the upper superior range, we saw a significantly low score in Digit Span, which can be sensitive to measures of short-term visual memory as well as concentration and attention.

The Information and Picture Arrangement subscales were also low compared to his otherwise high average. Information is a measure of long-term memory, and Picture Arrangement is more sensitive to understanding of protocol or responsible action in social situations where understanding of the cause and effect is important. These lower scores would indicate average abilities compared to other children, but quite a bit below Robert's average within himself.

To assist in sorting through any previously undefined learning deficits from attention deficit behaviors, I gave the standard and supplementary battery of the cognitive portion of the Woodcock-Johnson Psychoeducational Battery-Revised. These subtests are briefly described along with a pattern analysis.

Test Name	Grade Equivalent	Percentile
Memory for names	K.0 (6)	1
Memory for sentences	K.6	31
Visual matching	1.6	34
Incomplete words	K.5	20
Visual closure	5.3	91

Picture vocabulary	4.9	96
Analysis-synthesis	5.5	95
Visual-auditory learning	2.1	55
Memory for words	2.3	55
Crossout	3.3	84
Sound blending	1.7	46
Picture recognition	3.9	82
Oral vocabulary	2.2	58
Concept formation	1.4	39
Delayed recall-Memory for names	K.0(14)	3
Broad Cognitive Ability (based on the first 7 subtests)	2.1	56
Long-term retrieval	K.1	7
Short-term memory	1.4	40
Processing speed	2.1	60
Auditory processing	1.2	31
Visual processing	4.8	92
Comprehension-knowledge	3.3	84
Fluid reasoning	2.7	69
Broad cognitive Ability (based on subtests 8–14)	2.0	56

Generally the Woodcock-Johnson test indicates strong cognitive skills, but with many variations. The Broad Cognitive Ability of second grade level on the extended tests, as well as the standard portion, is at an average level. But there is a significant variation from highs to lows within the remaining subtests.

The summary interpretation from the Woodcock-Johnson test was that Robert had significant deficits in long-term retrieval of information based upon auditory input. He had short-term auditory memory and generalized auditory processing difficulties.

DIAGNOSTIC CONCLUSIONS

The evaluation of the data was that Robert did display significant criterion for the diagnosis of Attention-Deficit Hyperactivity Disorder. The diagnostic criterion requires that at least eight of fourteen items be present. These behaviors must have occurred before age seven with a duration of at least six months and not be part of a developmental disorder such as mental retardation.

My understanding of the data and descriptions provided by the home and the teacher indicated that Robert probably had at least thirteen or fourteen of these behavioral categories.

The diagnostic process also included obtaining rating scale information. Both the Conners and Achenbach scales were at or near a significant level for measures of hyperactivity. The Conners and McCarney ratings by the teacher were also at the significant level. The behavior seemed to occur at home and at school, as well as in other social settings. It was not behavioral or situational specific. Parenting inconsistencies and inappropriate educational placement were ruled out.

The next area of differential diagnosis delt with ruling out oppositional/defiant behavior or conduct problems. Robert did not seem to display the strong, almost evil opposition to authority with consistent lying and manipulation at the level needed to qualify for these diagnostic categories.

The last area of differential diagnosis involved learning or auditory memory difficulties. Robert did have some visual-motor problems as assessed by previous professionals. The current testing seemed to indicate that there were also auditory processing difficulties. The challenge was to assess whether a learning difficulty was preventing Robert from storing auditory-based information or whether an attention deficit was accounting for the problems in this area.

CASE SUMMARY

My conclusion, based on the assessment, was that Robert had Attention-deficit Hyperactivity Disorder concurrent with the possibility of an auditory processing dysfunction, as well as the previously known visual deficits.

CASE STUDY OF TREATMENT FOR A SEXUALLY ABUSED CHILD

PRESENTING PROBLEM

This case began in the month of September as I met with Mr. and Mrs. Stanley, who had been referred by their pediatrician.

A few weeks earlier the parents had returned home where a fourteen-year-old boy had been babysitting their daughter and son, ages six and two. As the father entered the room where the baby-sitter and the six-year-old daughter, Gayle, were playing, he sensed something was wrong. His daughter wouldn't look at him and seemed nervous. The baby-sitter said he and Gayle had been reading a book together. The father didn't think the explanation fit the situation and later questioned his daughter more fully. After a time, a hint of threat was described by Gayle, followed by more explicit details.

Gayle described genital and anal touching accompanied by fairly aggressive hitting and use of instruments to inflict pain. The baby-sitter had also threatened that Gayle's parents would be injured, die, or that her father would have to go away and never return. Further disclosures to the parents suggested Gayle's younger brother had also been abused.

These reports began to explain to Mr. and Mrs. Stanley why their daughter had undergone significant personality changes over the course of the summer months. Gayle had been a fairly compliant, optimistic, cheerful, and problem-free child. But beginning in June and July, she became more noncompliant, was disobedient, experienced nightmares, and showed outward signs of anger. Gayle was under the care of the baby-sitter about seven times over that summer. During this time, the mother also noticed that when she would go tuck Gayle in at night her daughter would go rigid, as if afraid of being hurt. It was much like a child might do if she was anticipating being hit or getting a shot from a nurse.

PHASE ONE: CRISIS INTERVENTION AND ASSESSMENT

Prior to the first appointment with me, there had been no police-instigated interviews. The pediatrician had contacted Child Protective Service (CPS) as the law required. The CPS caseworker had contacted the parents, determined this was a third-party incident, and informed the local police department. A "third-party" incident is one where the alleged perpetrator is someone outside of the home and who poses no continuing danger to the child.

The next step was for me to see the child. The parents informed their daughter that I was a doctor who would help her begin to feel better about what the baby-sitter had done. They had indicated this was not Gayle's fault, but it was something that needed to be talked about so everyone could get the help they needed.

I completed several assessment sessions with Gayle, using the playroom and various activities. These sessions revealed that there had been significant abuse. It involved rather brutal physical contact such as squeezing and hitting the genital areas. Gayle described and demonstrated the baby-sitter touching her genital area with severe force. At times I was concerned that Gayle did not express adequate pain or relate emotion during the recall of these events. On other occasions her responses seemed appropriate. But I did note the variation.

Developmentally, Gayle was clearly a bright, creative, and verbal child. She caught on to concepts quickly and showed a high level of sensitivity and awareness of adult reactions. This meant I could communicate at a higher level than average for a six-year-old. But I needed to remember that trauma tends to depress abilities, at least for a time.

Fairly quickly, Gayle's feelings of anger began to emerge. She began expressing anger toward the baby-sitter, saying things like, "I want to hit him in the nose and make it bloody." Puppets and regular dolls were used frequently at this stage. Gayle had demonstrated the type of touching by pointing to her own body and through the use of regular dolls. No anatomical dolls were used during those initial sessions.

Later, Gayle demonstrated with anatomical dolls how the baby-sitter put his hands on her brother's penis and anus. Gayle also described hiding in different places around her house, such as under the table and behind the sofa. She did this to try to escape detection and subsequent painful contact with the older boy.

PHASE TWO: SHORT-TERM TREATMENT

A police investigation took place at the same time I was conducting the assessment and validation phase of treatment. This included questioning of the baby-sitter. There was total denial and a very angry and defensive response from the baby-sitter's family. Gayle's parents remained supportive of their daughter in spite of veiled threats by the other family to sue or retaliate in some fashion. There were several instances of dead animals placed at the Stanleys' doorstep and blood splattered on their house. But no culprit was ever identified.

Over the next few months at least one additional victim was identified. Her report was validated by a police sexual assault investigator, as well as by another psychologist. The details of the other victim's disclosures seemed to corroborate Gayle's story.

In play sessions, Gayle acted out her anger by drawing with the paints and felt tip pens, calling the baby-sitter names and painting all over his face. While playing with the doll house, Gayle referred to the baby-sitter's threats saying that he told her God would hurt her if she ever told anything. Most of the time Gayle would only provide a few descriptive details, or expressions of what she was doing. Then she would quickly change the subject and and go on to another activity.

During the assessment phase I saw Gayle weekly. Each time I would talk to the parent who brought her, usually Mrs. Stanley. Early in the course of assessment, Mrs. Stanley revealed she had been abused by her older brother when she was a child. This information had never been revealed, and it took her daughter's trauma to bring it to the surface. Immediately, I scheduled sessions with the mother and we began processing her adult survivor issues. Later that winter I recommended she join a support group led by a female colleague. This proved to be quite helpful and supplemented the concepts and feelings we covered in her individual sessions. We ended up scheduling sessions with both Mr. and Mrs. Stanley to deal with parenting, legal, emotional, spiritual, and educational issues. These were in addition to the individual sessions with Gayle. Later I had sessions with her little brother and sessions with Mrs. Stanley. As the stressors mounted, Mr. Stanley experienced some burn-out and depression, so I spent time with him dealing with stress management ideas. Both parents were on medication for anxiety and depression for a short time.

Phase Three: Long-term Treatment

A month or so after treatment began, Gayle started acting out in more aggressive ways at home. This is very characteristic of a child experiencing the post-traumatic consequences of abuse. I told the parents this was very normal, and we discussed what would be appropriate discipline for such times.

Over the course of that winter and spring there were some additional details provided by Gayle that reflected severe physical, as well as sexual abuse. Most of Gayle's statements seemed valid, but I needed to be alert to elaboration and enhancement. Some of that did occur. I tried to identify consistent themes and characteristics and compare these features to established patterns of abuse. Most of Gayle's statements seemed consistent. Sometimes I could tell by her tone of voice and body language when she was adding some untrue details to her story. I would ask her, "Is that really what happened or are are you just making it up?" Usually I would get an acknowledgement and a corrected version. A few times I wasn't as sure about the truthfulness of her response. I just had to make a note and look for consistent patterns.

This case did seem unusual in that the abuser was only fourteen and the abuse seemed quite violent and aggressive. Also, the abuser's family was well respected and active in the church, and the boy was an excellent student with no other behavior problems. The police investigation turned up very little concrete evidence. Some things did match, however. For example, Gayle later described a black bag that the boy had used to carry some scary pictures and video tapes that were shown to Gayle and her brother. A search of the baby-sitter's room did turn up a bag matching Gayle's description. A collection of video tapes was also found, but no incriminating content was uncovered.

Gayle frequently had trouble sleeping and for months would come into the parents' room and get into bed with them. We worked toward gradually becoming more firm about requiring her to remain in her own room. This was after a great deal of desensitizing activity and spiritual intervention.

I eventually became concerned about a possible demonic or ritualistic component to the abuse. I was skeptical at first, but later wondered if this might be true. At that point, I suggested a more direct prayer intervention. Elders from their church prayed with and for Gayle and the family on several occasions. On one evening I went to the Stanley home and participated with a team of representatives from the church specifically to focus on spiritual issues. This did not produce immediate or dramatic results, but gradually Gayle was able to sleep without disturbance.

Gayle did not seem to have major problems with self-blame or guilt. While she did experience some physical trauma, there was no sense of long-lasting physical or emotional damage. Ongoing fear and anger were the biggest issues. In play sessions, Gayle would act out by throwing bean bags, Legos, or Tinker Toy parts. Often she would want to designate some object as Tommy (the baby-sitter) and "bomb" him out. I tried to help her channel the anger into nondestructive forms. Part of the reason for this was my own survival. Sometimes I would hold Tommy's car, plane, or puppet. When this happened, I was on the receiving end of those "bombs." On several occasions the frames of my "unbreakable" glasses were pressed into the ultimate test and came up on the short end of the deal!

One benchmark of improvement was Gayle's dreams. In the beginning she was often threatened, hurt, or victimized by Tommy or monsters in her nightmares. Later, she became the aggressor in the dreams and would beat up on the monster, ghost, or person. Evidence of Gayle's empowerment was taking place. We talked about how God was restoring Gayle to health and how He wouldn't let Tommy's actions keep her from being a normal child and adult.

Gayle had excellent support from her parents and extended family. There were no continuing issues with trust. It took a number of months before any caretaker or baby-sitter could be used outside of family members, but that was not a major obstacle.

Gayle's social relationships and friendships progressed naturally, for the most part. During her first grade year there were problems with a boy in her class who singled her out for pestering, teasing, and some inappropriate touching. It was learned that he had been abused, so there were a series of school conferences to work out the best way of handling that situation. Almost a year and a half after the abuse, the county prosecutor decided not to prosecute the case. It was a long deliberation with the final conclusion that there were too many liabilities to the case. The prediction was that Gayle and her parents would have to relive the pain with only a 50/50 chance of prosecution. The mother's history would also have to come out and that would complicate case presentation. By that time, I was recommending that Gayle should not testify in the case. She had come a long way, and the dynamics of the situation suggested it would be harmful for her to have to go through the trial.

After about eighteen months we began to meet only once or twice a month. Gayle also enrolled in a child victim's group conducted at a local mental health center. This turned out to be very beneficial. Gayle was able to tell her entire story and hear the stories of other children. The group ended up reviewing many of the same topics that Gayle and I had covered. But done in that setting, it added a new dimension of internalization for her. She was hesitant about going at first. She was told that we wanted her to try it for two or three times, and if, at that point, she was still uncomfortable, she wouldn't have to continue. After a couple of meetings she decided to stick with it. Besides, she didn't want to miss earning the points at each session and having a celebration party at the end.

Conclusion (Subject to Future Needs)

After about two years we terminated scheduled meetings. Along the way we had instituted several rituals or times of celebration. For example, after it was decided that there would be no trial, the family took a short vacation and conducted some family activities to declare "this reign of fear, worry, and unhappiness" over. The parents were careful to say there probably would be other unhappy times in their lives, but this chapter was finished. The use of appropriate rituals or celebrations was important to give the entire family certain stakes in the ground that they could point to and know that some problems had been solved, and some issues processed. Much like we might do when we doubt our faith, the victim and her family can look back at a date and say, "I know I have taken care of that issue, because that time when I was seven and we were at the Oregon coast we threw those rocks in the ocean and prayed."

Since the formal termination of counseling, I have talked to the parents several times. We have discussed signs to look for that would indicate Gayle and I need to meet again. There will be those times. But we have built an individual and family bond that will stand us in good stead for those future trials and temporary setbacks that can accompany each developmental stage.

CASE STUDY OF SUSPECTED CHILD RITUAL ABUSE

PRESENTING PROBLEM

A single parent, Terrie brought her six-year-old daughter, Lisa, to me for a second opinion regarding possible ritualistic abuse of the child. It was already known that the girl had been sexually abused. The acknowledged perpetrator had confessed to several counts of sexually abusing Lisa and several other children while they were in the home of a relative. However, after initiating treatment with another counselor, the six-year old began disclosing to her counselor and mother stories, experiences, and drawings that strongly suggested more severe abuse than had previously been acknowledged. The perpetrator denied all of the new allegations, and the police had nothing to work with but the report of this girl. Most of her statements and drawings had taken place only with her mother. A few disclosures had been made to the counselor. However, the well-meaning counselor had made some procedural errors from an investigative point of view, and Lisa was unable to reveal anything to investigators. Another professional opinion was needed to substantiate, if possible, the claims of the victim.

SOURCES OF INFORMATION

Evaluation was based on information from several background interviews with Lisa's mother, analysis of a fairly extensive series of pictures drawn by Lisa in her mother's presence, and transcriptions of conversations between Lisa and her mother (see examples in exhibit 1). These pictures were made during a period beginning the end of that summer and continuing until immediately prior to our first consultation. Other information came from copies of police reports and interviews between law enforcement officers and Lisa (done in preparation of the case).

In addition to the clinical interviews with Lisa, the mother completed various background information forms including a medical and family history. She also responded to the Child Behavior Checklist by Achenbach and the Personality Inventory for Children (PIC).

While working with Lisa, I had her give responses to several standardized and projective tests, including the Bender Gestalt, Draw-A-Person, and portions of the Thematic Apperception Test. Lisa also responded to portions of the Projective Story Telling Cards, and the Rorschach Response Protocol. Since Lisa was being home-schooled, there was no current classroom teacher who could provide additional observations. A Sunday school teacher from her church, who taught Lisa in a pre-kindergarten Sunday school class, completed the Walker Problem Behavior Identification Checklist, revised version.

Goals

The goals in this consultation were to establish Lisa's developmental degree and intellectual ability as well as to try to establish the nature and extent of the abusive trauma. The authorities wanted to know whether the disclosures regarding the ritualistic abuse were factual or fabricated.

Symptoms and Characteristics

The following descriptions and conclusions were contained in the final report.

Lisa has difficulty concentrating or paying attention. She is obsessed with things like blood, garbage, fire, earthquakes, bombs, etc. She is restless, tends to be very clinging or highly dependent on her mother, cries often, particularly when the mother is not present, has a strong fear of wolfs, dogs, bugs, bears, church, doctors, and dinosaurs. Dinosaurs used to be one of her favorite toys. She expresses fears that she has done something bad, is highly perfectionistic, seems to get hurt and be accident prone. Lisa sometimes talks about hearing voices from a "spirit friend," and acts impulsively.

Sometimes while sleeping the mother observes pelvic thrusts or twitches in her daughter. Lisa will occasionally bow down over and over. She expresses feelings of guilt, being tired, complains of bottom aches and pains, and of headaches and nausea. At times Lisa will stare at a fire in a compulsive manner. She reports her legs sometimes won't walk or allow her to stand. She has complained of vaginal pain. She will pick at her skin, nose, and sometimes at her vaginal area. There is occasional compulsive hand washing, nose blowing, and changing of her panties. Lisa will put Kleenex in her panties. She describes normal things in her environment as appearing to be demons, fires, dinosaurs, hot lava, earthquake, bears, and the devil. Lisa expresses a hatred of boys and men. She often takes three hour naps. She tends to horde things she doesn't need such as clothes, toys, sticks, rocks, business brochures, and papers. The mother further states that Lisa makes potions, ties up her toys, puts tape on the mouths of all her toys, constantly wraps up toys with cloth strips or puts blindfolds on her toys. She is always killing bad guys and suspending toys with ropes.

She talks about "poop" constantly and imagines eating poop. She wants to put mud on everything, talks about imagining what it would look like if her head or other body parts were cut off. She describes life-threatening circumstances. The talk in her sleep will sometimes include reference to "we will do this or that." She has trouble getting to sleep unless her mother is in the room. She talks about not wanting to live anymore, wants to be in heaven, denies any memory or recollection of having any tantrums or venting of feelings which occurred on a previous day. She doesn't remember feelings. She fears that her mother will not come back if she is left or that Lisa will be kidnapped if her mother is gone.These symptoms are most definitely found in a child experiencing severe emotional stress.

These symptoms are very indicative of children who have been abused and would quite strongly suggest a series of traumatic events. While I have not seen Lisa engage in most of these particular behaviors, and have only the mother's report to go on, these symptoms go beyond what one would expect from the kind of abuse to which a perpetrator has confessed. The abuse to dolls, the tying up, and the cutting, suggest some type of aggravated, repeated abuse. The intensity and pervasiveness of these symptoms would usually come from a form of trauma above and beyond "horse play" games of fondling, and touching which have been previously acknowledged by the perpetrator.

These characteristics are definitely those found in abused children. The lack of affect and the general depressed feeling is pervasive. It is almost as if the life essence has been removed from what was a very bright, normally developing, little girl.

On the other hand if the physical abuse described by Lisa did actually occur, there would have been multiple examples of scars and wounds. None were ever seen by the mother or documented by a physician. Perhaps these images and memories were only imprinted by the person or persons described by Lisa. At this point we cannot tell.

CASE SUMMARY

I reviewed all of Lisa's drawings and examined the extensive transcriptions that her mother made from tapes of the dialogue between herself and Lisa while the pictures were obtained. I could only assume these were accurate representations of what Lisa had said and done. I had very limited information directly from Lisa. Given these limitations of validation, Lisa did show a multitude of symptoms consistent with ritual abuse.

Her symptoms included: low self-esteem, clingy dependence, aggressiveness, acting-out, distractibility, tendency to be accident prone, resistance to authority, mood changes, being withdrawn, short attention span, baby talk, extensive psychosomatic complaints, sleeping disorders, fear responses, genital preoccupation, and provocative sexual behavior. There are complaints about vaginal or anal pain, detailed descriptions of sexual events, and references to perpetrators and other possible victims. Lisa has talked about and drawn potions, medicine, different kinds of clothing, and other people involved in violent ritualistic behavior. This activity involved hurting, cutting, chopping, and penetrating bottoms, vaginas, and penises. She describes witnessing other sexual or violent acts.

My opinion was that there was a strong possibility that Lisa had been exposed to more extensive abuse than had been formally documented to this point. I encouraged law enforcement personnel, the therapist, and the family to be duly alert. This was for the purpose of encouraging additional disclosures and to allow a safe environment for her story to unfold. There was also the possibility of continued risk. Everyone needed to be cautious, without communicating excessive fears to Lisa. There was every reason to wonder about additional perpetrators. There is also reason to be alert for dissociative features which may become more evident in months or years to come. Intensive therapy will be needed if that eventuality unfolds.

Exhibit 1
Examples of Lisa's Drawings

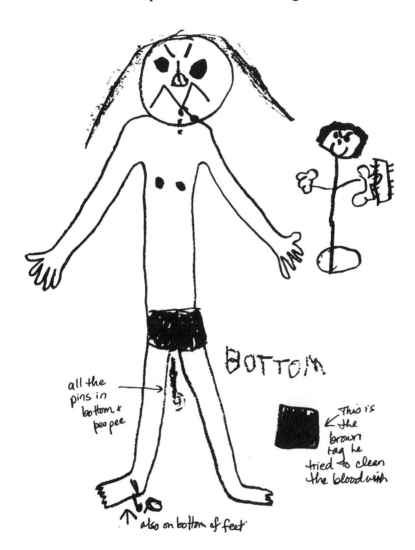

all the
pins in
bottom &
pee pee

BOTTOM

This is
the
brown
bag he
tried to clean
the blood with

also on bottom of feet

Drawing 1

Lisa's drawing of self indicating she was poked with pins in her vagina (pee pee/bottom) and on her feet. The perpetrator (small figure to the right) then used brown bags to clean up the blood.

(Notes are by mother.)

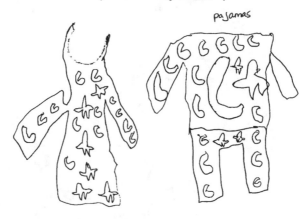

Drawing 2

Lisa's recall of pajamas worn by one of alleged abusers.

Drawing 3

Demon of fear that Lisa sees in her brain during nightmares.

(Original drawing was in vivid colors and black.)

This case illustrates the difficult and elusive nature of verifying instances of ritual abuse. After numerous sessions, I was able to obtain only a very few direct statements from the girl. The child's pictures were quite graphic. The examples shown were taken from the approximately 150 pictures she drew over about four months.

If nothing else, Lisa's extensive drawings and accompanying stories represent an unusual and bizarre imagination. She had no prior exposure to symbols or procedures found in ritualistic abuse. Where did all of these ideas come from? Did the abuse actually happen and the resultant inevitable scars mysteriously disappear? Or was she drugged and had these images and ideas imprinted in an attempt to create fragmentation or MPD? At the time of the evaluation, I could not be certain. Her statements to me were highly suggestive, but there was not sufficient data to make a convincing case. The only alternative was to continue to observe the child as she continued in therapy and see if more details would emerge through direct disclosure.

Appendix III

Sample Court Order

JOHN SMITH	*	**IN THE**
Plaintiff	*	**CIRCUIT**
v.	*	**COURT**
MARY SMITH	*	**FOR**
Defendant	*	**KING COUNTY**

* * * * * * * * * * * *

ORDER

UPON THE AGREEMENT of the parties it is ordered by the Court this _____ day of _____ , 19___ , as follows:

1. Grant L. Martin, Ph.D. (hereinafter Psychologist) is hereby appointed to conduct a parenting plan evaluation in the above-captioned case.

2. The parties are hereby ordered and directed to produce any information which the said Psychologist may require and to produce themselves and their children at such reasonable times and places as may be required by the Psychologist for the purpose of examination. The parties shall cooperate with the Psychologist in taking such tests as may be necessary to conclude the evaluation.

3. The Psychologist shall report his findings to the Court in writing not later than sixty (60) days from the date of this Order. Said report shall contain a recommendation with respect to the determination of residential, visitation and decision-making responsibilities that are in the best interests of the child(ren).

4. The cost of services rendered by the Psychologist shall be paid equally by the parties in a manner outlined by the Psychologist's services and agreement contract.

_____
Judge

Bibliography

Achenbach, Thomas M. *Manual for the Teacher's Report Form and the 1991 Child Behavior Profile*. Burlington, Vt.: Univ. Assoc. in Psychiatry, 1991.

Achenbach, Thomas M., and Craig S. Edelbrock. *Manual for the Child Behavior Checklist and Revised Child Behavior Profile*, Burlington: University of Vermont, 1983.

Anderson, N. T. *The Bondage Breaker*. Eugene, OR: Harvest House, 1990.

Azar, S. T., and D. A. Wolfe. "Child Abuse and Neglect." *Treatment of Childhood Disorders*, ed. E. J. Mash, R. A. Barkley, New York: Guildford Press, (1989): 451–489.

Bain, Lisa J. *Attention Deficit Disorders*. New York: Dell Publishing, 1991.

Baldwin, L. C. "Child Abuse as an Antecedent of Multiple Personality Disorder, Special Issue: Multiple Personality

Disorder." *American Journal of Occupation Therapy* 44 (1990): 978–983.

Barker, Philip. *Clinical Interviews with Children and Adolescents.* New York: W. W. Norton & Co., 1990.

Barkley, Russell A. *Attention Deficit Hyperactivity Disorder. A Handbook for Diagnosis and Treatment.* New York: The Guilford Press, 1990.

———. *Attention-Deficit Hyperactivity Disorder: A Clinical Workbook.* New York: The Guilford Press, 1991.

———. *Cognitive-Behavioral Therapy with ADHD Children.* ed. L. Braswell and M. L. Bloomquist. New York: The Guilford Press, 1991.

Blau, Theordore H. *The Psychologist as Expert Witness.* New York: John Wiley & Sons, 1984.

Braswell, Lauren, and Michael L. Bloomquist. *Cognitive-Behavioral Therapy with ADHD Children.* New York: The Guilford Press, 1991

Braun, B. G. "Multiple Personality Disorder: An Overview. Special Issue: Multiple Personality Disorder." *American Journal of Occupational Therapy* 44 (1990): 971–976.

Bricklin, Barry. *The Bricklin Custody Evaluation Report.* Penn.: Village Publishing, Inc., 1990.

———. *PORT Handbook: Perception-of-Relationships-Test.* Penn.: Village Publishing, Inc., 1990.

———. *Bricklin Perceptual Scales.* Penn: Village Publishing, Inc., 1990.

———. *The Bricklin Custody Evaluation Report.* Penn.: Village Publishing, Inc., 1990.

———. *Parent Awareness Skills Survey Manual.* Penn.: Village Publishing, Inc., 1991.

Brown, D. G. "Divorce and Family Mediation: History, Review, Future Directions." *Conciliation Courts Review* 20 (1982): 66–77.

Browne, A., and D. Finkelhor, "Impact of Child Sexual Abuse: A Review of the Research." *Psychological Bulletin* 99 (1986) 66–77.

Browning, D. S. *Religious Thought and the Modern Psychologies: A Critical Conversation in the Theology of Culture.* Philadelphia: Fortress, 1987.

Buzzard, L., et. al. *Readiness for Reconciliation*. Marrifield, VA: Christian Legal Society, 1987.

Collins, Gary R. *The Rebuilding of Psychology: An Integration of Psychology and Christianity*. Wheaton, Il.: Tyndale House, 1977.

Conners, C. Keith. *Feeding the Brain: How Foods Affect Children*. New York: Plenum Press, 1989.

———. *Food Additives and Hyperactive Children*. New York: Plenum, 1980.

———. *Conners' Teacher Rating Scales*. North Tonawanda, N.Y.: Multi-Health Systems, Inc. 1989.

———. *Conners' Parent Rating Scale*. North Tonawanda, NY: Multi-Health Systems, Inc. 1989.

Connors, C. Keith, and K. C. Wells, *Hyperkinetic Children: a Neuropsychological Approach*, Beverly Hills, CA.: Sage, 1986.

Copeland, Edna D. *Medications for Attention Disorders (ADHD/ ADD) and Related Medical Problems*. Atlanta: SPI Press, 1991.

Cozolino, Louis J. "The Ritual Abuse of Children: Implications for Clinical Practice and Research." *Journal of Sex Research* 26 (1989): 131–138.

———. "Religious Expression and Ritual Child Abuse." *Psychologists Interested in Religious Issues Newsletter* (APA Division 36) 14 (1989): 3–6.

———. "Ritualistic Child Abuse, Psychopathology, and Evil." *Journal of Psychology & Theology* 18 (1990): 218–227.

Crewdson, John. *By Silence Betrayed: Sexual Abuse of Children in America*. Boston: Little, Brown and Company, 1988.

de Young, Mary. "A Conceptual Model for Judging the Truthfulness of a Young Child's Allegation of Sexual Abuse." *American Journal of Orthopsychiatry* 56 (1986): 550–559.

Edwards, Dayan and Eliana Gil. *Breaking the Cycle: Assessment and Treatment of Child Abuse and Neglect*. Los Angeles: Association for Advanced Training, 1986.

Farnsworth, Kirk E. *Whole-Hearted Integration: Harmonizing Psychology and Christianity Through Word and Deed*. Grand Rapids: Baker Book House, 1985.

Feingold, Benjamin. *Why Your Child is Hyperactive*. New York: Random House, 1975.

Finkelhor, David. *Child Sexual Abuse*. New York: The Free Press, 1984.

———. *A Sourcebook on Child Sexual Abuse*. Newbury Park, CA: Sage Press, 1986.

Finkelhor, David, Linda Williams and Nanci Burns. *Nursery Crimes: Sexual Abuse in Day Care*. Newbury Park, CA: Sage Press, 1986.

Forsyth, W. *Cases of Difference Between Parents or Guardians*. Philadelphia: T. & J. W. Johnson, 1950.

Friedrich, William N. *Psychotherapy of Sexually Abused Children and Their Families*. New York: Norton, 1990.

Friesen, James G. *Uncovering the Mystery of MPD*. San Bernardino, CA: Here's Life, 1991.

Friedman, Virginia M. and Marcia K. Morgan. *Interviewing Sexual Abuse Victims Using Anatomical Dolls*. Eugene, OR: Migima Designs, Inc., 1985.

Gardner, Richard A. *Family Evaluation in Child Custody Mediation, Arbitration, and Litigation*. Cresskill, NJ: Creative Therapeutics, 1989.

———. *The Talking, Feeling, and Doing Game*. Cresskill, NJ: Creative Therapeutics, 1973.

———. "Differentiating Between Bona Fide and Fabricated Allegations of Sexual Abuse of Children." *Journal of the American Academy of Matrimonial Lawyers* 5 (1989): 1–25.

Gil, Eliana. *The Healing Power of Play*. New York: The Guilford Press, 1991.

Goldstein, Sam and Michael Goldstein. *Managing Attention Disorders in Children*. New York: John Wiley & Sons, 1990.

———. *Parent's Guide: Attention-deficit Hyperactivity Disorder*. Salt Lake City: Neurology, Learning & Behavior Center, 1990.

Goldstein, Sam and E. Pollock, *Social Skills Training for Attention Deficit Children*. Salt Lake City: Neurology, Learning & Behavior Center, 1988.

Gordon, Robert and Leon A. Peek. *The Custody Quotient*. Dallas, TX: the Wilmington Institute, 1989.

Gordon, Michael. *ADHD/Hyperactivity: A Consumer's Guide*. DeWitt, NY: GSI Publication, 1991.

Gould, Catherine. "Satanic Ritual Abuse: Child Victims, Adult Survivors, System Response." *California Psychologist*, 22 (1987): 9–15.

Haley, Jay. *Problem-Solving Therapy*. San Francisco: Jossey-Bass, 1976.

Halon, Robert L. "The Comprehensive Child Custody Evaluation." *American Journal of Forensic Psychology*, 8 (1990): 19–46.

Hancock, Marie and Karen Mains. *Child Sexual Abuse: A Hope for Healing*. Wheaton: Harold Shaw, 1987.

Heitritter, L. and J. Vought. *Helping Victims of Sexual Abuse: A Sensitive Biblical Guide for Counselors, Victims, and Families*. Minneapolis: Bethany House Pub., 1989.

Hicks, Robert A. *In Pursuit of Satan: The Police and the Occult*. Buffalo, NY: Prometheus Books, 1991.

Hodges, William F. *Interventions for Children of Divorce: Custody, Access, and Psychotherapy*. New York: John Wiley & Sons, 1986.

Hollingworth, Jan. *Unspeakable Acts*. New York: Cogdeon & Weed, 1986.

Hudson, Pamela S. "Ritual Child Abuse: A Survey of Symptoms and Allegations." *Journal of Child and Youth Care*, (1990): 27–53.

James, Beverly and Maria Nasjleti, *Treating Sexually Abused Children and Their Families*. Palo Alto: Consulting Psychologists Press, Inc., 1983.

James, Beverly. *Treating Traumatized Children*. Lexington, MA: Lexington Books, 1989.

Kendall, Philip C. and Lauren Braswell. *Cognitive-Behavioral Therapy for Impulsive Children*. New York: The Guilford Press, 1985.

Kirby, Edward A. and Liam K. Grimley. *Understanding and Treating Attention Deficit Disorders*. ed. A. P. Goldstein, L. Krasner, S. L. Garfield. Psychology Practitioner Guidebooks. Elmsford, NY: Pergamon Press, 1986.

Kluft, Richard P. ed. *Childhood Antecedents of Multiple Personality*. Washington, D.C.: American Psychiatric Press, 1985.

Loveless, Curtis M. "Sexual Abuse Allegations in Child Custody Cases—Some Practical Considerations." *Journal of the American Academy of Matrimonial Lawyers*, 5 (1989): 47–61.

MacFarlane, Kee and Jill Waterman. *Sexual Abuse of Young Children*. New York: The Guilford Press, 1986.

Marron, Kevin. *Ritual Abuse: Canada's Most Infamous Trial on Child Abuse.* Toronto: McClelland-Bantam, Inc. 1988.

Martin, Grant L. *Counseling for Family Violence and Abuse.* Dallas, Tx.: Word, 1987.

———. *Please Don't Hurt Me.* Wheaton: Victor Books, 1987.

———. *When Good Things Become Addictions.* Wheaton: Victor Books, 1991.

———. *The Hyperactive Child: What You Need to Know About Attention Deficit Disorder—Facts, Myths and Treatment.* Wheaton: Victor Books, 1992.

McIssac, H. *Family Mediation and Conciliation Service: Standards and Procedures.* Los Angeles, CA: Consiliation Court of L. A. Superior Court, 1984.

Nickerson, E. T. and K. S. O'Laughlin. "The Therapeutic Use of Games." *Handbook of Play Therapy,* ed. Charles E. Schaefer and Kevin J. O'Connor. New York: John Wiley & Sons, 1983.

Parker, Harvey C. *The ADD Hyperactivity Workbook for Parents, Teachers, and Kids.* Plantation, Fl.: Impact Pub., 1988.

Piers, E. V. and D. B. Harris. *Piers-Harris Children's Self-Concept Scale.* Los Angeles: Western Psychological Services, 1984.

Rapacki, Lyle J. *Satanism—The Not So New Problem,* Third ed. Flagstaff: Crossroad Ministries, Inc. 1988.

Raskin, D. C. ed. *Psychological Methods in Criminal Investigation and Evidence.* New York: Springer, 1989.

Richardson, J. T. et. al. *The Satanism Scare.* Hawthorne, NY: Aldine de Gruyter, 1991.

Ritual Abuse Task Force, Los Angeles County Commission for Women. *Ritual Abuse.* 1989.

Robin, Arthur L. and Sharon L. Foster. *Negotiating Parent-Adolescent Conflict: A Behavioral Family Systems Approach.* New York: Guilford Pub., 1989.

Rogers, Martha L. "Review of the Current Status of the Use of Statement Validity Analysis Procedures in Sex Abuse Cases in the United States." *Issues in Child Abuse Accusations,* 2 (1990): 69–75.

———. "Coping with Alleged False Sexual Molestation: Examination and Statement Analysis Procedures." *Issues in Child Abuse Accusations* 2 (1990) 57–68.

Ross, Dorothea M. and Sheila Ross. *Hyperactivity: Current Is- sues, Research and Theory.* New York: Wiley, 1976.

Russell, Diana. *The Secret Trauma: Incest in the Lives of Girls and Women.* New York: Basic Books, 1986.

Schaefer, Charles E., Karen Gitlin and Alice Sandgrund, eds. *Play Diagnosis and Assessment.* New York: John Wiley & Sons, 1991.

Schutz, Benjamin M. et. al. *Solomon's Sword: A Practical Guide to Conducting Child Custody Evaluations.* San Francisco: Jossey-Bass Inc., 1989.

Sgroi, Suzanne. *Handbook of Clinical Intervention in Child Sexual Abuse.* Lexington: C. D. Heath and Co., 1982.

Smith, Lendon H. *Your Child's Behavior Chemistry.* New York: Random House, 1975.

Sparrow, S. S. et. al. *Expanded Form Manual, Vineland Adaptive Behavior Scales,* interview edition. Circle Pines, Minn.: American Guidance Service, 1984.

Van Benschoten, S. C. "Multiple Personality Disorder and Sa- tanic Ritual Abuse: The Issue of Credibility." *Dissociation: Progress in the Dissociative Disorders* 3 (1990): 22–30.

Van der Kolk, B. A. *Psychological Trauma.* Washington, D.C.: American Psychiatric Press, 1987.

Van Ornum, William and John Mordock. *Crisis Counseling with Children and Adolescents.* New York: Contiuum, 1990.

Wakefield, Hollida and Ralph C. Underwager. Techniques for Interviewing Children in Sexual Abuse Cases. Paper presented at the fifth Annual Symposium in Forensic Psy- chology, San Diego, CA. 1989.

———. *Accusations of Child Sexual Abuse.* Springfield, Ill.: C. C. Thomas, 1988.

Walker, Leonore E. "Psychological Assessment of Sexaully Abused Children for Legal Evaluation and Expert Wit- ness Testimony." *Professional Psychology: Research & Practice* 21 (1990) 344–353.

Wender, Paul H. *The Hyperactive Child, Adolescent, and Adult.* New York: Oxford Univ. Press, 1987.

Woodcock, R. W. *Woodcock-Johnson Psychoeducational Battery Revised.* Allen, TX: Teaching Resources, 1989.

Ziskin, Jay. *Coping with Psychiatric and Psychological Testimony.* Marina del Rey: Law and Psychology Press, 1981.

Subject Index

About the Author

GRANT L. MARTIN, PH.D.

Grant L. Martin, a licensed psychologist and marriage and family therapist, is a counselor with CRISTA Counseling Service, where he has served for over 18 years. He is also an adjunct professor in the graduate counseling program at Seattle Pacific University. He has published many articles in professional journals and Christian magazines and is the author of nine books, including: *The Hyperactive Child: What You Need to Know About Attention Deficit Hyperactivity Disorder, When Good Things Become Addictions, Counseling for Family Violence and Abuse,* and *Please Don't Hurt Me.*

Dr. Martin received a B.A. degree from Westmont College, an M.S. degree from the University of Idaho, and a Ph.D. from the University of Washington. Formerly a clinical professor at Western Washington University, Dr. Martin has also served as a team leader and researcher at the Child Development Center at the University of Washington. He is currently a member of the American Psychological Association and is national vice president and executive board member for the Christian Association for Psychological Studies (CAPS).

He and his wife Jane live in Seattle. They have two sons: Bryce and Lance.